Substance Abuse
in Adolescents and
Young Adults

Substance Abuse in Adolescents and Young Adults

A Guide to Treatment

JOSEPH NOWINSKI, Ph.D.

Associate Adjunct Professor of Psychology
University of Connecticut
Director of Psychology, Elmcrest Psychiatric Institute

W. W. NORTON & COMPANY • *NEW YORK* • *LONDON*

First Edition

Library of Congress Cataloging-in-Publication Data
Nowinski, Joseph.
    Substance abuse in adolescents and young adults : a guide to
treatment / Joseph Nowinski.
        p.   cm.
    "A Norton professional book" — P. facing t.p.
    1. Substance abuse — Treatment.   2. Teenagers — Substance use.
3. Young adults — Substance use.   I. Title.
    [DNLM: 1. Substance Abuse — in adolescence.   2. Substance Abuse —
therapy.   WM 270 N9474s]
RJ606.D78N89   1990
362.29′0835 — dc20   89-70965

ISBN 0-393-70097-6

W. W. Norton & Company, Inc., 500 Fifth Avenue, New York, N.Y. 10110
W. W. Norton & Company, Ltd., 37 Great Russell Street, London WC1B 3NU

1 2 3 4 5 6 7 8 9 0

For Maggie and Joe
and their generation
with affection

Foreword

For the past decade, therapists have noted a marked increase in the number of children and adolescents sent for treatment and the increased severity of their symptoms. During this same era, there has been an explosive growth of drug use in the same group.

For many youngsters, drugs and alcohol have become the quick fix or magic bullet for self-treatment of their alienation, low self-esteem, inadequacy, and fears about the future and independence. However, the very use of these substances starting in early adolescence alters the youngsters' ability to complete the tasks of adolescence, master self-doubts, and establish a positive sense of identity. The result of this interaction is an adolescent trapped in a self-defeating pattern of substance use to compensate for a reality which is unsatisfying while at the same time not doing anything to alter the reality.

Should treatment of these youngsters be focused on traditional 12-step methods or should they be seen as adolescents using drugs/alcohol as their means of acting-out? Dr. Nowinski begins the process of sorting out for us the various and diverse problems presented by the adolescent substance abuser. We must be knowledgeable about the 12-step recovery process but also aware of the developmental process of adolescence. Only by synthesizing these two areas can we begin effective understanding and treatment of these difficult patients. This book now gives us the tools we need to develop an effective strategy for treatment.

Anthony A. Ferrante, M.D.

Contents

Introduction:
The Symptom That
Became an Illness

There was a time, not so long ago, when the public view of alcoholics and other addicts was not much different from its view of vagrants and criminals. The skid-row bum, the vagabond, and the mugger: all were images commonly associated first with alcoholism and later with drug addiction. Most professionals held views that were little different. The stigma associated with addiction contributed not only to denial of the problem in those afflicted with it, but also to efforts by family members to cover up the problem and to reluctance on the part of professionals to treat it directly. Addiction as a problem of human living was relegated to the psychological closet, along with other problems that were too threatening to be seen as they were, such as child sexual abuse. In those days addicts had few persons to turn to for help or understanding, outside of fellow addicts. Addicts, not unlike victims of abuse, were often blamed for their own problems, which were attributed to their poor character or lack of willpower.

Although we have become enlightened to some degree about adult addiction, with positive results in terms of acceptance and treatment, the outlook is not yet so optimistic when it comes to youths who abuse alcohol and other substances. Professionals and the lay public alike hold many negative views about adolescent addicts, most of which are erroneous and unnecessarily pessimistic. I recall, for example, how some colleagues reacted to my decision to concentrate in this area and to create programs specifically for the treatment of substance abuse in adolescents and young adults. "Oh, my!" was the typical response; "What a challenging group to work with." In the mental health professions, the word "challenging" is a euphemistic way of saying; why would anyone want to do that?

In truth, the work hasn't always been easy; but then, family therapy, sex therapy, and marital therapy haven't always been easy either. On the other hand, the rewards of the work are extraordinary. The typical 14-, 16-, or 18-year-old who enters treatment is a young person with cloudy, saddened eyes, or a face drawn tight with anger and tension. These teenagers are humorless, confused, and lost. Even the most arrogant are transparently afraid. To see them a few weeks later—alert, smiling, and having fun—is a pleasure for a therapist. And this is not an unusual outcome by any means.

* * *

It is a new phenomenon in the mental health field to find adolescent substance abuse identified in records as a primary diagnosis. It's also new to find programs designed specifically for the treatment of substance abuse and addiction in young people. This represents not only a breakthrough in treatment, but also a breakdown of some long-standing barriers that have separated the traditional mental health professions from the recovery movement that dates to the founding of Alcoholics Anonymous in 1935.

Historically, the mental health professions have not enjoyed the best of relations with recovery programs such as AA or its sister organizations. Even today many professionals know surprisingly little about these programs or about the Twelve Steps and Traditions upon which they are based. Trained in an academic/research milieu, and grounded in the medical model and scientific determinism, mental health professionals have been slow to overcome their biases against recovery programs which emphasize faith and acceptance, which seek treatment in a fellowship of peers, and which identify truth with the collective wisdom of the group. Favoring behavioral, cognitive, or psychodynamic models, therapists have been turned off by what they regard as an overly simplistic approach based on spirituality and characterized by cliche slogans like "Easy Does It" and "One Day At A Time." As a result, recovery programs have enjoyed closer relations with organized religion than they have with organized mental health. AA meeting schedules, for example, have typically listed more places of worship than mental health clinics or psychiatric hospitals.

For their part, individuals committed to working 12-step recovery programs have been skeptical of both the ideas and the methods of psychology and psychiatry. Many have felt that their substance abuse problems were minimized, ignored, or dismissed as mere "symptoms" by medical or psychological clinicians. Horror stories abound of failed attempts to treat addiction through medication (resulting in vicious cross-addictions), of years of misdirected efforts at trying to cure addiction through insight therapy, and of disappointing work with therapists who naively assumed that addiction would spontaneously disappear once some other issue was resolved.

Despite differences in philosophy—compounded no doubt by distrust based in ignorance—there has been some movement in recent years toward greater cooperation and understanding between the recovery movement and the mental health establishment. Part of this may reflect sheer necessity: as 12-step programs have proliferated, applying their principles to all sorts of compulsive behavioral and emotional problems, ranging from sex to aggression to eating, even the most skeptical professionals find it difficult to ignore the appeal of the 12-step model, even if they don't embrace its philosophy or believe in its effectiveness. Beyond that, the bridge between the mental health professions and the recovery movement has grown stronger as some professionals have begun to educate themselves about 12-step programs and then come to respect and even join them. From the other side, meanwhile, there has been a growing recognition that, while a 12-step program may be the cornerstone of recovery, it does not address all of the personal and interpersonal issues that recovering persons need to face, and that psychotherapy therefore has something legitimate to offer.

* * *

Cooperation between the recovery movement and the mental health professions can be facilitated by increasing understanding of the differences that have separated them in the past. These differences are rooted in divergent philosophies, which in turn are reflected in divergent approaches to treatment. The mental health professions by tradition have been grounded in the "medical model." In its application to problems of human behavior and emotions, the medical model is popularly known as the "psychodynamic model." According to the medical/psychodynamic view, overt behavioral and emotional problems—depression, truancy, sexual dysfunction, aggression, etc.—are considered symptoms, much the same way that a fever is viewed as a symptom in medicine. From this perspective, the goal of diagnosis is the identification of the underlying illness. The whole concept of psychiatric diagnosis, in fact, is based on the premise that mental "illnesses" underlie dysfunctional behaviors and emotions. What lies on the "surface"—namely behavior and emotions—are mere symptoms of the illness beneath the surface. Psychotherapy and pharmacotherapy, therefore, are aimed at curing the underlying illness, the expectation being that the "symptoms" will then disappear, just as a fever disappears once the underlying virus that causes it is successfully treated.

In terms of the psychodynamic model, substance abuse has been considered to be a symptom of something else: something more fundamental, like depression, irrational thinking, unresolved oedipal conflicts, or manic-depressive illness. Even quasi-behavioral or so-called systems approaches have adopted this view, regarding substance abuse as symptomatic of marital conflict, sexual frustration, etc. The "primary problem" that substance abuse was thought to be a symptom of has depended largely on the therapist's theoretical biases; in each case, however, the substance abuse itself was looked on as a symptom of this more primary problem. Therapists have been inclined to focus on this other problem and have historically resisted focusing on substance abuse itself.

If professionals have had a hard time recognizing adult substance abuse as an illness in its own right, their resistance to accepting it as an illness in adolescents has been even stronger. Like most people, many professionals have had a hard time accepting the very idea that a teenager could be an addict. Like our culture as a whole, the mental health establishment has underestimated the extent of adolescent substance abuse and denied the reality of adolescent addiction. Substance abuse in young people has been minimized, shrugged off jokingly, or rationalized as a normal (and therefore temporary and benign) "phase" of adolescence. When it has been recognized by professionals, it has typically been regarded (again) as a symptom of something else.

In contrast to the medical/psychodynamic model, the recovery movement was founded on the notion that addiction is an illness in and of itself, and that it must be treated directly and primarily. It views any diversion from this approach—for example, considering substance abuse a symptom—as naive at best and destructive at worst. From the perspective of the recovery movement the psychodynamic model is "enabling"; that is, it allows a substance abuse problem to continue by shifting the focus away from it.

The recovery movement differs from the psychodynamic approach not only in its view of addiction but also in its approach to treatment. If the psychodynamic approach models medicine in thinking of problems as symptoms, it also models it in seeing the therapist as the provider of treatment, just as the doctor provides the cure for a medical illness. Insight, reframing, hypnosis, circular questioning, and paradoxical communication are but a small sampling of the psychotherapist's armamentarium, the equivalent of the physician's medicine chest. When the right intervention is applied, therapists believe, the problem will be "cured," once and for all.

The recovery movement views things differently. It places responsibility for treatment (recovery) on the patient (addict). It regards any attempt to shift responsibility, for example to the therapist, as missing the point and enabling the addiction to continue. It identifies recovery as coming not from treatment by an expert, but from support by peers suffering from the same illness. The 12-Step program is simple, straightforward, and devoid of jargon. It is regarded as generic: equally effective for all who can embrace it and accept responsibility for their own recovery. Finally, it regards recovery as a lifelong, day-at-a-time process, instead of something that can be achieved through a cure.

Traditionally, there has been little room for spirituality in psychological or psychiatric approaches to diagnosis and treatment. Not so in the recovery movement, which is deeply spiritual, where honesty is valued above all else, and where recovery is thought to be dependent in part on faith in a "higher power." Mental health professionals who have had a hard time reconciling these concepts with their own views and approaches may continue to be alienated from the recovery movement.

Adolescent psychiatric facilities have existed for a long time, but hospital-based adolescent substance abuse programs are new. Cooperative relationships between the mental health establishment and the recovery movement are also new, still tentative, and still marked by more mutual distrust than is good for the patients both want to serve.

Large gaps remain with respect to issues such as diagnosis, the use of psychotropic medications in treatment, and the value of psychotherapy. Still, collaboration is beginning. The gap is closing, and hands are beginning to join. If we can build on this, establishing trust that's based on mutual respect, we may be able to create truly innovative programs that effectively help the vast numbers of youths who fall victim each year to substance abuse and addiction.

* * *

The reader will find the word "tribe" used in this book, both to refer to the various peer groups that exist within the adolescent subculture and also to describe a model for group treatment of adolescents and young adults. In Native American culture, the tribe was regarded as an organic social entity, not unlike a person or an animal. According to this view each and every member of the tribe plays a significant role — and makes a significant contribution — to the "life" of the whole.

A treatment program is not unlike a tribe: it is organic, and each member plays an important role. With this philosophy in mind, I would like to acknowledge and express my gratitude to all those people who, like myself, played parts in creating the Manor House programs for teens and young adults at Elmcrest Psychiatric Institute, and especially to those who have put their hearts and souls (not to mention their hard work) into it: Art, Mary K., Donna, Pam, Judith, Lisa, Jane A., Janine, Jane C., John F., Ursula, John C., Phil, Roy, George, Janet, Joan, Joanne, and Wayne, to mention a few. You all know who you are; I hope you know how much you've meant. I also want to express my gratitude to Tony Ferrante for providing me with the opportunity to be creative, and for supporting Manor House through its developmental process. Finally, I want to thank my editor, Susan Barrows, for her enthusiasm and thoroughness. Thanks to her the reader has far fewer commas to wade through.

Substance Abuse in Adolescents and Young Adults

1

Patterns of Adolescent Substance Abuse

The first time I met Amy I remember thinking that she didn't look like a girl in trouble with drugs. Intellectually I knew better, of course; still, I was fairly new at this, so when I saw her sitting there in the hospital reception area, blonde and freckled and rosy complexioned (and barely 15), my initial reaction was disbelief. Surely she had to be the exact opposite of anyone's stereotype of an addict, adolescent or otherwise. She stopped chewing her gum and looked up when I introduced myself. She gave me a tentative smile as I extended my hand, followed by a much less tentative one as I smiled at her. "Hi!" she said. I realized then that her smile was bright but her gaze was vacant.

Amy had started drinking and using marijuana at age 11, and by age 12 she was a regular user of both. At 13 she started using hallucinogens, mostly LSD, and then cocaine. She also used "pills," only some of which she could name. Most she could describe only vaguely: "black pills," "red pills," etc. Her favorite drug, by far, was LSD. During the interview she explained that a non-user (meaning me, obviously) just couldn't understand what a wonderful drug LSD was.

By the time she was 14 Amy had tried almost every mood-altering chemical you could think of, except for heroin, which for some reason she'd singled out as dangerous. Between the LSD and the cocaine she quickly lost all ability to concentrate or focus her energies. First she stopped doing any schoolwork, then she stopped going to school. Though she hadn't payed much attention to it at the time, she gradually lost all of her old friends, replacing them with a new peer group whose main interest was getting high. Her relationships — meaning boyfriends — were increasingly brief, and though she hadn't realized this consciously either, she'd taken to dating only those boys who could supply her with the drugs she wanted.

The thing that frightened me, listening to this young girl recite a chemical history that filled up two pages of notes, was the reckless abandon with which she'd thrown herself into her drug abuse. I asked her if it ever frightened her, taking unknown substances from unknown sources. She gave me a puzzled look and shook her head. I asked her how much LSD she was currently using. "As much as I can get," she replied with a giggle. "What does that mean?" I asked. "It means," she explained with mock patience, "that I get as much as I can, and then I use it up as fast as I can." I asked her if she'd been having any problems remembering things. She nodded, seemingly amazed that I should have guessed. "I usually don't know what day it is, or what I did an hour ago," she said with another giggle, which left me cold.

As Amy's drug use worsened, the quality of her life steadily deteriorated. She lost interest in virtually everything except getting high. Meanwhile, her personality started changing. Her parents noticed this, but, like most parents of adolescent addicts, they didn't know what to make of the things they saw. They knew that their daughter's once excellent grades had been slipping steadily for more than a year. They'd noticed that she'd become quieter, to the point of being withdrawn. She didn't like to talk about where she was going or who she was with. She would more or less slip in and out of the house, gradually becoming a peripheral member of the family. Still, they figured this was just a normal adolescent "phase." Other parents they knew shared similar frustrations and reported similar problems. Once or twice Amy's mother talked to her about drugs, but Amy shrugged off the concern with a nonchalant denial. Privately, Amy's mother mourned the fact that she felt like she'd lost her daughter — that Amy had essentially become a different person. Amy's father also talked to her about drugs. Amy laughed and told him not to worry, she wasn't into anything crazy like that. So her parents consoled each other, shared their anxieties in private, and hoped that time would help.

Rick's downfall was cocaine. Tall, muscular, and darkly handsome, he was the kind of 17-year-old whose physical appearance roused envy in most of his peers. Despite his good looks, though,

Rick had had his share of troubles. His father, an alcoholic and heroin addict, had fled the family when Rick was 12, never to be heard from or seen again. His mother had struggled along ever since. Most of the time she was just too tired (or depressed) to put much effort into talking to (or supervising) her son. Though intellectually gifted, Rick suffered from a learning disability that turned school into one continuing series of frustrations. Without supervision, he simply stopped going. He was one of those boys who are too eager to grow up and who as a result become caricatures of men. I liked him, but I could see that he had a big chip on his shoulder, along with a temper to match.

At 14 Rick started drinking. He was popular with the girls, and he partied often and hardy. He derived some satisfaction from winning drinking games at parties, and in an ironic way found pride in his ability to drink more than anyone else. This, plus his exaggerated toughness, formed the basis of his rough imitation of manhood.

Rick experimented with other mood-altering chemicals as well, but he liked alcohol best and stuck with it until, at 16, he discovered cocaine. Following his pattern with alcohol, Rick binged on the drug, and by the time he was 17 he was using it daily, consuming roughly a gram at a time. A couple of months before coming to see me he'd started freebasing.

To support his growing habit, Rick began stealing and selling small appliances from the store where he worked. Within a few months, he estimated, he'd stolen over $1,500 worth of goods. One night, when he was feeling strung out but had no money and couldn't wait until he sold something, he stole some money from the cash register. The store owner, who'd been suspicious of Rick for a while, caught him red-handed. At the police station, Rick confessed to everything, was booked, and spent a few nights in jail while his mother came up with bail money and found a lawyer.

As I talked with Rick and his mother I became aware that he, like Amy, had also changed a great deal over the past couple of years. His mother had noticed these changes, but like Amy's parents she hadn't known what to make of them and had little time to deal with the possibilities they suggested. Expressing guilt over not watching him more closely, she pleaded with me to take her son into treatment. Rick, meanwhile, sat across the room, glaring and looking angry, as well as intensely uncomfortable because of the withdrawal I suspected he was experiencing. He didn't want to go to jail, he said (resentfully) when I asked him; but he wasn't very interested in drug rehabilitation either.

For the first two weeks Amy more or less drifted through treatment, never being terribly difficult but never being terribly motivated either. As this pattern continued it became apparent that she had little chance of staying sober by herself. Her cravings were still strong. She hadn't yet connected, on a gut level, with the Twelve Steps; and she seemed totally incapable of resisting even the slightest peer pressure. We felt certain that, once she left the safe confines of our program, she'd use again. She ended up going voluntarily to a halfway house, and at last contact was doing well there.

Rick's anger and rebelliousness nearly got him kicked out of our program. Twice he was put on probation, and at one point he was just one incident away from being shown the door. He was confronted several times a day, first by staff and later by peers and staff, on his aggressiveness and intimidation. I remember watching some of these confrontations and thinking that he invited them and used them as evidence of his manhood. That chip on his shoulder was big as the Rock of Gibraltar. The "confrontation" that finally got to him, though, was really just an innocent, almost passing remark made by one of the girls in the program. It happened during a "family night" discussion. All she said was that it was probably harder for Rick to be gentle than it was for him to be tough. I can still see the look in his eyes when she said that.

Rick left the program with a better attitude than he came into it with, but he still refused to consider the halfway house we wanted him to enter. He felt he could stay sober by going to AA or NA meetings. He didn't want counseling either. He showed up at our door three months later. He was using cocaine again, and marijuana and alcohol, too. When I went in to talk to him our eyes met. His embarrassment was obvious. I could still see that chip on his shoulder, too; but now there was also a trace of fear mixed in with the arrogance. Fear can be humbling, and humility is important to recovery; therefore, I wasn't dismayed. He was readmitted to the program, and after a period of evaluation he went on to a long-term treatment program and, I hope, to recovery.

Brian sat across the table from me, looking tired and nervous.

Though his face and hands were clean, his long brown hair was disheveled and knotted, his clothing wrinkled and dirty. He'd been brought to the appointment with me by a "friend": a young girl who, from what I could see, obviously cared a great deal about him — enough to literally take him off the street and persuade her parents to put him up overnight until he could see me. Later on, I gave them a few minutes alone to say goodbye; then I walked her to her car, to get his clothes. She avoided looking at me, but I could plainly see the tears in the corners of her eyes. After she handed me the pile of clothing there was a brief, awkward moment of silence between us. Then I found my voice and thanked her for what she'd done for Brian. She nodded, still not looking at me, and got in the car.

Despite some tentative and transparent efforts at seeming nonchalant, Brian was clearly desperate. He'd been kicked out of his house six months earlier, following a year of intense rebellion and conflict with his parents. The last straw came when he was arrested for possession of marijuana. When his parents gave him the tough love choice — get treatment or leave — he left.

For the first couple of months things were okay; in fact, for those first months Brian was very happy. He moved in with friends and got a job. He stopped going to school, got stoned every day, and partied every night. Eventually, though, he started feeling bored and dissatisfied. That's when things started going downhill.

To his chagrin, Brian discovered that there was nothing he could do to change the environment he was living in. His friends' partying went on, and as it did the quality of their collective lives got worse. The apartment got dirtier and dirtier, the parties louder and louder. He'd wake up in the morning to find strangers sharing his bedroom. Personal possessions started disappearing, including money. It wasn't long after that that they stopped paying rent — because they were spending all their money on drugs and booze. When the landlord threatened to call the cops, they simply packed their things and left.

At that point Brian made an important — perhaps lifesaving — decision: he chose not to go along with his friends. Instead, he wandered from place to place, staying with friends he'd had when he was still in school — a week here, a few days there. He still got high every day, but managed to use somewhat less. This nomadic lifestyle lasted for another month; then he lost his job, and things fell totally apart.

When I saw him Brian hadn't spoken with his parents at all for nearly three months. I called his home from the hospital and got his mother. I explained that Brian had been brought there by a friend and that he was talking with me about admitting himself to our drug program. I wanted to know how she and her husband would feel about that. I could hear her voice break as she replied that it would be fine with them.

Brian did well in the program. I remember a comment that his father made after Brian had been with us for three weeks. "I never thought I would see this much change," he said. "If you had told me three weeks ago that my son would be sitting here, looking the way he does, talking about getting help from a Higher Power, and telling me about how he's decided to go for further treatment, I'd have said you were crazy."

PREVALENCE OF ADOLESCENT SUBSTANCE ABUSE

If you're reading this book, chances are you don't need convincing that substance abuse and addiction among adolescents and young adults represents the major social problem of our day. Still, it can be helpful to summarize some of the hard facts and the realities that support such a strong statement.

In 1985 it was estimated[1] that over two and a half million, or roughly 12 percent of the adolescent population in America, were current users of marijuana. Nearly double that number admitted to having tried marijuana at least once. Nearly seven million, or 32 percent of persons between the ages of 12 and 17, were current users of alcohol, and again nearly double that number had tried alcohol at some time. Five percent of youths were daily users of one or both of these mood-altering chemicals. Meanwhile, another survey—this one of high school seniors in 1986[2]—revealed that 13 percent of males, and 11 percent of females admitted to using cocaine at least once in the previous year.

If these numbers seem shocking, consider the fact that they are probably underestimates. Why? Because many of the most serious substance-abusing adolescents probably weren't in school at the time the surveys were done, having dropped out before their senior year. If estimates are correct—that between seven and ten percent of people who use mood-altering chemicals (including alcohol) will go on to become addicted to them — then we are talking, conservatively, about a minimum of one million future alcoholics, not to mention the hundreds of thousands who will become addicted to marijuana, cocaine, or other drugs. The cost to society implied in these statistics, in terms of both rehabilitation and lost productivity, is nothing less than staggering.

The current drug problem among America's youth had its roots in the late 1960s, and it's probably safe to say that it followed the rapid increase in the use of prescription as well as illicit mood-altering drugs by adults. In 1968, only 19 percent of the adolescent population claimed to have tried marijuana at least once by age 18[3]; by 1974 this had increased to 53 percent. At the same time, the historical trend has been toward use of drugs at younger and younger ages. American high school students of the class of 1974 who indicated that they'd tried marijuana said they first used it at an average age of 16[3]; by 1984 the average age for first use had dropped to 12.

It has been possible to study trends in drug use among youths since the National Institute on Drug Abuse (NIDA) began sponsoring annual surveys of the nation's high school seniors. These trends are summarized in Table 1.

These data have limitations. First, the more severe cases of substance abuse are underrepresented due to absenteeism. As many as 20 percent of high school seniors have either dropped out or are chronically absent.[3] Second, we have little reliable data on the prevalence of substance abuse in the years prior to the NIDA surveys. What little data we do have supports the idea that prior to the late 1960s prevalence rates were lower.

Table 1: Percent of Seniors Using in Previous 12 Months

SUBSTANCE	1976	1986
Alcohol	86%	85%
Marijuana	45%	39%
Cocaine	6%	13%
Hallucinogens	9%	6%
Stimulants	16%	13%
Sedatives	11%	5%

Source: National Institute on Drug Abuse, 1987 (2).

PATTERNS OF SUBSTANCE
ABUSE IN ADOLESCENTS

A number of studies have examined the issue of how substance abuse progresses in adolescents. One study compared adolescents in treatment to adults in treatment,[4] and found that the adolescents were much more likely than the adults to begin their substance abuse career with something other than alcohol. This finding squares with clinical experience, which suggests that more adolescents than adults have "atypical" drug histories, meaning that they are less likely than adults to follow a uniform progression of use, starting with alcohol, progressing through marijuana and cocaine, and ending in narcotics. Also, adolescents are quicker than adults to initiate and extend poly-substance abuse. For adolescents, in other words, even more so than for adults, new substances are added to the list of those actively abused. Much adolescent substance abuse, in fact, is poly-substance abuse, whereas adults tend to focus on one or two "drugs of choice."

Notwithstanding the fact that adolescents are prone to atypical chemical histories, it is still possible to generalize somewhat about the course of substance abuse in young people. Studies have shown that the most common progression is as follows:[5,6]

- Non-use
- "Non-problematic" alcohol use
- Marijuana use
- "Problematic" alcohol use (abuse)
- Use of hallucinogens, amphetamines and other "pills"
- Use of cocaine
- Use of heroin

The percentage of adolescent non-users is remarkably small, with as few as 25 percent of teens as young as eighth grade reporting that they never use alcohol at all.[7] As a youth moves through this progression, substances are added rather than substituted. There are, for example, relatively few adolescents who use marijuana only. Eighty-four percent of current cocaine users also use marijuana. Marijuana appears to act as a "gateway" drug, with fully 98 percent of persons who have tried cocaine reporting that they tried marijuana first.[8] This supports the conclusion that, at least for adolescents, progression to the next level of substance abuse — from marijuana to problem drinking, or from problem drinking to the use of pills or cocaine—does not mean that other substances have been given up. In addition, once an adolescent has experimented with one illicit substance—marijuana—the likelihood increases that he or she will experiment with others.

There are times, particularly when doing clinical assessments and interventions with adolescents, when it is useful to know about common patterns of progression. It can be helpful in dealing with denial or when making treatment recommendations. It is especially important to know that marijuana use typically precedes cocaine use, that it usually continues after the onset of cocaine use, and that an adolescent who is abusing cocaine is probably also abusing marijuana and alcohol. Similarly, most "pillheads"—adolescents whose preferred drugs are barbiturates ("downers") or amphetamines ("uppers")—have most likely progressed through marijuana use and have had periods of alcohol abuse as well.

The clinician who works with adolescents needs to appreciate the fact that they are much more experimental than adults. The adolescent substance abuser, largely out of sheer immaturity and a youthful (and irrational) sense of invincibility, will more readily try anything that promises to create a new emotional experience or "high." This is why adolescents and young adults are more inclined toward poly-substance abuse and the use of hallucinogens and inhalants, which are much less frequently abused by adults.

FROM ADOLESCENCE TO ADULTHOOD

Table 2 summarizes the prevalence of substance abuse in a cross-sectional survey of Americans in different age groups, ranging from adolescence to adulthood.[1]

In interpreting these data it is important to note that this is not a longitudinal study; in other words, the data tell us nothing about what those who are now 12 to 17 will be doing when they are 18 to 25, or 26 and older. Rather, it compares usage rates for a group of youths aged 12–17 to another group aged 18–25, and to a third group aged 26 and over. On the other hand, the study does inform us that substance abuse in both adolescents and young adults is higher than it is in the rest of the adult population. Of course, one could be optimistic and hope that the data will prove to be predictive: that as the younger cohorts age they will use fewer drugs and less alcohol. However, the

Table 2: Percent of Current Users by Age*

SUBSTANCE	12–17	18–25	26+
Alcohol	32%	72%	60%
Marijuana	12%	22%	6%
Cocaine	2%	8%	2%
Inhalants	4%	1%	0.5%
Hallucinogens	1%	2%	0.1%

*Current User = Used once or more in past 12 months.

more likely explanation is that the data reflect changing patterns in substance use, toward more use at earlier ages.

MYTHS VERSUS REALITIES

Data available from surveys help to put the issue of substance abuse among adolescents and young adults into perspective. It is, in reality, a major problem: adolescents and young adults rival or surpass the adult population in their use of mood-altering chemicals. Adolescent addiction is also a reality. Many adults, including health and mental health professionals, find it difficult to apply the concept of addiction—or chemical dependency—to teenagers and young adults. When they think of "addicts," they imagine middle-aged men and women, not 15-year-olds like Amy. When they think of adolescents and young adults, they imagine parties and good times, not addiction, overdosing, date rape, and suicide. Yet these are also the realities of adolescence. It is a dangerous tendency for adults, and especially parents of teens, to overly romanticize adolescence, while minimizing the breadth and depth of stressors and substance abuse among this population. These are forms of denial and enabling that all too often allow problems to worsen and become chronic. The idea that "it can't happen here" applies to few, if any, communities in contemporary America. The statistics cited here do not define only the inner cities of America. Data collected by the Connecticut Alcohol and Drug Abuse Commission,[9] in the author's home state, which enjoys one of the highest per capita income levels in the nation, are not substantially different from those reported in national surveys.

The problem, then, is real. Adolescent substance abuse is pervasive, and it may not be the passing phase that parents would like to believe it is. Adolescent substance use is not harmless; it can and does lead to dependency that can easily undermine potential and destroy lives. The leading causes of deaths among youths are accidents and suicides both of which are highly correlated with substance abuse.[10] In the past 20 years, the incidence of suicide among youths has doubled in this country, while alcohol and drug-related fatal car crashes are more common by far among youths than any other age group. Few adolescents today have not known at least one friend who was killed or seriously injured in a car crash in which substance abuse was a contributing factor. Few do not have at least one friend who has been in treatment for substance abuse, and most have known at least one peer who has attempted to hurt himself (or someone else) while under the influence of a mood-altering chemical.

SUMMARY

Adolescent use and abuse of mood-altering chemicals are epidemic, to the point where substance use among high school students is the rule rather than the exception. Data indicate that, as compared to a generation ago, substance abuse begins at an earlier age. As compared to adults, moreover, substance use progresses into poly-substance abuse more quickly in young people. Contrary to stereotypes, teens can be addicted to drugs. Hard data on rising incidences of adolescent suicide, fatal car accidents, and admissions to rehabilitation centers point to a social problem of major proportions.

2

Causes of Adolescent Substance Abuse: A Multidimensional Model

Rather than thinking about the "causes" of substance abuse in young people, it is more productive to think in terms of "risk factors": of social, personal, and familial factors that predispose youths to abuse mood-altering chemicals. The more risk factors dominate a young person's life, the more likely it is that he or she will get into trouble with drugs or alcohol. On the other hand, there is no absolute certainty of this—no simple one-to-one correspondence between risk factors ("causes") and substance abuse ("effect").

To understand adolescent substance abuse we need to understand first of all the cultural context in which it occurs. This, in a sense, is the first risk factor, and it applies to most youths, for America has become a drug oriented society; in other words, our ethics with respect to the use of mood-altering chemicals are basically permissive and sympathetic. The past two generations have witnessed a proliferation in the development and use of both licit and illicit mood-altering chemicals. We use drugs—those we obtain from physicians as well as those we obtain in liquor stores and on the street—to enhance feelings of well-being and to help us cope. Adolescents are not very different from adults in this regard. The adolescent subculture, despite differences in form, has a great deal in common with its adult counterpart; this is true across the socioeconomic spectrum.

Americans—adolescents and adults—use mood-altering substances "instrumentally": with willful intent, in order to manipulate emotional states and influence behavior. Much of this use goes on in social contexts. Adult cocktail parties and happy hours may not look like

12

college or high school beer bashes, but their superficial differences may be less important than their functional similarities.

Social use of substances, from alcohol to cocaine, is facilitated by their ready availability. Though some parents and teachers continue to be surprised that drugs are as available as they are, the fact is that 90 percent of high school seniors report that marijuana would be "very easy" or "fairly easy" for them to obtain.[1] Among this same group, 61 percent, 49 percent, and 48 percent reported, respectively, that amphetamines, barbiturates, and cocaine were also readily available to them. Another study, of eighth graders, summarized its findings as follows:

> The results indicate that by eighth grade students have some understanding of the chronicity of substance abuse . . . a more than incidental degree of involvement with substances, and a tendency to be nonchalant about it.[2]

Still another study summarized its findings regarding the prevalance of drug use among teens in this way:

> While counselors and school personnel perceive drug taking as disordered behavior, from the high school peer perspective this may not be so. It is the norm.[3]

Studies such as these reveal a fact of adolescent life that is not much different from the facts of adult life in America: that substance use is more the rule than the exception, that substances play a central role in social interactions, and that their use is considered normal and acceptable behavior.

At its most basic level, teen substance use is hedonistic. Most adolescents list their primary reasons for using as curiosity and to have fun.[4] Getting high leads the list of reasons why adolescents use substances, either alone or in social contexts. The same is true for adults — they use substances to feel good. They get high (or stoned, or drunk) in order to enjoy the emotional, perceptual, and/or cognitive effects that substances create. They actively pursue these effects, using alcohol, for example, for its disinhibiting and intoxicating effects, cocaine and amphetamines for their energizing and euphoric effects, tranquilizers and barbiturates for their relaxing effects, and marijuana, LSD, and other hallucinogens for their effects on thinking and perception.

① Hedonistic pleasure and ② behavioral disinhibition are two reasons why we use substances. Equally important — and more dangerous — is the role that mood-altering chemicals have come to play as a means of coping with dysphoric emotions, such as anxiety, loneliness, grief, boredom, and anger. This is "compensatory" use, meaning the intentional use of chemicals to minimize or avoid dysphoric emotional states. One could argue that we have become, collectively, a society that is phobic of anxiety, grief, or any dysphoric emotion, just as we've become preoccupied with enhancing and sustaining euphoria. The power of this cultural ethic on youths can't be overestimated: We quite literally are teaching our teens, by our actions, to avoid negative feelings and to cope with them through chemicals as opposed to more natural means. Meanwhile, the development of chemical technologies for the treatment of emotional disorders continues to produce more and more effective tranquilizing and anxiety-reducing substances, many of which lead to the same kind of tolerance associated with alcoholism. Withdrawal and abstinence from these substances can be as painful and difficult as is withdrawal from alcohol, cocaine, or narcotics.

THE ADOLESCENT SUBCULTURE

Virtually all cultures condone some use of mood-altering chemicals; however, their use has traditionally been tightly controlled. It is supervised substance use, and is often connected to rituals which bear social and/or religious significance. Selected adults define and monitor the circumstances under which use is deemed appropriate. They also invest that use with meaning beyond simple hedonism or compensation. They do this through ritual and tradition. Historically, permissible substance use has been associated with certain age-linked rites of passage, with important social events, ③ and with celebrations and ceremonies.

Contemporary American culture — collectively the family, the community, and organized religion — has deteriorated significantly in the past half century. As a result, our adolescents live within a culture that not only has a pro-chemical ethic, but also is detraditionalized to the extent that controls are decidedly lacking. On the broadest level, these circumstances represent one "cause" of adolescent substance abuse; in other words, they are a risk factor. Most adolescent substance use today does not occur within defined family, social, or religious circumstances. On the contrary, as the above studies suggest, it occurs in the context of a subculture of peers that is unsupervised, which improvises its own rituals, and which assigns its own meanings to substance use. It is, at its worst, a caricature of adult society; and, like all caricatures, it is prone to excess.

Despite the sociocultural risk factors to which they are exposed, not all adolescents abuse substances chronically or become addicted. Perhaps miraculously, many pass through adolescence—and even through periods of substance abuse—and emerge relatively unscathed. Of course, this is not true for all of them.

If chronic substance abuse in adolescents can't be accounted for totally by the pro-chemical culture we live in or by the excesses of the adolescent subculture, then what is to blame? Rather than being conclusive, these factors, like all the others presented in this model, should be viewed as contributory. It typically takes more than simple exposure to the adolescent scene to cause addiction. What follows is a discussion of some of the additional factors that place young people at risk for abusing mood-altering chemicals.

THE ADOLESCENT PERSONALITY

Adolescents are by nature inclined to take risks. Much of the romance of adolescence—and the nostalgia that many adults have for it—revolves around the zany (and risky) exploits of teenagers. Many of these exploits, from diving off of rocks, to driving fast, to experimenting with drugs, are as dangerous as they are exciting. Perhaps it's sheer energy that motivates adolescents to take risks that adults shrink from, but the chances are that it also has something to do with the psychology of adolescence.

Adolescents live in the here-and-now much more than adults do. Developmentally speaking they are somewhere between childhood and adulthood, not only biologically but also in terms of cognitive development: things like the ability to plan and anticipate. This is the cause of anguish for many parents of teens, who frequently find themselves more concerned than their children are about the consequences of their actions, about getting into college or making a living.

Their limited perspective on time contributes to adolescents' diffi-

culties in delaying gratification — another source of parental conster-
nation. They are more like big children than small adults in this
regard. Substance abuse worsens this. It weakens the will, promotes
immediate gratification, and dulls the ability to think ahead. These
are all personal qualities (and psychological abilities) associated with
maturity. Children are relatively incapable of them, and even adults
vary a great deal on these dimensions, as most adolescents certainly
do.

Mood-altering chemicals offer immediate gratification, and even
relatively mature adolescents will regress under the influence of
drugs, weakening in their capacity to anticipate dangers and resist
immediate pleasure or relief. The adolescent who is immature to
begin with is that much more vulnerable to progressing from experimental or social use of drugs to habitual use in order to feel good or
to avoid feeling bad, without regard to consequences. In time alcohol
and/or drugs become this adolescent's main source of recreation, of
coping, or both. This was the case with Amy, the first adolescent
described in Chapter 1. She was a decidedly immature young woman,
even before she got into drugs, and she became virtually childlike
afterward. She had never developed very far in terms of planning,
thinking ahead, or organizing, and her substance abuse was effectively blocking any growth at all in these areas. That's why she was able
to remain drug-free only within a structured inpatient setting and was
a strong candidate for quick relapse as soon as that structure was
removed. She needed to do a great deal of catching up, developmentally, in order to have any chance of sustaining recovery.

It's important to note, in Amy's case, that her substance abuse was
motivated primarily by simple hedonistic desires: She liked feeling
high. At least in the beginning, it was not compensatory; that is, it
was not aimed at reducing anxiety or any other dysphoric emotion. It
was perpetuated, and got worse, partly as a result of her immaturity.
She'd been a pampered, overprotected child, which did her no favors
once she was exposed to a peer group that promoted substance use
and provided easy accessibility to all sorts of drugs. Accordingly,
treatment in her case was somewhat different than it would be in
cases where substance abuse played a stronger compensatory role. In
either case, however, one goal of treatment is to help the young
person develop the abilities to think ahead, to plan, and to delay
gratification on the basis of a broader perspective on time.

A second aspect of the adolescent personality concerns rebelliousness: that tension which naturally exists between teens and authorities and which reflects of the underlying dynamic of individuation. This basic developmental process is the pathway that leads from childhood to adulthood. If it is successful, individuation ends in identity and autonomy. One key dynamic in individuation is the development of willpower. Willpower—basically, knowing what one wants and thinks, independent of what others might want or think— is vital to maturity. At the same time, willpower that develops without the concurrent development of the ability to plan and delay gratification—self-control—is dangerous; both are necessary, and teens who develop willpower without self-control are apt to be reckless and to get into trouble.

The drive for the development of willpower comes from within. It is inexorably tied up with the need for independence, and therefore usually involves opposition of some form. The development of self-control, in contrast, is largely a function of family and cultural influences. The parent's response to individuation is therefore critical to its outcome, and particularly to the development of autonomous (adult) functioning. The parent who resists excessively the adolescent's developing will invites either increased rebellion or else surrender, while at the same time promoting immaturity. The overcontrolled adolescent fails to develop an adult-like will and does not regard him or herself as an autonomous individual. Despite outward appearances, and even rebelliousness, these adolescents remain highly vulnerable to peer pressure. Psychodynamically they are likely to surrender their ego to that of someone else. Typically they will seek to achieve a pseudo-independence (and pseudo-identity) by substituting a peer—for example, a boyfriend or a peer leader—for the overcontrolling parent.

The other (and equally dysfunctional) response to individuation is represented by the parent who abdicates responsibility in response to the adolescent's expression of will. Working in concert, parents and culture provide the values and boundaries (limits), the traditions and rituals, that are essential to the development of self-control. Self-control, in turn, acts as a counterbalance to willpower in the mature adult. Parents who fail to provide reasonable rules, as well as limits based on reasonable expectations, in effect abdicate their parental responsibilities. Similarly, the society that has abandoned its traditions, its rites, and its rituals has abdicated its responsibilities with respect to socialization and character development. The result is adolescents who are left without the means through which to temper their developing wills—in short, a new generation that is detached from the old and essentially out of control. Distortions in the personality development of so many youths today is attributable in part to the breakdown of culture.

When individuation is successful, on the other hand, the personality that emerges during adolescence and young adulthood represents an amalgam of what is modeled from parents, what is modeled from the culture, and what is learned from personal experience. At its best it is a character that is marked by willpower and integrity, and which is guided by ethics, values, and ideals that serve the social interest.

Christine was the youngest, by far, of five children. Her next older sibling, a sister, was in her late twenties, married, with two young children. Chrissie, as she was called, was 15. She'd been raised by a mother who was a strict, rigid, and overbearing woman of 60, and a father who'd been a quiet alcoholic all his life and who, at 63, was very much feeling its effects. Though Christine's mother had been a strict parent to all her children, it seemed she was even more so with Chrissie. Predictably, when Chrissie hit adolescence, the stresses in the family became acute.

What I remember best about Christine was a comment she made to me about herself. I was talking to her about substance abuse treatment, and at one point in our conversation she remarked that she had little reason for going on. I asked her what she meant. She replied that nothing seemed to be working out for her. "I don't like the way I look, or who I am," she said despondently.

"What don't you like about the way you look?" I asked.

"I don't like my face, my hair," she replied, "and I never have anything nice to wear."

I thought Chris had rather pretty hair, and said so; meanwhile, her clothes, I commented, may have been simple, but they were clean and attractive and looked good on her. She smiled gratefully, glancing up at me, and nodded in thanks. I knew, though, that what I thought was a lot less important than what she thought her peers thought.

Through ninth grade Chris had been a good student and, in many ways, a model teenager. She got mostly A's and B's, played in the school band, and was active in the drama club. Then, in tenth grade, things between her and her mother took a turn for the worst. As she explained it, it became increasingly difficult—almost impossible, in fact—for Christine to please her mother. "No matter what I do," she complained, "Mom always seems to pull the rug out from under me." I asked her what that meant. She claimed that her mother expected total obedience. Even the slightest infraction, the slightest deviation from expectations, was met with severe punishment, generally in the form of excessive restrictions. It was also my impression, from what I heard, that Chrissie's mother was having a lot of trouble accepting both her daughter's budding sexuality and the fads and styles of her peer group. Differences of opinion—in truth, virtually any effort on Chris' part to establish her individuality—precipitated severe criticism. "She thinks I'm a slut because I went with my boyfriend alone to the movies," said Chris. "And she accuses me of hanging out with perverts just because my friends look different from the way she did when she was our age."

The result of this constant conflict was that, within the past year, Chris' grades in school had plummeted. She'd dropped out of all her co-curricular activities, and her initial experimentation with alcohol and drugs had developed into something closer to a habit. By the time I saw her she had several symptoms of dependency to alcohol, notably tolerance. Her substance abuse, I felt, was at least partly an act of rebellion against her mother; at the same time, I was convinced that Chris was drinking in a compensatory way: to make up for her anger, her anxiety, and her damaged self-esteem.

Mark's arrogance and self-centeredness got him into a lot of trouble during his treatment, though ironically it also contributed to his being a leader among his peers. The son of educated, professional parents, Mark had been raised with few limits and outside of any traditions; as a result he'd developed little respect for authority. He had a strong will but little self-discipline and no sense of social responsibility. Though in deep and obvious trouble with substances, he nevertheless questioned every aspect of treatment. Even though he'd been kicked out of one school and suspended from another, for example, he complained often and bitterly about the unfair rules and regulations of our program.

Mark's parents had abandoned their parental role as limit-setters when he hit adolescence. Why? As they later explained it, having been children of the sixties, they felt obliged to acknowledge their own experimentation with drugs. This had the effect of undermining their own confidence with respect to opposing their son's self-described "recreational" use of marijuana and alcohol.

In their desire to be non-authoritarian and open, Mark's parents went so far as to allow him to have parties at home, where both knew very well that marijuana and alcohol were being used. When I questioned them about this, they explained that Mark needed to develop his own values about drug use (presumably through experience alone), and that by allowing him to party at home they at least could be assured of where he was. If ever there was a false sense of safety, I thought, surely this was it!

In the course of Mark's treatment it became critical to get his parents not only to take a stand on drug use but also to effectively set limits (and impose consequences when necessary) on their son. He desperately needed to develop some self-control, to balance his impulsive and powerful will, if he were to have any hope at all of maturing and remaining drug-free. As long as Mark's parents believed that limits and consequences were somehow demeaning to a child as intelligent as their son, they were flirting with disaster.

PEER PRESSURE

Sensitivity to the peer group is another factor that needs to be considered in the etiology of adolescent substance abuse problems. Adults, of course, are also sensitive to the norms of their chosen peer group; adults, like adolescents, experience anxiety at the prospect of disapproval from peers and typically seek their approval. Much parent-adolescent conflict is in fact conflict over loyalties: over parental approval versus peer approval. The individuation process moves forward in the context of this dynamic tension between family and peers.

Adolescents, it goes without saying, are keenly sensitive to group norms. It's a rare adolescent who has the ego strength to stand apart from peer norms or to resist peer group expectations to any great extent. Adolescents' self-consciousness reveals their acute awareness of peer norms for appearance, behavior, and attitudes. Much of their moodiness results from their constant struggle to win and keep the approval of their peers.

The point has already been made that the adolescent subculture is a substance-using subculture which promotes the hedonistic use of mood-altering chemicals. Using alcohol, marijuana, cocaine, and other drugs instrumentally, especially for "recreational" reasons, is an accepted social activity among teens and young adults. To the extent that their peer group advocates and/or condones substance use, adolescents are at risk for abuse and addiction.

③ ADOLESCENT ALIENATION

Stereotypes aside, adolescents are not identical. They differ, among other ways, according to the particular subgroup (or "tribe") they belong to. "Preppies," "jocks," "intellects," and "heads," for example, have different styles of dress, different values, different social structures, rites, and languages. Within these tribal groups, teens differ, as a function of their preadolescent experiences, in their sensitivity to peer group norms and expectations: to "peer pressure." Those adolescents who are the most insecure, or who have the least self-esteem, are more vulnerable to peer pressure. They are more apt to seek peer approval even if that approval must come through antisocial or immoral behavior.

Alienation from traditional religious and social values puts young people at ever greater risk for substance use. Youths in these circumstances are more likely to experience "peer group drift" — movement toward a peer group that is more heavily involved in substance abuse — especially if they are under stress, suffer from low self-esteem, have poor relationships with their parents, are living in a family in which others are abusing substances, or are alienated from religious values[5] and/or traditional social roles.[6]

As it's used in this book, the term alienation refers to a disaffection with culture — a disconnection from parental and societal values and ideals, traditions and rituals. Alienation can be described as a spiritual dimension inasmuch as it includes rejection of the values and meanings that motivate people and guide their behavior, and which by tradition are transmitted from generation to generation through the family, organized religion, and the community. There is an affective component to alienation; it is not an emotionally neutral state. Alienated teens are angry teens. Alienated teens act out of a sense, often unconscious, of betrayal by those whose values they reject. In one way or another, every alienated young person is someone who has been neglected: by the family, by society, or both.

Values are passed down from generation to generation principally through two social institutions: culture (sometimes represented by organized religion) and the family. Parents, through their words and actions, are the primary transmitters of social values. They are supported, however, by the culture, including the extended family, the community, and organized religion. Collectively these social institutions are the vehicle for the transmission of culture: of rules of conduct (ethics), of priorities (values), and goals (ideals). They accomplish this through traditions, rites, and rituals.

Contemporary America is a detraditionalized society, in which the family, community, and organized religion compete with the adolescent subculture for the development of adolescent spirituality. That subculture has grown stronger and more influential as the elements of culture have grown progressively weaker. Increasingly, the peer group is the dominant factor influencing the individuation process. It is winning the competition for the hearts and minds of young people. Today's adolescent subculture is beyond a doubt stronger, in comparison to the family, the community, and religion, than it has ever been. It exists virtually apart from these traditional social institutions. To make matters worse, many parents have simply accepted this, as well as the power of the peer group. They seem to feel that it is inappropriate for them to supervise their adolescents' peer relationships or limit them in any way. In one of the cases cited earlier, Mark's parents balked at imposing rules or limits or at supervising their son's relationships. They literally allowed the peer group to use their home for unsupervised activities that included substance abuse. According to their reasoning, it was unacceptable to "impose" their values on Mark. Yet this is exactly how adolescents develop values! In effect, Mark's parents were abdicating their responsibilities as ethical/spiritual leaders. While they thought it would be harmful to impose limits, the balancing influence that their values and limits would have provided was precisely what their son needed in order to grow.

Parents cannot afford to abandon their responsibilities in the spiritual dimension. The development of a healthy identity is dependent upon striking a balance between personal desires and willpower, on the one hand, and self-control and social values, on the other. The

peer group and parental structure and leadership are equally important in the individuation process. To the extent that parents model
values such as social interest over self interest, of compassion over
vindictiveness, and of charity over selfishness, they raise children
who will not fall victim to the excesses of the peer group, such as
cultism or gang activity. On the other hand, if they do not model
these values, or if they absent themselves from their children's moral
development, they set the stage for alienation and its consequences.
In assessing adolescent substance abuse, the influence of parental
modeling, specifically with respect to moral leadership, is an important factor to consider.

STRESS

The next risk factor to be discussed concerns stress and its relation
to substance abuse in adolescents. There are many sources of stress,
and the experience of stress itself appears to represent an interaction
between external factors — "stressors" — and internal ones — "coping
skills." The person who has experienced the greater number of life
changes (stressors), including losses, illnesses, and traumas, is said to
be under more stress. At the same time, the individual who has less
ability in coping will experience any one stressor as more stressful; he
or she is said to be more "stressed" than someone who is better at
coping. Symptoms of stress include nervousness and anxiety, irritability and agitation, insomnia, difficulty concentrating, sleep disturb-
ances and appetite disorders, and compensatory substance abuse.

Several studies have replicated this finding: that a dysfunctional
family environment and stressful life events correlate with increased
substance use in adolescent.[3,5,6,7] In one study,[3] adolescents were
ranked in terms of their substance use using the following scale:
abstainer, alcohol user, marijuana user, or polydrug user. A sample
of high school students was compared to a group of teens in treatment for substance abuse. When the samples were compared on
scales measuring life changes (i.e., exposure to stressors), the results
showed that the group in treatment had indeed experienced the greater number of life changes, and therefore presumably these youths
were under greater stress. Across the four groups, the abstainers, as
predicted, had on average experienced the fewest life change events.

The alcohol and marijuana users as groups were similar, but higher than abstainers and lower than the group in treatment, in terms of life stress.

A second study[6] used a self-report measure of anxiety and stress, which was administered to high school students and, for comparison, to a group of adolescents who had been referred for treatment of alcohol and drug abuse. The findings once again supported the hypotheses that teens referred for treatment have the higher stress levels, and that stress is therefore correlated with substance use. Additional findings of interest were, first, that the highest substance-abusing adolescents also scored lowest on measures of self-esteem and, second, that there was a positive relationship between substance use and a home environment that was perceived (by the adolescents) as "hostile." This study found that 40 percent of adolescents in treatment for substance abuse reported having been beaten or physically abused in their homes. Abuse is obviously a stressor. As many as 36 percent of this group had made at least one suicide attempt, and nearly three out of four reported serious family problems: arrests, violence, parental alcohol or drug abuse, or mental illness in one or both parents. The relationship between sexual abuse and substance abuse in teens has not yet been thoroughly explored, though preliminary indications, based on clinical experience, are consistent with the above — in other words, supportive of the connection between substance abuse, stress, and child abuse.

Not all adolescent substance abusers come from severely dysfunctional homes; neither are all of them physically or sexually abused. However, abuse is only one source of stress; and stress, as one risk factor for substance abuse, should never be underestimated. As with adults, stress is the major motivating factor for compensatory substance abuse in young people. Teens and adults alike are likely to turn to substances as a means of coping with chronic, inescapable stress.

INSECURITY AND LOW SELF-ESTEEM

In Chapter 3 we will look at some of the ways that substance abuse affects the developmental process in adolescents, but first we must consider the reverse: how a developmental deficit can contribute causally to substance abuse. One developmental process that very much relates to substance abuse is the process by which children and adolescents build self-esteem. Not only is self-esteem negatively affected by substance abuse, but low self-esteem also contributes to the likelihood of substance abuse.

The process that leads to the development of self-esteem (or fails to lead to it) is a dynamic one that begins early. Self-esteem (or, more simply, self-confidence) is based on mastery: on success in overcoming obstacles and conquering challenges. Like individuation, the motivation for the development of self-esteem comes from within. Infants, children, teens, and adults (if they are healthy) naturally seek out challenges and respond to frustration with added effort. Success enhances self-esteem and ultimately leads to a generalized belief in the individual's capacity to overcome obstacles and solve problems. Failure, in contrast, leads to lowered self-esteem and expectations for failure. Chronic failure and frustration end in despair and hopelessness — what is sometimes called "learned helplessness."[8]

Parents play an important role in the development of self-esteem. Through guidance, instruction, and help, the effective and involved parent promotes self-esteem. This is true not only in infancy and childhood, but also in adolescence and even later.

Security has its deepest roots in affection and nurturance, and parents' ability to provide for this fundamental psychological need is critical to healthy development. Insecurity — feelings of chronic anxiety — has its origins in a lack of affection and nurturance. The secure individual is one who is able to comfort him or herself in times of stress, as well as to seek comfort and support from others. The secure individual has a basically trusting attitude toward others. The insecure individual is fundamentally distrustful. He or she is apt to grow into an adult who is demanding, jealous, and possessive.

Low self-esteem and insecurity are powerful motivators — "trigger emotions" — for compensatory substance use. In the teen years, self-esteem becomes increasingly affected by social factors. Abilities and talents play an important role in determining self-esteem at this time. Every teenager is an individual in search of something to feel special about (and proud of), be it personal attractiveness, talent, social skill, or intelligence.

SUMMARY

This chapter has presented a multidimensional model of adolescent substance abuse. If our goal is to decrease the problem of adolescent substance abuse and to provide effective help for those young persons who fall victim to it, then we need to begin by understanding something about the scope of the problem and the factors that seem to be associated with increased likelihood of substance abuse.

Our society actively promotes the instrumental use of mood-altering substances. In a sense society's values are at least partly responsible for the current crisis of substance abuse among our youth. Another factor is the continuing detraditionalization of our society. Given the pervasive availability of drugs and alcohol in the adolescent subculture and the fact that it exists largely apart from the adult culture, the easier choice for youths today, by far, is to say "yes" rather than "no" to drugs.

In designing interventions, as well as prevention programs, it is more productive to think in terms of "risk factors" than "causes." There is probably no simple, linear, causal relationship that can adequately explain substance abuse (or lend itself to an equally linear intervention). Rather, there are many risk factors, ranging from the cultural level, to the family level, to the personal level. The more risk factors dominate a young person's life, the more vulnerable he or she is to using mood-altering chemicals, first instrumentally and later habitually. On the other hand, the more we can effectively eliminate or reduce risk factors, the less of a problem we are likely to have (as a society) and the more hopeful we can be about the lasting effects of treatment.

3

Substance Abuse
and Adolescent
Development

In order to design treatment programs that will be effective for young people, it is important to begin with an understanding of adolescent development and of how substance abuse affects the developmental process in youths. Based on this knowledge, traditional treatment approaches can be modified, or "translated," in ways that will make them viable for youths.

Substance abuse has profound effects on the developmental process. Some of the issues that will be examined in this chapter include the effects that substance abuse has on personality development, on social learning and cognitive development, on the development of coping skills, and on self-esteem.

SUBSTANCE ABUSE AND
PERSONALITY DEVELOPMENT

It is common wisdom in the addictions field that addicts stop growing—in other words, maturing—when addiction sets in. This idea, of "arrested development," has been clinically useful in the treatment of adult addicts and has application as well in dealing with adolescent substance abusers. What happens, for example, when substance abuse begins at age 10 or 12, instead of age 18 or 20? This is an important question. When adults in treatment were compared to adolescents in treatment,[1] it was found that, whereas the mean age at which the adults started abusing substances was 15, for the adolescents it was less than 12. Developmentally there are huge differences between 11- and 12-year-olds, versus 15- and 16-year-olds. While

27

both groups may suffer from developmental arrest, the impact on the younger group is decidedly different.

Developmentally, adolescents exist in a grey area, a limbo of sorts somewhere between childhood and adulthood. They are members of a separate subculture, which is highly developed and includes its own rites, norms, and language, and which is insulated from the larger society of adults by an unwritten code of secrecy. A great deal of personality development occurs during adolescence. Prior to this — through infancy and childhood — the individual is closely identified with his or her parents, and particularly with the parent of the same sex. The child's sense of individuality is limited. A kind of benign symbiosis connects parent and child, even at times when the child is seemingly rebellious or oppositional. Possessing a uniquely human and highly developed ability to learn through observation (modeling), the child learns to talk, walk, even think like the parent. Ironically, even those children who are outwardly oppositional are usually modeling a similar personality trait in a parent. Similarly, those children who frustrate their parents with their shyness usually have parents who also experience social anxiety.

Adolescents' personalities reflect their ambiguous social status as half-child, half-adult. At times they can be surprisingly adult-like, at other times remarkably childish. Societal and parental expectations and rules for adolescents are different from those for children, but they aren't the same expectations we have for adults. At times they are unclear or inconsistent. To a substantial degree (often much more than parents realize) adolescents conform — or attempt to conform — to these expectations. Put more simply, teenagers often act the way we implicitly tell them to act, through the expectations we consciously or unconsciously hold for them.

Clinically it is important to recognize the inevitability, and essential normality, of the adolescent status as half-child, half-adult. It is a crucial developmental stage, the outcome of which has a profound impact on adult relationships and personality. Teenagers' personalities are consistent with this: They have needs and desires that are sometimes childlike, sometimes adult-like; and their moods are fluid and unpredictable. The habitual use of mood-altering chemicals during this time of life creates developmental lags and inconsistencies. In treatment it is important to address this duality in the personality of the adolescent and to provide what is needed for the "child" to grow into a healthy "adult."

Whereas the child's identity is derived substantially from its parent's and could even be said to be merged with it, in adolescence the major identity issue is individuation: separation and the emergence of autonomous will and internal control of behavior. The outcome of successful individuation is an identity or "self" that is characterized by willpower and self-control. The successfully individuated adult feels and acts as an equal to his or her parent, whereupon the parent-child relationship changes. The unsuccessfully individuated person invariably develops a personality that is fundamentally "immature": either excessively willful or excessively dependent.

The peer group plays an essential role in the individuation process. The peer group not only contributes directly to personality development — through its norms and expectations — but also acts as a catalyst for the development of will and separation from the parent. Developmentally the peer group represents a transitional object of attachment: a stepping stone to autonomy. It is a bridge between the parent and self, the self being the mature adult personality: that constellation of attitudes, tastes, beliefs, values, etc., that make up our concept of who we are.

The core of the self is the "will": the individual's capacity for making choices and decisions and for acting independently even if that means acting contrary to parental or peer group expectations. Will emerges from the individuation process. The peer group facilitates its development by providing the leverage needed to enable the young person to stand apart from the parents. When an adolescent abuses substances, however, and particularly when that abuse becomes habitual, the individuation process is compromised. Maturation essentially stops, and the development of will is severely impaired. Addiction totally defeats the will at its seminal point in development.

While the peer group in many ways takes center stage throughout the adolescent and young adult years, it is easy to underestimate the important and ongoing role that parental and cultural influences play in development. True maturity requires not only will but also self-control. Whereas will develops primarily out of involvement with the peer group, the development of self-control — the capacity to plan, to persevere, and to delay gratification — is heavily dependent on parental and cultural influences. It begins in childhood, a time in life when self-control is largely dependent on external factors (rewards and punishments). It proceeds through adolescence, which is when self-control has the potential to take a developmental leap and become a function not just of external factors, but of internal ones, including values and priorities. Achieving this level of moral development is vital to recovery from addiction.

Whereas the adult addict may have developed some degree of will-power prior to addiction (which can be recovered in and after treatment), the addicted adolescent never had an opportunity to develop a will of his or her own. Part of adolescents' denial, however, is an illusion of free will: the false belief that they are "choosing" to be involved self-destructive behaviors like drug abuse, when in reality it's the drug that is making their decisions.

Through peer group drift, the influence of peer attitudes, values, and norms becomes not only more distorted but also more powerful as the adolescent moves from social use to habitual substance use. That part of the adolescent's developing personality representing peer influences no longer reflects mainstream values or expectations; instead it tends to become contaminated with extreme and unrealistic attitudes and beliefs that are dysfunctional in the larger society. Behaviors such as stealing and lying, selling drugs, or prostituting for drugs may be condoned and even encouraged within this group. In even more extreme cases, antisocial or satanic ideologies may dominate the developmental process.

Instead of moving forward with individuation, developing will-power and self-control, values and ethics, the substance abuser falls victim to immediate gratification, impulsivity, and hedonism. The result is an immature self-centeredness. As substance abuse deepens the peer group replaces the will, promoting further regression among its members. Collectively they become progressively more immature, more infantile. Along with the ability to delay gratification, the capacity to plan and to make independent judgments worsens over time. These are youths who are easily manipulated and exploited, despite their veneer of worldliness. Many fall victim to prostitution, pornography, and drug dealing, all the while thinking they've got it made. A kind of symbiosis develops within the abusing peer group, one in which there is a group personality but no individual personalities. When separated from this group — for example by being put into a rehabilitation program — habitual substance-abusing adolescents feel lost. They have little sense of themselves apart from the group, and though they are alienated from adult norms and rules they are incapable of effectively running their own lives.

SOCIAL LEARNING

Two things happen to adolescent substance abusers that retard their social development. The first has to do with their alienation from the mainstream adolescent subculture. Once they are identified as chronic drug users or drinkers, and as they begin to "drift" socially toward other habitual users, these youths are ostracized by mainstream peers. They are stigmatized, and they suffer the same kinds of consequences that other stigmatized persons do, including those who are identified as having a mental illness or who have physical handicaps. All of these groups pass through adolescence as outsiders. They don't participate in mainstream activities and don't benefit from those experiences. They live more or less on the outside, looking in. One consequence is that they don't work their way through the same developmental tasks — dating, for example — at the same time or in the same way as the majority of their peers. Whatever "relationships" they do have are built around using, and their main form of "recreation" is getting high. In treatment their social skills are found to be sorely lacking as compared to the average adolescent or young adult. They are awkward in relationships and have little or no idea about how to have fun or pursue an attraction without the help of alcohol or drugs.

As substance abuse moves toward addiction, preoccupation with use sets in, and this compounds the deficit in social learning that characterizes the adolescent substance abuser. As life becomes more and more centered around getting high, the abusing adolescent pays less attention to anything else that is going on around him or her. Old hobbies and favorite activities are dropped. The attention span shortens, and the youth sees the world through a haze. Under these circumstances little learning (or development) can occur, and the adolescent moves tediously, if at all, through developmental stages. In recovery there is much catching up to do, as the following case illustrates.

Mark was nearly 20 when he overdosed on cocaine. He'd been drinking and smoking pot steadily since age 11, and had gotten into coke about a year before. One night, while partying in his usual way with his using friends, he experienced the scare of his life. It began with a rapid, pounding heartbeat that went on and on and on. Then he began sweating — profusely. At first he felt only a tightness in his chest; then it started to hurt. That panicked him. With the help of a friend he made it home. For hours he lay in bed, unable even to close his eyes. His parents were finally wakened by the sounds of his sobbing. Though they'd long suspected that their son was using marijuana, they had no idea that he'd gotten into cocaine. They took him to the emergency room; the next day he saw me and a day later he was in treatment.

After being in treatment for several days — and having his body essentially clear of chemicals for the first time in nearly 10 years — Mark started to talk about himself. One of the first interests he expressed in sobriety was a desire to go through his baseball card collection! At first I was shocked; then I discovered that he'd asked his parents to bring him some comic books to read in his free time. Meanwhile, his favorite activity in creative therapy was drawing cartoons based on Saturday morning television shows. Psychological testing revealed that these interests were not the result of limited intelligence but of retarded development.

In sobriety, adolescent substance abusers express confusion and anxiety over basic social skills, such as initiating contact with the opposite sex, making new friends, or interviewing for a part-time job. They lack appropriate assertiveness and conversational abilities and have little idea of how to relate to peers without the aid of substances as the primary social agenda. These deficits need to be recognized and addressed in treatment. Strategies for doing this will be presented later.

COGNITIVE AND MORAL DEVELOPMENT

One developmental process that is arrested by substance abuse is the capacity to think in abstract terms. Cognitive growth appears to stop once substance abuse becomes habitual. For most adolescents this means that thinking gets "stuck" at the concrete level. This undermines moral development, which rests on the ability to make ethical choices according to abstract concepts such as justice, social responsibility, etc. Normally this begins to occur in early adolescence and continues well into adulthood. Even otherwise mature adults, who have a good grasp of other abstract concepts, may not develop an abstract moral view.[2,3]

What it means to be morally "concrete" is that behavior is guided primarily by immediate consequences, rather than by ethical principles. Moral decisions are made on the basis of simple concepts, such as equity ("an eye for an eye") and reciprocity ("I'll scratch your back if you'll scratch mine"). The primary motivation for "good" (ethical) behavior is perceived consequences in a given situation. This has been called "control through constraint."[2] At this level, concepts of "right" versus "wrong" or "good" versus "bad" rest primarily on what behavior is rewarded versus punished; they have relatively little to do with concepts like fairness, justice, or even social welfare (the best interests of the group or community). Children could be described as morally concrete: Their "moral" behavior is largely situational — in other words, dependent on expected consequences in a particular situation. Children lack abstract moral concepts — principles that remain constant across situations — to guide behavior.

Not surprisingly, research has found that children's "moral" behavior is relatively unstable across situations. Placed in a situation where expectations for punishment are low, children will be inclined to cheat or lie more than they will if they expect to be punished for these behaviors.[3] This is not a sign of weak moral character in children, as much as an indication of their level of development.

This is very significant for adolescent and young adult substance abusers, who think and act much more like children than like adults (or even like typical adolescents) with respect to morality and ethics. They operate on a concrete level, much the way children do. If they believe that they can get away with using in a particular situation — without specific physical, social, or legal consequences — they are likely to do it. If they have advanced to making decisions on the basis of ethical concepts at all, it is likely to be on the basis of equity and reciprocity.

A less mature level of moral development — and of behavioral control — then, is one that is dependent on external consequences. In a sense this is not "self"-control at all, if by that we mean control that is based on moral values and ideals. It is important to recognize that substance-abusing teens and young adults tend to be developmentally arrested at this level, and that they consequently will respond to control by constraint (i.e., external consequences). Long-term recovery, however, demands abilities (and maturity) beyond this. Treatment programs that rely too heavily on control of behavior via rewards and punishments may fail to promote developmental growth, and therefore invite relapse as soon as the external constraints (in short, the program) are removed.

There are more mature levels of behavioral control and moral development. The first is "control through cooperation."[2] At this level the welfare of the group is balanced against individual desires in making ethical decisions. It may be "wrong" to sell alcohol to minors, for instance, because that is associated with increased traffic fatalities. In this context, group norms control behavior more than situational expectations (or even personal agreements based on reciprocity), and ethical behavior becomes defined as behavior that promotes the integrity and welfare of the group. This type of control can and should be promoted in treatment programs, since it represents a step forward from control based on expected consequences and extends the individual's perspective beyond discrete relationships. Recovery, for example, is a shared (group) goal and responsibility; therefore, recovering persons have obligations to each other as well as to themselves.

A third level of moral development is what could be called true self-control. This happens when behavior is determined not solely by expected consequences, or even by peer group norms, but by values and ideals[2,4] that may transcend the group itself. At this developmental level personal conduct is mediated largely by abstract moral concepts (justice over equity, equality, the rights of the minority, freedom of expression, etc.). Many such values are integral to the Twelve Traditions of Alcoholics Anonymous.[5]

Moral development appears to proceed partly as a result of internal factors, such as the ability to think abstractly, and partly in response to social influences, principally modeling. This is where parents and culture enter the picture. Parental attitudes and behavior are the outward manifestations of underlying ethics that are modeled by children during adolescence. Parental moral development, in fact, may place a ceiling on the moral development of the child (unless the child is exposed to alternative models that have an impact). For this reason, among others, work with adolescents in recovery requires concurrent work with their families. If this is not possible, then stronger efforts must be made to influence the moral development of adolescents, for example by exposing them to an alternative "culture" as is described in Chapter 15.

COPING SKILLS

Substance abuse and coping ability ("resilience") have a reciprocal relationship: Inadequate coping skills are a risk factor for substance abuse, which in turn impedes the development of nonchemical means of coping. Stressors abound in everyday life. They range from minor frustrations to major threats, losses and traumas. The healthy individual possesses a range of cognitive and behavioral skills with which to deal with the anxiety, sadness, confusion or discomfort that stress creates.

Coping abilities are not all learned during adolescence; some have their origins in childhood and even infancy. Affection, nurturance, and comfort from loving parents or other adults are important in the development of security, which plays a significant role in coping. The secure individual is more resilient in the face of stress, more willing to confront challenges, and more persevering in the face of frustration. Conversely, the insecure individual is more motivated to avoid challenges and to despair when frustrated. Secure individuals are able to comfort themselves, to seek comfort through social support, and to find solace in spiritual beliefs. It is not surprising that adolescents who fall victim to substance abuse are typically alienated from their parents and from spiritual values.

Self-esteem develops throughout life as a function of mastery. The individual with high self-esteem is self-confident, having built a "track record" of success, including success in handling stressful events and circumstances. The person with low self-esteem is again at risk for substance abuse, as a way of fleeing stress rather than coping with it in other ways.

Substance abuse not only can stem from inadequate coping skills but also contributes to further impairment in this area. During adolescence, additional learning takes place with respect to coping. Coping strategies that are more cognitively oriented, such as problem-solving and assertiveness, are developed in adolescence. The adolescent who comes to rely on substances to anesthetize stress will not learn much about these more sophisticated ways of coping. They will depend more and more on chemicals, instead of on their brains, to get them through tough times.

One of the leading causes of relapse in recovering persons is stress that is inadequately managed.[5] It becomes essential in treatment, therefore, to help the recovering adolescent build a repertoire of coping skills, ranging from learning to seek and use social support and comfort, to discovering and cultivating spirituality, to using cognitive strategies like problem-solving, to being more (and more appropriately) assertive.

INTELLECTUAL DEVELOPMENT

That substance abuse leads to impaired intellectual and academic development goes without saying. Declining school performance is frequently a key indicator of progression from social to habitual substance use. A significant proportion of substance-abusing adolescents, however, had learning problems prior to their abuse. Not uncommon is a history of attention deficit and hyperactivity disorder or generic learning disabilities. Damaged self-esteem may be the operative factor here in inviting compensatory substance use.

Substance abuse appears to impair the individual's ability to learn. It undermines the capacity to concentrate, as well to retain information. Therefore, any treatment approach must account for the individual's educational needs, and either provide for or at least monitor that dimension of recovery.

SELF-ESTEEM

Adolescents are nothing if not self-conscious. The reader who recalls his or her own adolescence will certainly remember the keen, almost painful self-awareness of those years. Emotions ran high — or low — depending largely on how you felt you looked that day and whether you felt accepted or rejected by your peers. Despite the fact that adolescent styles and fads can exert such a powerful influence that a group of adolescents can appear to be in uniform, beneath the surface every adolescent is striving to define him or herself as an individual as much as he or she is striving to find a niche in society.

Self-esteem is a multidetermined part of the ego. The central dymanic in its development — mastery — has already been discussed.

Self-esteem rises and falls, becomes stable or labile, as a function of success versus failure in a range of situations: physical, social, and intellectual. It also depends on acceptance (versus rejection), first by parents and later by peers. Achievement, skill, and interpersonal attractiveness, therefore, become increasingly important bases for self-esteem during adolescence and young adulthood. The peer group is the arena for this. Being stigmatized, ostracized, or ridiculed by peers during these years has severe damaging effects on self-esteem. These youths are often depressed and unconsolable; they may be self-destructive. Understanding and overcoming these rejections may be the key to recovery for some young people. Not surprisingly, low self-esteem that leads to a self-fulfilling prophecy of peer rejection is often rooted in parental rejection, neglect, or abuse.

Substance abuse also damages what for most adolescents is an already sensitive and fragile body image. Adolescents harbor many naive and misguided ideas about the physical effects of substance abuse, for example on fertility. Almost all of them feel guilty on some level about their abuse, and many may be ashamed of their substance-related behavior. Anonymous sexuality and prostitution, lying, and stealing are some of the things that substance abuse can lead to. Part of the recovery process, for adolescents as well as for adults, involves coming to terms with one's irresponsible, illegal, or immoral behaviors, and the shame, guilt, and damage to self-esteem that they create.

SUMMARY

Habitual substance abuse in adolescents leads to arrested development in many areas. The effects of substance abuse in these formative years are pervasive. Depending on when their substance abuse began, adults in recovery may still manifest some aspects of arrested development; however, whereas the adult is likely to recover former abilities in recovery, the recovering adolescent faces many unmet developmental tasks. Treatment for the adolescent, then, is more a matter of "habilitation" and growth than of rehabilitation. As much as possible, treatment should aim not only to sustain abstinence from substance use but also to remediate developmental deficits. It needs to provide the kind of structure that can effectively replace impaired ego development and lack of self-control; in short, it must provide opportunities for accelerated developmental growth.

4

The Addiction Process

The common denominators among adolescents who abuse substances are low self-esteem and poor ego development. Whether their substance use had its roots in simple curiosity or in desperation, regardless of whether it started out as pleasure-seeking or as a means of blotting out grief, depression, or some other negative emotion, all substance-abusing youths in the end suffer from diminished self-esteem and impaired self-control. These are young men and women who are impulsive, alienated, and filled with self-hatred.

Addicted adolescents are a mass of contradictions. Though they may appear from the outside to be almost intolerably self-centered, privately these young men and women hate themselves. They crave attention and acceptance, yet typically they alienate all but those who are most like themselves. They may wear their arrogance on their sleeves and regard themselves as immortal and omnipotent; yet they cannot control even the simplest of impulses. Adolescent substance abusers are a caricature of adolescence itself. Even more than their peers, they lack a future perspective, cannot delay gratification, possess little willpower, and are vulnerable to peer pressure. To help them, it is necessary first to understand how they became this way.

This chapter presents a model for understanding the process of addiction on a psychodynamic level. Addiction is an insidious, progressive process that typically begins with experimental or social use, which is virtually normal within the adolescent subculture, as it is within the larger adult culture. The next step is when the teenager begins to use substances purposefully to manipulate his or her emotions: to seek out specific emotional or behavioral effects associated with chemical use. This is "instrumental" use, and it can in time become habitual use. At this point substance use starts to become the focus of the adolescent's lifestyle. Former interests drop away, new friends replace old ones, and life gradually "accommodates" to the mechanics of use—to obtaining and using mood-altering chemicals. In the final stages of addiction substance use is a compulsive act, needed in order to induce a subjective state of normality. Accommodation is complete, to the extent that the addict's life is controlled by mood-altering chemicals. He or she must use in order to ward off the dysphoria of withdrawal. Understanding the dynamics of these various stages in the addiction process is useful in diagnosis and treatment planning.

For purposes of discussion the process of addiction can be usefully divided into five stages: experimental use, social use, instrumental use, habitual use, and compulsive use. Let's examine each of these stages in terms of what is happening inside the adolescent. In the next chapter we will focus more on the overt: on what is showing up in terms of behavior and symptoms at each of these stages of use. As we do this, it's important to keep in mind that while these stages of use are qualitatively different, the borders that separate them are not sharply defined. Essentially, it is continued use that causes the adolescent to gradually deepen his or her level of involvement and become entangled in the cycle that ends in addiction.

THE EXPERIMENTAL STAGE

The primary motives for experimental use of substances are curiosity and risk-taking, both of which adolescents possess in abundance. At times, peer pressure plays a role in experimental use. Adolescents have their own rites of passage, most of which have as their theme the defiance of some parental restriction or limit. So, teenagers will smoke cigarettes, buy pornography, dive into ponds from overhanging cliffs, wear outrageous clothing, drive cars too fast, have sex when they're not supposed to, etc. Psychodynamically, experimental substance use fits in here.

Experimental substance use can be identified by the fact that the emotional impact of use—the mood-altering effects of the chemical—are secondary to the adventure itself that use involves. When asked how the substance made them feel, experimental users may not be able to recall very well; on the other hand, they may recall vividly the thrill associated with the experience. At this stage, frequency of use is occasional at best, but use may occur alone as well as in a social context.

In societies like ours where mood-altering substances are prevalent, experimental substance use is virtually a norm among adolescents. It can place adolescents at risk, however, if they are exposed to adult models who use substances regularly on any of the other levels described here, or if they discover, through experimental use, an emotional effect that they later pursue.

THE SOCIAL STAGE

The context of substance use at this level is strictly social. This is drinking and drugging that may take place at parties or in parking lots, but which is invariably a social event. Curiosity, thrill-seeking, and defiance may all play a motivational role in social use, depending on the adolescent and the peer group; but the primary motivation is social acceptance.

The peer group facilitates social use. Liquor, marijuana, cocaine, etc., are typically shared freely or else sold to friends at cost (as opposed to being sold for profit). Adolescents and young adults often use mood-altering chemicals simply to fit in with the crowd. Adult motives for social use of substances are not much different. When was the last time you attended a party where not even alcohol was available? Have you ever felt uncomfortable not drinking when everyone around you was?

Not only is social use of substances facilitated by the peer group, but substance use in turn serves as a social facilitator. This marks the adolescent's introduction to instrumental substance use. Adolescents are not much different from adults in this respect either; they too use substances to "loosen up" in social situations where they might otherwise feel tense or to disinhibit behavior that they would normally suppress. It is not only socially accepted but actively promoted.

What many adults don't realize is that what constitutes "social" drinking and drug use within the adolescent subculture is nothing like "social" drinking or drug use among adults. Today's adolescent subculture exists almost entirely apart from (and unsupervised by) the adult culture. As a result largely of adolescent immaturity, norms in the adolescent subculture tend to be little more than caricatures of adult norms; in other words, adult norms taken to excess. Therefore, whereas it would be unusual, at an adult party, to find people drinking beer by the pitcher instead of the glass, mixing drinks randomly, or playing "drinking games," this is not uncommon at high school and college parties. Whereas adult drinkers tend to develop tastes that they stick to, adolescents and young adults will often drink or use almost anything that's available. If an adult were to do that, you might suspect addiction; if an adolescent does it, it may be "normal," i.e., not clinically significant. By the same token, if you were to learn that a middle-aged neighbor went to two parties last month, and got sick each time as a result of alcohol and marijuana use, with a terrible hangover the next day, you might be inclined to think this person had a problem. But what if it's a high school senior or a college sophomore? The fact is that this kind of using is not uncommon within that subculture.

It's in the social stage that the young person first gets in touch with the emotional and behavioral impact that substances can have. This sets the stage for the next level of involvement. They experience a mood swing, or a behavioral effect, and then return to normal. Subjectively—and this is very important—they feel normal ("like themselves") after use, except perhaps for the occasional hangover. Since they remain functional, this level of use is rarely if ever identified as risky by adolescents or even by adults. Warnings or cautions are typically ignored. The ubiquitous defense of denial enables teens and young adults to dismiss negative consequences associated with substance abuse, even while friends are admitted to rehabilitation centers or die in car accidents. Many parents still don't associate social use with danger, except perhaps as it may relate to driving. Social use is protected by the adolescent code of secrecy, and to a large extent it is enabled by adults who regard it as normal and acceptable. No one believes that the most negative of consequences will happen to them.

THE INSTRUMENTAL STAGE

In the instrumental stage, the adolescent learns, through a combination of trial-and-error experience and modeling, to use substances purposefully to manipulate emotions and behavior. He or she discovers that alcohol and drugs can affect both feelings and actions. The teenager gets acquainted with the mood swings that alcohol and drugs can produce, as well as the behaviors they can influence, and begins to use substances purposefully to suppress feelings or enhance them, to inhibit behavior or disinhibit it.

The key word at the instrumental stage of use is "seeking": the young person has moved beyond social use—where the primary motivation is peer acceptance, and where the context for use is social—to the point where he or she actively seeks out the specific emotional and/or behavioral effects of drugs. Social use sets the stage for instrumental use, providing the trial and error experience that leads to seeking. The two types of instrumental substance use are hedonistic use and compensatory use. They reflect somewhat different motivations.

Hedonistic Use

The main reasons that adolescents give for initiating drug use are curiosity and pleasure-seeking. Teenagers do lots of things out of curiosity, including risky things that most adults would think at least twice about. Adolescents are also hedonistic. They like to have fun, even if that, too, is risky at times.

Hedonistic use of mood-altering chemicals is just that: pleasure-seeking. It is characterized by experimentation and bingeing. It is substance use that typically begins in a social context, but which progresses to private as well as social use. It is motivated by the desire to get high, to disinhibit behavior (for example, sexual behavior), or both.

At the instrumental level the adolescent may experiment in an effort to discover how a variety of substances affect moods and behaviors. The difference between this and simple experimentation, however, is the objective. In simple experimentation, the goal is to satisfy curiosity; it is driven by the urge to take risks, period. At the hedonistic stage, in contrast, experimentation is directed; it is seeking behavior that is aimed at discovering new ways of feeling good. Toward this end many substances and combinations of substances may be tried out.

Subjectively, the adolescent is selectively reinforced for instrumental substance use. He or she experiences a mood swing, then returns to normal. If the affective experience is positive, use is reinforced. Typically there are few negative consequences to deal with. Of course, there are those unfortunate ones whose first experience with a substance, such as cocaine, is fatal; and there are those who take LSD once and suffer frightening and unpredictable flashbacks for the rest of their lives.

A very important point, from a psychodynamic perspective, is that at the instrumental stage the adolescent continues to return to a subjective state of normality and relative comfort after getting high. Except for the occasional transient hangover, subjectively there is little or no discomfort or "withdrawal" following use. Instrumental use, in other words, is use that is not yet driven by any discomfort associated with non-use. As substance use deepens, this changes.

Shelley's parents were both hardworking and successful people who'd had little involvement themselves with drugs and who drank only socially. Though they loved their only child a great deal, they'd made the mistake of thinking that they could delegate parental responsibilities to others. So, they paid for therapists, paid for a year of treatment at a "motivational institute," even paid for an expensive private school, all to no avail. Growing up essentially unsupervised, Shelley became willful. Her will, however, lacked the tempering influence of self-control, so she was impulsive and moody. Despite her airs of indifference and independence, she was deeply insecure and easily influenced by peer pressure.

When I met her I was struck by how socially smooth Shelley was. Her personality had a veneer of maturity that thinly masked her true immaturity. She'd exercised poor judgement in getting recklessly involved with cocaine, and, at 16, was showing signs of chemical dependency. She craved the drug at times, had dreams about it, felt irritable when she couldn't get it, and slipped into depressions that she couldn't account for. Her father had noticed that her already poor attitude about school, as well as her outbursts at home, had gotten decidedly worse over the past year.

When I asked her father to join us, Shelley's demeanor changed instantly. The smoothness disappeared and she became testy and oppositional, challenging whatever her father said either verbally or through her expression. He talked about how her peer group had changed recently, and how much he and his wife disliked the new friends that Shelley had made; she made faces. They didn't like her sleeping out as often as she did, he said, or disregarding even the liberal house rules they'd established; she groaned loudly and rolled her eyes.

Shelley's involvement with drugs had begun to cross the border separating hedonistic from compensatory use, which will be discussed shortly. The distinction is mainly useful as a heuristic device. It does not define mutually exclusive categories of drug users; on the other hand, it is useful in treatment planning.

Shelley's cocaine use began largely out of a desire to have fun. Her immaturity—the result largely of a lack of limits—enabled it to move quickly to the habitual level. She liked having fun, was impulsive and reckless; when she discovered that cocaine made her feel good—very good—she dove into it with her usual abandon. As she used cocaine more she gravitated toward a group of peers who partied often, and who also liked the drug. It was only after she was already experiencing significant signs of addiction, however, that Shelley could admit she might have a problem, and then only reluctantly. In treatment she was difficult. She resisted following rules, and it quickly became apparent that she was dependent on external forces—rewards and consequences—for whatever "self-control" she had. After six weeks of inpatient treatment she still had not progressed to the point where her behavior was motivated in any way out of an appreciation for the greater good of the group, much less on the basis of healthy personal values. Accordingly, she was referred to long-term residential care.

In the instrumental stage, intoxication and other mood-altering (and behavioral) effects are actively sought out. Parents and teachers may begin to notice some behavioral and personality changes at this point: Grades may become somewhat erratic, absences may increase, and motivation for school (and other activities) may decrease. Often, conflict with parents and siblings intensifies. There may be resistance to house rules and rebellion against parental and school limits. Parents frequently are confused about the meaning of these changes: Do they point to a problem or are they "normal" adolescent difficulties? As a rule of thumb, adolescents can be expected to get along reasonably well with their parents, teachers, and siblings, most of the time. They can also be expected to participate in the family and to live up to their potential in school. They can be expected to be active and happy, most of the time. The more consistently that they are not this way, the more likely it is that there is some problem, perhaps involving substance abuse. In Shelley's case, her underachievement and moodiness when she first started using drugs heavily were in and of themselves nothing new, though her father had noticed that both were more extreme than they had been in the past.

Compensatory Use

The second type of instrumental substance use is called "compensatory," meaning that it is the intentional use of mood-altering chemicals as a means of coping with stress and uncomfortable feelings. The goal is the suppression of emotion: anger, anxiety, shame, guilt, loneliness, sadness, boredom, etc. Even adolescents who do not start off using substances as a means of coping with negative emotions eventually discover this use for mood-altering chemicals. What starts out as fun and social evolves into a means of coping: of getting through a bad day, of forgetting an argument with a girlfriend or boyfriend, of relieving boredom or reducing stress. In other cases, substance use begins as a compensation.

Harry came in wearing a black leather jacket, a black leather "rebel" hat cocked down over one eye, and tattered jeans. The back of his jacket was emblazoned with emblems of heavy metal rock groups and symbols of drug glorification. Looking at him you would have thought he'd be in deep; in truth he was only in the early stages of use that was primarily compensatory in nature.

Harry's parents had divorced when he was 10: he was now 15. His father, still an active drug addict, wanted to get back together with his ex-wife and, as he put it, "reunite the family." To do this he enlisted his son's help in two ways: First, he swore Harry to secrecy about his ongoing drug use; second, he asked Harry to help him obtain heroin and cocaine and to shoot up.

Harry, caught hopelessly in a web of divided loyalties, tried his best to handle a situation over which he had no control. With his face lined deeply with stress, and his eyes revealing an almost desperate pain, he told me about how he'd made drug runs for his dad, about how he would help him fill the syringe (because he was shaking too much to do it himself), and how once he'd even pushed the plunger down after his father had finally struck a vein. He didn't feel he could tell anyone about this, least of all his mother.

Harry was paying an incredible emotional price for his efforts to be loyal to his father. He was clearly depressed, and at one point confided that he occasionally thought about suicide. Twice, he said, he'd sat alone in his room, late at night, making shallow cuts in his wrist with a pocket knife. He showed me the scratches.

Remarkably, despite his stress Harry's involvement with drugs had not yet become habitual. He did use, however, and the motivation for his use was clearly compensatory: He drank and smoked marijuana in order to relieve his anxiety, guilt, and desperation. In his own words, he used so that he could "stop thinking and feeling."

I felt certain that without intervention Harry would end up being either an addict or a suicide statistic. Mercifully, he'd managed (so far) to stay away from his father's drugs of choice, but he was getting stoned several times a week; when he drank, it worsened the very depression he sought to relieve. Treatment, I knew, would mean helping him get disentangled from his parents' relationship, separate himself from his father without guilt, and find better ways of coping.

Compensatory use is functionally different from hedonistic use, but outwardly the adolescent may look the same. One sometimes has to look closely to see the emotion that is being dealt with through compensatory substance abuse; at other times, as in Harry's case, it's painfully obvious. It may be anger or depression, brooding resentment or chronic anxiety, boredom or guilt. Once substance abuse is stopped, these emotions quickly emerge, and if unchecked can drive the individual back toward use.

As is so often the case, it is only when negative consequences have accrued that substance abuse is typically suspected at all. While few adolescents are either purely one or the other — hedonistic or compensatory users — clinically it is important to identify primary motivations for substance use and to differentiate primarily hedonistic from primarily compensatory use. The adolescent who is using mood-altering substances substantially as a means of coping must be taught coping skills in addition to recovery skills. The adolescent whose use is primarily hedonistic must learn alternative ways of experiencing pleasure and satisfaction.

THE HABITUAL STAGE

Habitual substance use differs from instrumental use not just in frequency of use but in its underlying motivation, for it is in the habitual phase that symptoms of dependency start to appear. Habitual use marks the boundary separating purposeful use from compulsive use; it is the gray area in which the battle for control is fought, and where chemicals begin running the individual's life. Whereas the key word in the instrumental stage is seeking, here it is "accommodation": The abuser's lifestyle becomes progressively centered around using as a means of coping and recreating; meanwhile, former relationships, interests, and activities gradually fall by the wayside.

When substance use becomes habitual, "peer group drift" occurs. Old friendships fall away and are gradually replaced by new ones—with people who are heavier users. Clothing, language, interests, and attitudes also change, so as to conform with the new peer group.

In the examples given earlier, Harry's drug use began as compensatory; Shelley's, on the other hand, had started out as hedonistic. As her cocaine cravings became more severe, however, and as withdrawal symptoms (agitation, depression, paranoia) worsened, she began using alcohol and marijuana to help relieve her discomfort. This kind of substance use is called "medicinal." Even addicts whose use starts out as purely hedonistic will eventually be driven to medicinal use if their use becomes habitual. This is because habitual users, unlike instrumental users, gradually find that their emotional state does not return completely to normal anymore after using, even after the hangover passes. Instead, their emotional state, once they are no longer high, settles at a level that is something less than normal. They may feel irritable, restless, or mildly depressed. They may find it difficult to concentrate, sit still, or sleep soundly. It is these withdrawal symptoms that motivate them to use medicinally. They will either use more of the substances they are already becoming addicted to or else try to compensate for the discomfort with some other substance.

As adolescents progress from instrumental use of substances to the deeper stage of habitual use, they begin to use substances on a more and more regular basis, often daily. Subjectively, many begin to sense their impending dependency and react to it by establishing various self-imposed "rules" or "limits." They will, for example, determine not to use certain drugs except on weekends, only so much of a substance, or only some substances and not others. They may decide to not use certain combinations of substances or to avoid using in some situations. Then, they begin breaking their own rules: They get high before school, not just after school; they use cocaine after deciding to use only marijuana; they use freebase after deciding to use only powder; they get drunk and black out after deciding to have no more than two beers. This is the internal struggle for control that ends in addiction. As the battle is lost, adolescents begin to justify their use or to minimize it: They "decide" to break their former rules or compare themselves to peers who are even heavier users. Habitual users sometimes convince themselves that substance use makes them happier, helps them cope better, or enables them to perform better in some situation.

Subjectively, habitual users begin to crave their drug(s) of choice and to become preoccupied with getting high. They think about using more or less all the time: while they're in school, while they're playing basketball, while they're at the movies with friends. They find it hard to think or talk about much else. Aside from spending a great deal of time getting high, they start taking pleasure in sharing "war stories" about their adventures and exploits while stoned or high. They get irritable and out of sorts when deprived of their substances, and don't enjoy being places or doing things that don't involve substance use in some way. This is what is meant by the term "accommodation." The habitual user's lifestyle becomes more and more centered around use.

Habitual users can usually be easily identified, being known within the larger adolescent community by such nicknames as "burnouts" or "deadheads." This is the group whose main form of recreation and socializing is getting high—whose primary "relationships" are with chemicals.

Two events occur during the habitual stage that drive the user toward addiction. The first is the fact that the user no longer returns to a subjective feeling of normality after substance use. The mood swing, in other words, has started to change. It no longer swings back to normal but stops someplace short of normal. This leads to cravings and symptoms such as anxiety, depression, or irritability, which pushes the user toward further use or toward medicinal use of other substances.

The second event is "tolerance." This refers to the fact that the effects of mood-altering chemicals gradually diminish the more they are used. This is sometimes referred to as "habituation." Habitual substance users find, over time, that they just don't get as high on a couple of lines of cocaine, on a couple of joints, or on a couple of drinks, as they once did. This motivates them to use more of the same substance, a stronger form of the same substance, or new substances in order to get high. This is tolerance, and it is one prime symptom of addiction.

THE COMPULSIVE STAGE

In this final stage, substance use is a compulsive behavior. Accommodation to use is now complete and total. The addict is preoccupied with use, to the extent that getting high (or planning for it) is literally all that he or she thinks about and does. The attention span for anything else is limited or nonexistent. School, work, hobbies and interests all take a back seat to substance use. Relationships — with parents, friends, boyfriends and girlfriends — become stressed to the breaking point as a result of neglect, manipulation, or both, and either end or settle into alienation. The only "relationship" the addict has is with his or her drug(s) of choice.

Compulsive substance use is use that is totally out of control: The battle has been lost. Yet the addict may still not accept it. Instead of being humbled by defeat, he or she may flee into arrogance and grandiosity. In truth, chemicals are now running his or her life, and any defense is born of desperation.

Subjectively, the problems that develop in the habitual stage worsen. Tolerance grows worse; meanwhile, the mood swing once associated with substance use has been replaced with a state of chronic anhedonia. That is what makes use compulsive: The addict feels bad when he or she isn't high and is driven to use by that nagging discomfort. Substance use is now necessary in order to achieve a subjective feeling that's anything close to normality, and even that falls short.

At the compulsive stage preoccupation is so extreme that the adolescent will hide his or her supply of drugs, even from so-called "friends". The idea of running out is so aversive that the individual will go to great lengths to maintain his or her sources and secure their supplies. Girls will become the girlfriends of dealers in order to secure their supply; boys and girls alike may begin dealing, not just to make money but to guarantee their own supply.

Even during this final stage, and despite their total defeat, addicts may make occasional efforts to control their use. Each progressive failure, of course, only makes self-esteem that much worse. At some point defenses may break down. When this happens the addict is

overwhelmed with shame and hopelessness, and may become suicidal. Few addicts, in fact, have not contemplated suicide, and many
have acted on these thoughts in one way or another.

The victim of addiction is not only obsessed but is obsessively self-
centered. This is one of the more noticeable personality changes
associated with addiction. Parents readily acknowledge that the child
they now live with is not the same child they used to know. Friends
will say much the same thing and often are angry at the addict as a
result of being lied to or used. The addict, meanwhile, is alternately
depressed and aggressive, irritable and apathetic.

The arrogance of addicts — adult or adolescent — represents an unconscious defense against the loss of control they are experiencing
over drugs. They are desperate, but all they reveal is rebellious indifference. In compensation for being unable to control their use, they
may become very controlling over others, very demanding, exceed-
ingly defensive, and blaming. This is the point at which they most
often enter treatment. The clinician needs to be prepared for it.

SUMMARY

Once an adolescent has progressed to habitual use of mood-altering substances the clinical picture is largely the same, regardless of
the initial or underlying motivation for substance use. Determination
of the relative contributions of hedonistic pleasure-seeking versus
compensatory coping as primary motivations at the instrumental
level of use is significant for treatment planning. Initially, however,
treatment goals are similar for all habitual users, and clinically they
look pretty much alike. All have experienced developmental deficits
as a consequence of their chemical use, and all have to start at the
same point in the recovery process. Differences among addicts typically become apparent only after sobriety has been achieved and
recovery has begun. These differences can be important, but they
should not be the focus of early treatment.

5

Diagnosis of Adolescent Substance Abuse

How can a clinician differentiate substance abuse from addiction, or substance use that constitutes abuse from "normal" adolescent experimentation? What are the key signs and symptoms, and how does one identify them? Obviously, the solution would be simple if we could just ask the young person and expect to get straightforward answers. However, this is unlikely. The diagnosis of serious substance abuse or of chemical dependency is based on signs and symptoms and is arrived at indirectly based on responses to factual questioning. To accomplish this, diagnostic interviewing for adolescent substance abuse must be carefully structured and skillfully conducted.

The goal of the diagnostic interview is to determine the level at which substance abuse is occurring: experimental, social, instrumental, habitual, or compulsive. Signs and symptoms of dependency should correlate with the level of chemical use. For example, if there is evidence of preoccupation with use, then responses suggesting that use is limited to the social stage would be called into question. Based on information obtained from the diagnostic interview and supplemented by information from collateral sources (teachers, parents, etc.), a diagnosis and initial treatment plan are generated.

Tom was brought in for an evaluation after he was suspended from school when two teachers smelled alcohol on his breath. All of Tom's teachers had noticed a progressive deterioration in his appearance, as well as personality changes, over the past several months. A junior, he'd started the school year getting his typical B's and an occasional C; lately, however, he'd been failing almost every subject. His absentee rate was not exceptionally high, but he was often late and was suspected of sneaking off grounds during study periods. At home,

51

where he lived with his divorced mother and younger sister, he'd become more and more aggressive, uncooperative, and rebellious. Though he'd never been a model child, his mother complained that she'd never had so much difficulty with Tom as she was having now. His sister, she said, positively hated him and accused him of stealing from her. When confronted about his behavior, from his disregard of house rules to his poor grades, Tom would either curse his mother or walk out of the house. Once or twice she feared he might hit her or his sister.

At first his mother attributed her problems with Tom to her divorce. Her ex-husband, she said, was an active alcoholic. Three times she had separated from him, until, finally, she decided to divorce; three times, therefore, the children had suffered through the pain of separation. Though neither child had had what she would consider to be a good relationship with their father—he was alternately abusive and neglectful—she assumed that Tom in particular must be experiencing some reaction to losing his Dad, even though the two had seen each other only a couple of times in the last year.

Tom's mother knew that her son drank, and she suspected that he smoked pot too; but she assumed that he did this only at parties with friends. She'd spoken to him about it and voiced her disapproval; however, since she'd never gotten very far with Tom's father on this issue, she didn't pursue it with much conviction with her son. She just hoped the divorce would help matters.

Tom, I learned during our interview, had recently been arrested for shoplifting. He admitted to me that his sister was right: He had stolen from her, and from his mother too. He was failing all but one class in school and was planning on dropping out. His substance use, which had started out with alcohol and marijuana, had progressed to cocaine. Recently he'd tried freebasing. The day he was caught drunk in school he was also stoned on marijuana. He was using both of these substances to cut down on the discomfort he felt after using crack.

Tom said he hadn't ever tried to stop using cocaine; therefore, he didn't know if he could. When I pressed him on it, he reluctantly admitted that he probably couldn't stop, even if he wanted to. He had few signs of tolerance to alcohol or pot, but clear signs of tolerance to cocaine. Moreover, he was using some mood-altering chemical virtually every day, at all times of the day. By his own admission he would use as much cocaine as he could get his hands on. When he freebased he experienced headaches, as well as rapid heartbeat, profuse sweating, and chest tightness. Afterwards, he was very irritable.

My diagnosis in Tom's case was cocaine addiction, combined with habitual alcohol and marijuana abuse. Because he was out of control (addicted), I told Tom that he would need intensive impatient treatment initially, followed by either intensive outpatient treatment or extended residential care, depending on how he did in primary treatment.

In diagnosing compulsive substance use (addiction), the clinician must look for evidence in three areas: tolerance, loss of control, and continued use despite clearcut negative consequences related to use. With adolescents, inpatient treatment is generally indicated whenever use has become habitual, not just when it is truly compulsive, and some intervention is indicated even when use has become instrumental.

THE DIAGNOSTIC INTERVIEW

Introductions

It is easy to overlook the importance of correctly opening a diagnostic interview or, for that matter, the importance of how one meets any new client for the first time. With adolescents, the issue of "who is the client" needs thought. Is it the teenager? Is it the parents? Is the court or the school the "client"? Is it somehow the whole family that is the "client"?

In some ways the therapist serves all of these interests, but he or she must clearly serve one of them first. This does not mean that the therapist working with an adolescent cannot do family therapy; on the other hand, the therapist must be prepared for the possibility that the "best interests" of each party may be different. The family, for example, may or may not be a "therapeutic" environment for the recovering teen. At other times it makes a great deal of sense to treat the entire family as the client, as when dealing, for instance, with enabling and codependence, which will be discussed later. When interests become blatantly incompatible, however, the parents or family may need a separate therapist.

To emphasize the fact that the adolescent is the primary client, it is advisable to meet with him or her individually first. Always begin the interview with the appropriate introductions. In the waiting room I like to introduce myself to the adolescent or young adult first, and then ask him or her to introduce me to any other family members present. I then ask the adolescent to join me in my office, explaining to family members that I will see them later.

Getting some basic information—names, ages, occupations, etc. of all family members—is a good icebreaker. Get this information down on paper, for ready reference when meeting later on with the family. The first substantive discussion to take place concerns confidentiality: who can have access to what kind of information the adolescent shares, and under what conditions. Information relative to substance use that is communicated in the context of treatment for substance abuse is privileged, even if that information is communicated by a minor. Stating this fact clearly from the outset (and explaining that it will be related to the parents as well) can facilitate disclosure during the diagnostic interview. If the interview is being conducted for a specific purpose—to advise a court regarding treatment, for instance—this purpose needs to be stated, along with exactly what information will and will not be subject to disclosure. Finally, procedures for release of information should be briefly reviewed. Taking the time to go over these ground rules will facilitate open communication and avoid potential complications later on. Most importantly, it communicates something to the teenager: that you intend to deal with him or her straightforwardly and with respect.

It is important to verify with the teenager that he or she knows why the interview is taking place, which is to help assess an alcohol or drug problem and make recommendations regarding treatment. Don't assume that this has been communicated. Occasionally a parent, or even a referring professional, may not have made this clear. If that's the case, explain the purpose of the interview and who will know the results.

When interviewing an adolescent for the first time, it is also important to have, in advance, some information about the circumstances surrounding the referral. Negative consequences that may be related to substance use—problems in school or with the law—should be noted. This information can usually be obtained from a parent, a school psychologist or social worker, or another adult in supervisory role relative to the youth, such as a referring probation officer. Finally, when interviewing for substance abuse, assume that the adolescent is actively using mood-altering chemicals on some level, has at least experimented with others, and will understandably be motivated to understate his or her level of involvement with chemicals.

The Presenting Problem

Following introductions and ground rules, begin the diagnostic interview proper, starting with the adolescent's own account of the circumstances that led up to the interview. It's helpful to open this discussion with a general question, something like: "Why don't you tell me about what's happened, and why you're here today?"

The tone of this kind of question clearly assumes that a problem exists. The therapist is better off being direct (and presumptive) about this than being too indirect, thereby coming across as naive and gullible. If the adolescent plays coy, prompt him or her by mentioning something you already know from your other sources, then say that you'd like to hear about this in his or her own words.

Questioning the adolescent about the circumstances surrounding the assessment will provide some initial insights into denial versus acceptance of a substance abuse problem, as well as openness to treatment.

Family Constellation

After getting some information about the presenting problem, the next step is to describe the family constellation. Genograms are convenient for this. In the genogram presented in Figure 1, generations move from past (top) to present (bottom).

The top line in this diagram represents the grandparents of the adolescent (JOSEPH) being assessed. The second line represents Joseph's parents and their siblings (i.e., Joseph's aunts and uncles), and the bottom line lists Joseph and his siblings. It is not important at this point if Joseph does not recall all of this information; what is important is to get down as much of it as he is aware of. Figure 1 represents the most basic of genograms; however, even at this level it can help to "orient" the clinician in an intergenerational sense.

Once the basic genogram or family tree is outlined, begin elaborating on it by following up with questions about parent-child relationships and sibling relationships, including the young person's percep-

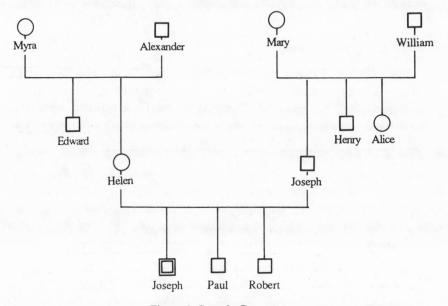

Figure 1. Sample Genogram

tion of his or her parents' relationship. If the parents are divorced, perceptions about what their relationship was like before the divorce are useful. Clinically, what is most important at this point is not whether all of these data are absolutely accurate, but whether the adolescent believes them to be true. Uncovering issues such as abuse or neglect, at this early point, will be important when it comes to making treatment recommendations later on. Useful questions to ask at this point are:

- How do you get along with your parents?
- Which parent do you have the most conflict with? What do you fight over?
- How do your parents reward you? How do they punish you?
- If your parents are separated or divorced, do you have regular contact with the one you don't live with? How do you get along with that parent?

- How do your parents get along with each other? What kinds of things do they disagree or fight over?
- How often does your mother (father) drink? How often have you seen them drunk?
- Have you ever drank with your father (mother)?
- What other chemicals (substances) does your father (mother) use? Do they smoke pot? Use cocaine? How often?
- Do either of your parents use medicine for stress or "nerves"? How often? Have you ever tried their medication?
- Does anyone in your family have a drinking or a drug problem? Who? Have they ever gotten treatment for it? How are they doing now?
- What kinds of drugs do your siblings use?
- Have you ever gotten drunk or high with your brother (sister)?
- Have you ever sold drugs, or has someone in your family sold drugs?

The Chemical History

The next step in the diagnostic assessment is to get an initial chemical history from the adolescent. While this information should be supplemented during the family assessment with data obtained from parents, it is important to get it directly from the adolescent at first. When gathering these data, always give the adolescent the opportunity to volunteer more information. Don't move too quickly from question to question. Leave pauses in the conversation, and maintain good eye contact.

The goal in the chemical history is to ascertain the kinds of substances the adolescent has used. Table 3, or one similar to it, can be used for this purpose. A place has been left at the top of Table 3 to indicate those substances that the adolescent has not used. These should be listed to verify that they have been asked about, and that the adolescent has specifically denied any use at all. Don't assume, in other words, that an adolescent has not used a substance unless you specifically ask about it. In general, adolescents who admit to using substances farther down in this scale will also have used all those substances higher up on it. For example, if the clinician knows in advance that there has been some cocaine use, it's best to assume that there has also been some use of alcohol, marijuana, etc. There are

Table 3: Form for Recording Use

SUBSTANCE	FIRST USE	LAST USE	12-MONTH USE	CURRENT USE
Non-Use				
DEPRESSANTS				
Alcohol				
Inhalants				
Barbiturates				
HALLUCINOGENS				
Marijuana				
LSD				
Mushrooms				
PCP				
STIMULANTS				
Amphetamines				
Cocaine (powder)				
(crack/freebase)				
Other				

exceptions to this pattern of progression, but they should be confirmed through questioning.

It is important to get all of the above information for each substance. This part of the interview can be started with a comment like, "I need to get some information on all of the different kinds of substances you've used, even if you've only used them only once or twice."

The first column to be completed is the one in which the adolescent tells you when (at what age) he or she first used a substance. Start with alcohol and work your way down the list. This will help you to determine the breadth of substance use. Keep in mind that most adolescent and young adult substance abusers are poly-substance abusers. It will be the unusual client who will be abusing only a single substance.

The next question is the last time the adolescent used each substance. He or she may have used marijuana and cocaine two days ago, had some drinks a week or two ago, and used LSD only twice, the last time a year ago. This is a typical pattern for an adolescent who has progressed from alcohol to cocaine use.

Twelve-month use, meaning the total number of times the adolescent has used each substance in the last year, is useful in discriminating social from instrumental and habitual use. It's important to give the adolescent time to think about this. Exact numbers are somewhat less important than the pattern than those numbers reveal.

Finally, current use needs to be estimated. Typically, this can be done in terms of how many times per week, or per month, the substance is now being used. Again, allow enough time for the teenager to think it through. Look for a pattern of increased use of a substance following an attempt to decrease use of another ("substance substitution").

After completing this chart, take a few minutes to reflect it back to the adolescent. Summarize his or her own chemical history, beginning with when it started, what substances it started with, how it progressed, and where it is now. Finish with a summary of the teen's current "substances of choice." Finally, solicit additional information. Ask the adolescent directly if there's anything you've missed or anything that needs to be corrected. Do not, however, argue with the adolescent about his or her responses or accuse him or her of lying, even if you believe this to be true. At this point it's best not to offer any opinion regarding addiction, as it may contaminate the next part of the interview.

Level of Use

Once the chemical history has been obtained, it is necessary to estimate where the adolescent is on the addiction continuum for each substance he or she is currently using. This dimension is as follows:

Non-use (abstinence)
↓
Experimental use
↓
Social use
↓
Instrumental use
↓
Habitual use
↓
Compulsive use

Each of these phases is associated with certain signs and symptoms.

EXPERIMENTAL USE

Motivated primarily by curiosity or thrill-seeking (and sometimes rebelliousness), the actual mood-altering effects of substances are less important than the thrill that's associated with the taboo act. Use may occur alone, but more typically it takes place in a social context. Use is infrequent, may be impulsive, and may involve bingeing as well as poly-substance use.

SOCIAL USE

Primary motivations are social acceptance and social facilitation ("fitting in"). Relaxation and disinhibition are the main mood-altering effects surrounding social use, which occurs in a social context, with small groups of friends or at parties. Bingeing is common and may be intentional: The youth may set out to get drunk, stoned, or high. Blackouts, passing out, and hangovers are common negative consequences associated with social use among youths. In these cases it is usually peer group pressure and peer group norms that are driving the abuse, which is therefore situational. This behavior is common at high school and college parties. Instrumental learning — about the effects of various chemicals on affect and behavior — begins in the context of social use.

INSTRUMENTAL USE

At this level substance use is seeking behavior. What is intentionally pursued are the emotional and/or behavioral effects of alcohol or drugs. Use may take place in social situations or alone. The adolescent is learning, through trial and error experience and modeling, about the effects that substances have on feeling states and behaviors.

There are two varieties of instrumental use. The first is pleasure-seeking and disinhibition — in short, hedonistic use. Alcohol, for example, can be used to disinhibit aggressive and sexual behavior. Cocaine and other stimulants lead to powerful feelings of euphoria and self-confidence. Marijuana and other psychedelics alter perception and thinking. Combinations of substances may be experimented with to see what effects they have. The important point to remember is that adolescents whose substance use is mainly hedonistic in nature are intensely interested in discovering new and better ways to feel good or experience something new.

The second type of instrumental use is compensatory, that is, the use of substances to inhibit behavior or suppress emotions. Intense and unrelenting anger, resentment, loneliness, guilt, shame, grief, boredom, or anxiety can all motivate compensatory substance use. The same kinds of substances may be used as for hedonistic reasons; only the motivation is different. However, the emotions that drive compensatory use make it the more common pathway to addiction.

Outward signs of instrumental use are typically minimal. Other than the occasional hangover, accidents, bad trip or blackout, negative consequences may be minimal. Absenteeism may increase slightly, and grades may become slightly erratic. None of these signs, however, is terribly obvious, and parents (and teachers) may therefore never attribute them correctly to substance use.

HABITUAL USE

As substance use becomes chronic, symptoms of chemical dependency gradually appear. Substance use becomes the primary means of recreation, of coping, or both, and the youth's lifestyle changes (accommodates) to use. The peer group changes toward a group that uses more, and more often. The habitual user is frequently high for days or weeks at a time.

Objectively, the habitual user becomes progressively less functional. Grades slide dramatically. Absenteeism and tardiness increase. Conflict with parents and siblings also increases, and the youth withdraws from the family. He or she becomes more rebellious, more irritable and moody, and uncooperative. Parents and teachers usually notice changes and suspect substance use. However, they may still hesitate to act decisively, or may attribute the problem to the wrong cause, such as depression.

It is during habitual use that the symptom of tolerance develops and the first serious negative consequences of substance use typically occur.

Tolerance has already been discussed; it refers to the need to use progressively more of a substance in order to produce the same mood-altering effect. Tolerance to alcohol and marijuana appears to develop relatively slowly, as compared to tolerance to substances like cocaine, especially in its freebase form. Contrary to the belief that adolescents don't abuse long enough to develop tolerance, many do. The prevalence of bingeing among teens and young adults may partly account for the rapid buildup of tolerance in this age group.

When assessing for tolerance, it is important to focus not on how much, in absolute terms, is being consumed, but on the mood-altering effects of use. The clinician needs to determine if the same amount of a substance is producing less of an effect than it used to; if so, then a tolerance has been built.

Since the concept of tolerance itself may be confusing to a teenager, specific rather than abstract questions need to be asked. Questions that can be helpful in determining whether tolerance has developed are:

- Does it take more beers (joints, lines. etc.) to get you high now than it used to?
- How many joints (drinks, etc.) does it take now to get you good and high, as compared to a year ago?
- How much _____ do you use at a time now, versus when you started using it?
- Do you find that you just don't get as high now, as you used to, on one drink (one joint, etc.)?

During the diagnostic interview one should try to determine to which substances tolerance has been developed. If tolerance to any substance can be demonstrated, the adolescent is probably addicted to it.

A second symptom of addiction is continued use of a substance despite *negative consequences* related to use. Being arrested for possession of marijuana, getting suspended from school for being drunk, steadily declining school grades, being arrested for drunk driving, losing a job because of chronic lateness: all of these are examples of negative consequences of substance abuse. When an adolescent continues to use after such consequences have occurred, the clinician should suspect habitual use bordering on addiction. Whenever a list of negative consequences exists, substance abuse should be suspected and investigated as the primary cause of the problem.

Negative consequences can be grouped into five areas: physical, social, legal, academic, and psychological. Some examples of each are listed in Table 4.

Table 4: Common Negative Consequences of Substance Use

Physical Consequences:
  Passing out (with or without injury).
  Blackouts (with or without injury).
  Increasing sickness (flu, colds, etc.).
  Headaches, stomachaches.
  Sweating, rapid pulse, chest tightness or pain associated with use (especially cocaine).

Social Consequences:
  Complaints, jokes, or remarks made by friends about use.
  Conflicts with boyfriend/girlfriend over use.
  Rejection by "social" users (the mainstream peer group).
  Peer group drift: the adolescent socializes almost exclusively with heavy users.

Legal Consequences:
  Arrests for possession, driving while intoxicated, disorderly conduct, etc.
  Probationary status.
  Arrested for stealing, breaking and entering, etc. related to substance use.

Academic Consequences:
  Declining grades.
  Increased absenteeism.
  Dropping out.

Psychological Consequences:
  Aggressiveness (alcohol, stimulants)
  Lethargy (alcohol, marijuana, barbiturates)
  Agitation (cocaine, hallucinogens, stimulants)
  Depression (cocaine, alcohol, marijuana)
  Paranoia (cocaine, marijuana)

COMPULSIVE USE

The border separating habitual use from addiction is not a sharp one. The symptoms of addiction differ from those of habitual use largely in degree. Character and spirituality gradually dissipate in addiction, and the personality changes, yielding to the so-called "addict" personality: grandiose, defensive, self-absorbed, manipulative, and arrogant. There is a steady deterioration in personal appearance, and the list of negative consequences associated with substance use grows longer. Social functionality is minimal, and ostracism from the mainstream peer group is complete.

Subjectively the addict feels bad more or less all the time. A dysphoric emotional state becomes the "norm," pushing the addict toward substance use all the more. In desperation the addict seeks relief through increased use or poly-substance use. Cocaine addicts, for example, often begin using large amounts of marijuana or heroin to ward off withdrawal.

The main symptoms of addiction — of loss of control over use — include preoccupation with use, the inability to stop use, and the increasing use of one substance in response to decreasing use of another. Preoccupation refers to the fact that addicts are literally obsessed with using. They think about little else, talk about little else, and do little besides using. They will do virtually anything to obtain and protect their supply of chemicals. They develop "relationships" with paraphernalia.

The addict cannot stop using his or her drug(s) of choice, and becomes irritable and depressed when deprived of them. Decreased use of a drug of choice is invariably accompanied by increased use of an alternative substance. Rapid use — "chasing the high" — reflects the urgency of the addict's need.

The concept of addiction can be a difficult one for youths to embrace. Like adults, teens associate the word "addict" with skid row bums and broken down alcoholics. On the other hand, they under-stand the idea of loss of control much better. Most adolescents, even when addicted, are blessed with relatively good health. One usually has to look closely to see many negative physical effects — aside from accidents — of substance use in this age group. More obvious, at least with young persons, are the spiritual effects of addiction. There is a sadness, a tiredness, an air of defeat about them. These young people lack the enthusiasm and capacity for fun that healthy youths possess. Of course, inwardly the addict is scared. Nothing is more frightening, after all, than the idea of being out of control of our lives, which is what the addict is. By communicating, directly and nonjudgmentally, that they understand the nature and scope of the problem, counselors can communicate hope to the addicted youth.

The diagnostic interview ends with a diagnosis, which needs to be shared with the adolescent. In doing so, it is important to use con-crete language, supported by specific examples. The word "addic-tion" can be avoided, in favor of a phrase like "out of control," when presenting a diagnosis of chemical dependency to a teenager and his or her family. As much as possible the diagnosis should be supported by information that has been provided voluntarily by the adolescent him or herself.

SUMMARY

This chapter outlined a process for conducting a diagnostic interview with an adolescent suspected of substance abuse. The data obtained here are often sufficient to make an initial diagnosis and to decide what kind of treatment is necessary. In general, the more deeply the young person has moved into habitual use—and certainly if there are any signs of loss of control—the more intense the treatment needs to be. At this level there is little if any chance that the adolescent will be capable of stopping unless he or she is temporarily removed from the home/school environment.

6

Functional Assessment

The diagnosis of substance abuse or addiction completes the first part of the assessment process. The next part — the functional assessment — aims at identifying strengths and weaknesses within the adolescent that will be relevant to treatment and recovery. The objective in treatment, of course, is to build on strengths while working toward remediation of liabilities and deficits. Some of these deficits will have predated the substance abuse problem and may have contributed to it; others will be at least partly the result of substance abuse. Assets, in contrast, represent areas that the counselor can rely upon to support growth and recovery.

EDUCATION

Education is one of the most important assets available to the adolescent. Success (versus failure) in school plays a decisive role in determining alternatives that have lifelong implications for the young person. School performance typically deteriorates as substance abuse progresses. As the teenager becomes a habitual user, concentration diminishes, gaps in knowledge grow wider, and failure is virtually inevitable. Most habitual users eventually drop out of school.

It is important, when assessing the adolescent substance abuser, to estimate his or her intellectual (academic) potential. This can be done through a brief history of school performance and learning problems. The objective is to estimate potential, independent of impaired performance. To do this, divide the educational history into early grades (K through 5), middle grades (6 through 8), and high school. For each period, ask both the adolescent and the parent questions such as these:

- What was _____'s attitude, in general, toward school during grades _____ through _____?

- How did _____ perform in school then? What were his/her grades like?
- What were _____'s best and worst subjects?

Summarize the educational history as follows:

- Does _____ have any reading or comprehension problems?
- Was _____ ever identified as having learning problems, such as being a "slow learner" or having a "learning disability"? If so, when? What was the nature of the problem? Was any remediation attempted? With what results?
- Was _____ ever identified as having an "attention deficit" or a "hyperactivity" disorder? If so, when? What, if any, treatment was _____ given? Was medication used? If so, what kind, and for how long? Was there an improvement in behavior? In grades?

The clinician should try to estimate the adolescent's potential by asking him or her to identify the grades (years) when he or she they did best in school. School performance levels prior to habitual substance use can be taken as a rough estimate of academic potential. The grade at which performance began to seriously decline provides an estimate of when learning effectively stopped, and therefore of the size of the academic gap that needs to be closed.

LIFE SKILLS

Substance abuse takes the adolescent out of the social/developmental mainstream. While peers are socializing, playing, and working, the substance abuser is absorbed with using. Consequently, much of the social learning that normally goes on during adolescence and young adulthood is missed by the teenage substance abuser. The product of this learning—what could be described as "life skills"—include such things as communication, recreation, and relaxation.

Communication skills can be assessed by the way the adolescent relates to the interviewer. What is the level of vocabulary used? Can the teenager express him or herself clearly? How outgoing is he or she? Is he or she excessively awkward or shy? Finally, is his or her language age-appropriate?

Social skills are probably as important to success as is raw intellectual ability. The teen who cannot express him or herself adequately, or who is exceptionally shy or socially inappropriate, will be at a decided disadvantage in recovery unless progress is made in these areas. Another important life skill is the ability to be appropriately assertive (as opposed to passive or aggressive). This may need to be assessed more gradually over the course of treatment, through observation of interactions with counselors and with peers.

Life skills also include practical abilities such as job interviewing skills, budgeting, dressing appropriately, etc. These areas need to be assessed. They will be either personal assets or areas in need of remediation.

Two final areas that should be assessed are the youth's skills relative to recreation and relaxation. Both are vital to psychological health, and unhealthy individuals typically are lacking in one or both of these areas. Basic questions to ask are:

- What do you do to relax?
- What do you do for recreation and fun?

Don't be surprised if the adolescent substance abuser has to struggle to find answers to these questions or gives answers that refer to a time before he or she got involved with alcohol or drugs.

It's important, as part of a functional assessment, to try to identify interests that might be rekindled through treatment. This may take some doing. Help the teenager or young adult come up with a specific list of several recreational activities and hobbies that could be pursued. Equally important is to help the adolescent replace substance use with alternative methods of dealing with stress; therefore, the clinician needs to work with the teen to develop a list of activities that he or she might turn to for relaxation and stress reduction.

EMOTIONAL ADJUSTMENT

The teenager who cannot adequately control his or her emotions, who cannot learn to express them appropriately, or who can't deal with certain emotions effectively, will be at risk for substance abuse.

To the extent that the issue of dealing with painful emotions is not addressed in treatment, the risk of relapse following treatment will be high.

Compensatory substance use is typically associated with, or "triggered" by, certain dysphoric emotional states, particularly anger, grief, anxiety, boredom, loneliness, and depression. The counselor should try to identify these emotional triggers. One adolescent, for example, may report that he drinks when he feels "pissed off" (angry); another may say that she snorts cocaine because it makes her feel less "down" (depressed).

Jack's substance abuse had its roots in a drug oriented high school culture where it was common, beginning in sophomore year, to abuse alcohol and marijuana and to experiment heavily with substances like LSD and cocaine. In addition, anxiety served as an emotional trigger for Jack's compensatory substance use. "I was always nervous about everything," he recalled during our assessment interview. "My parents can tell you about that. I was always worried about things, very serious about everything. Like school. I've always worried over every little test — even when I knew I'd probably get an A." That was before Jack discovered alcohol and pot. After that he didn't worry so much. His grades went down, but so did his anxiety. Eventually, he became addicted to marijuana and abused LSD sufficiently that he suffered from frequent flashbacks.

If possible, try to identify the emotional triggers for substance use using the adolescent's own words if possible. If that becomes difficult, try using some prompts. Ask the teenager, for instance, if he or she uses when feeling . . .

| Sad | Frustrated | Mad | Depressed | Lonely |
| Angry | Unhappy | Bored | Uptight | Nervous |

Also try to identify any significant losses that may point to unresolved grief. Timmy, a handsome, sturdy, but obviously desperate and drawn-looking young man of 17, related to me how he'd been drinking a case or more of beer every day for the past year. During that time he'd dropped out of school and was arrested twice for breach of peace. It was only after I questioned him further that it came out that his drinking had stared shortly after his girlfriend was killed in a car accident.

Once emotional triggers are identified, the next step is to identify the kinds of situations in which these emotional triggers are pulled. Get specific examples of circumstances when the adolescent feels angry or sad, frustrated or bored, and subsequently has used. For Timmy it was thinking about his girlfriend; for Jack, it was thinking about a test. Develop a detailed scenario, with the help of the adolescent, of the sequence of events that leads to substance use. Sometimes the situations that trigger use are social ("fighting with my parents"); at other times they may be more personal and solitary ("lying in bed thinking about my ex-boyfriend"). The key is to draw the connection between the situation, the dysphoric trigger emotion, and substance use. Understanding this connection plays a vital role in treatment and relapse prevention.

SELF-ESTEEM

Despite the emotional ups and downs of adolescence, the well adjusted adolescent is basically a happy person. One need only observe a group of teens interacting freely to appreciate their vast capacity for fun. Conversely, the teenager who is chronically unhappy is a troubled adolescent, who may turn to substance abuse to compensate for his or her unhappiness. Chronic depression may be a sign of abuse or neglect, of unresolved grief, or of low self-esteem.

Self-esteem is a broad concept, but basically it has to do with attitudes toward the self: approval versus disapproval, acceptance versus rejection, pride versus shame. Self-esteem is built through mastery and acceptance and is an aspect of the self that is always in development, either increasing or decreasing.

Self-esteem can be assessed through questioning and observation, and appearance is a good place to start. Self-acceptance is usually a reflection of perceived acceptance by significant others, including parents and peers. Questions like the following are useful in assessing self-acceptance:

- Does the youth appear to take care of his or her appearance? Are his or her clothes clean? Hair washed?

- Does the young person have any complexion problems; if so, are they being attended to?
- Does the youth appear to suffer from any form of appetite or eating disorder (anorexia, obesity, bulimia)?

Self-esteem is based in part on mastery, and reflects perceived talents and abilities. The counselor should seek answers to these questions:

- What does the teenager believe he or she does well?
- What is the teen most proud of about him or herself? Least proud of? Is there a balance between perceived assets and perceived liabilities?
- What are the youth's goals in life? What does he or she think his or her potential is? In other words, how many alternatives does he or she perceive?

Self-esteem is also built on acceptance — by self and significant others. Estimate the degree to which feelings of guilt, shame, or rejection may be undermining self-esteem:

- What kind of negative (traumatic) experiences have been associated with substance abuse?
- Did any experiences of abuse (physical or sexual) predate substance abuse?
- Was the young person subject to neglect, parental rejection, or abandonment at any point in his or her life?
- What kinds of acts might the youth feel guilty or ashamed about?

Self-esteem is invariably a focus of treatment. This initial assessment is intended to identify sources of low self-esteem and highlight areas for therapeutic work.

SPIRITUALITY

Spirituality, as the word is used here, has less to do with religious beliefs per se than it does with personal values and ethics. The "spiritual" person, in this sense, is a person whose life is characterized by meaning. This is a person who possesses positive values, who is motivated to achieve prosocial goals, and whose relationships are guided by a sense of ethics. When one or more of these elements is missing, psychological adjustment is poorer. Research has found, for example, that personal qualities such as these are associated with greater resistance to stress. This has been referred to as psychological "hardiness" or "resilience"[1]; it is also close to what people in the recovery field think of as spirituality. Some of the key values associated with hardiness (or spirituality) are hopefulness (optimism), a belief that even negative events may have a positive hidden meaning, and commitment (perseverance). Values that are emphasized by the recovery movement include faith ("Let go and let God"), compassion ("There but for the grace of God go I"), and humility. Adolescents who drift into substance abuse, who are drawn to various cults, or who join antisocial gangs and become capable of the most grotesque violence, typically begin as alienated, hopeless, and faithless youths. In a word, they lack spirituality.

Because it may play a role in the etiology of substance use, and because it almost certainly does play a role in recovery, the issue of spirituality — of values and ethics — can't be neglected when assessing the adolescent substance abuser. Spirituality can (and should) be addressed by the therapist. Emotionally, the most common signs or symptoms of spiritual difficulties are feelings of chronic boredom, shame, or alienation. Boredom suggests a lack of direction, values, or meaning; alienation suggests a more active, angry rebelliousness. Both feelings, as well as guilt, are common emotional triggers for substance use. Similarly, the adolescent who feels shame or self-hatred in consequence of some transgression or act of victimization, but who has found no way of coming to terms with these feelings, may very well discover that they can be anesthetized through substance use.[2]

A brief history of involvement in organized religion is a useful starting point for assessing spirituality because it leads more or less naturally into a discussion of personal values and priorities and to concepts such as faith and hope:

- Of what religion are the parents?
- Has the family been religiously active as a unit? If participation in religious services stopped, when did it stop, and why?

Next, teens must be asked about their current beliefs with respect to a "higher power." First of all, do they believe in such a power? If so, what is their conception of it? Is it understanding? Forgiving? Comforting? Have they ever prayed? If so, what have they prayed for? Do they feel that here is a meaning to life in general, and to theirs in particular? Do they have hope that life can be happy and fulfilling for them? Do they ever find comfort, in times of stress, in faith?

When interviewing adolescents, ask them what they think are the most important things in life. What qualities do they value and respect most in others? Whom do they admire most, among their peers and among the adults they know? What is it about these people that they admire? How would they like to be more like them?

Last, ask the adolescent about his or her life goals. Exactly what these are is less important than whether or not they exist. Ask the proverbial question: What would he or she like to be doing five years from now? Does he or she have a plan for getting from here to there? Can he or she picture him or herself happy and satisfied at some point in the future? What images are associated with this fantasy?

The adolescent or young adult who is spiritually bankrupt will have little investment in recovery, which is, after all, a lifelong endeavor and something that requires hard work in exchange for its rewards. Recovery from addiction and substance abuse depends in part on valuing sobriety, on believing in the personal potential that sobriety can liberate, and on building upon personal assets.

SUMMARY

This chapter outlined a process for conducting a functional assessment. The goal is to identify personal resources that can be used to advantage in treatment, as well as areas which will need to be addressed remedially in treatment. When this is combined with the diagnostic data obtained relative to substance abuse, plus the family assessment that is described in the next chapter, a definitive treatment plan can be developed.

7

Family Assessment

If treatment with adolescents is to be effective, the process of diagnosing substance abuse must be extended to include a family assessment. This chapter describes a method for assessing families to determine the role that family dynamics have played in the development of a substance abuse problem, and to assess the impact that substance abuse has had in turn on family dynamics.

Counselors must guard against any tendency to assume that all adolescent substance abusers have identical family backgrounds or that dysfunctional family dynamics are the sole cause of substance abuse problems in adolescents. Typically, substance abuse and family dynamics interact and influence one another. Family dynamics may predispose an adolescent to substance abuse; but it is equally true that family dynamics change in response to active substance abuse in an adolescent child. In treatment planning it's important to examine both sides of this coin.

FAMILY DYNAMICS AND SUBSTANCE ABUSE

Effects of Parental Substance Abuse

Though more definitive research needs to be done, there is a gathering body of evidence indicating that parental substance abuse places children and adolescents at risk on several levels. On the simplest level, parental use of alcohol and drugs, even at the instrumental level (and regardless of whether it is for hedonistic reasons or as a means of coping with stress), is problematic because it models the very behavior that is getting the adolescent into trouble. Studies of adolescent substance abusers tend to report that one or both parents are frequently involved in substance abuse of some form.[1]

The effects of parental modeling are often underestimated, despite

74

the fact that perceived use of alcohol and drugs by adults correlates significantly with use by adolescents.[2] In assessing the family, it is important to determine the role that parental modeling may be playing in the adolescent's substance use. Factors that should be assessed include the range and duration of parental use (i.e., a parental chemical history), the function of use (pleasure-seeking, coping, or both), and the level at which the parent is involved, from social use to compulsive use. This is best approached in a straightforward manner, by asking directly about parental use of alcohol and other substances. It is useful to ask the adolescent about this first, during the individual assessment, and then to ask the parent(s) during a separate interview.

On another level, there is a growing body of research that points to a correlation between parental substance abuse and any number of problems in children and adolescents. These problems range from inferior scholastic achievement[3] and learning deficits,[4] to behavioral problems such as aggression[4] and emotional problems such as anxiety and depression.[4,5] Clinical experience suggests that these academic, behavioral, and emotional problems in turn set the stage for compensatory substance abuse in the adolescent.

Depending on how old a child is, parental substance abuse will have different effects on his or her psychological development. Parents are not affected identically by substance abuse. It's safe to assume, however, that there will be some regression in the substance-abusing parent, with some concomitant deterioration of adult functioning. This means that the parent who is abusing substances will act more or less like a child and will lose some of those abilities associated with adulthood: the ability to delay gratification, to plan, to exercise self-control, etc. This will affect his or her capacity to effectively parent: to provide for a child's emotional and psychological needs.

Parenting is largely a function of each parent's own developmental limitations. Those who are not very secure individuals—who were deprived of basic nurturance themselves as children—will become impulsive, anxious, and either neglectful or overly controlling as parents. They are at risk for becoming physically, sexually, or emotionally abusive.

Parents who are relatively more mature—who at the very least possess some basic sense of security—will be capable of providing nurturance, comfort, and support to their own infants and children. However, those who lack self-esteem are vulnerable to becoming jealous of their children. They may withdraw from the parent-child relationship, becoming aloof and distant; alternatively, they may react against their child's developing mastery by becoming critical and rejecting. Parents who possess some degree of healthy self-esteem, in contrast, can build self-esteem in their children.

Finally, the parent whose own development was compromised at the stage of individuation will resist his or her adolescent child's efforts to individuate. The poorly individuated parent will be either excessively rigid or laissez-faire and detached. Typical dysfunctional parenting styles at the stage of individuation are overprotection and harsh rejection, both of which aim to deny the development of differences and autonomy.

The addicted parent, debilitated in spirit and will, will inevitably fall victim to his or her own developmental limitations. The consequent effects on children are therefore worse than they would otherwise be. These effects will not be identical for all children of addicted parents; however, whatever effects there are will be negative.

The child's most fundamental psychological need is for security; therefore, young children of addicted parents are at risk for insecurity, which can easily persist into adulthood. This is particularly true if the addicted parent is the mother. If, on the other hand, parental addiction develops after childhood—and assuming that the parent provided needed nurturance, affection, and comfort to the young child—then the child of an alcoholic parent will not necessarily be an insecure individual.

Both parents affect the development of self-esteem, and substance abuse in either one usually has deleterious effects on the child's or adolescent's developing sense of mastery and self-confidence. Throughout childhood and adolescence, parents facilitate the development of self-esteem through acceptance, encouragement, and guidance. The substance-abusing parent, however, may not be in a position to provide these things.

Substance Abuse and Child Abuse

Rob, at 17, had already accumulated enough trouble to last the average person a lifetime. He had an arrest record longer than his arm: twice for driving while intoxicated, for driving an unregistered vehicle, malicious mischief, assault, breaking and entering, and larceny. He'd had two car accidents, the last of which had resulted in a fractured skull and impaired hearing. He was, according to his mother, totally out of control. He was also drinking every day, beginning first thing in the morning.

After tolerating an abusive marriage for nearly 15 years, Rob's mother had finally divorced his father. He was a man who drank heavily and who abused and neglected his wife and children, physically and emotionally. Rob witnessed much of this and suffered personally from it as well. Despite it all, after living with his mother for a while, he decided to move in with his father. That lasted a short time and ended in a hurried departure that Rob stubbornly refused to discuss with anyone. His substance use had started at age 12; by age 14 he was a habitual user; and by 16 he was an alcoholic. Having to overcome the effects of both abuse and addiction meant that he had a long, hard road ahead of him.

Monica entered our substance abuse treatment program at age 13. Dark haired and slight, she had a child's face and body, which she chose to hide beneath heavy makeup and sexy clothes. That, of course, was the tip-off: Monica had been abusing alcohol and marijuana since age 11, which was when her stepfather began sexually molesting her. On admission to our center she was experiencing significant withdrawal symptoms. She was physically quite uncomfortable for the first couple of days. It was during this time that we discovered and reported the sexual abuse. We also discovered, in a routine search of luggage, evidence of involvement in cult-like activities with satanic overtones.

We learned that Monica had told her mother—twice, in fact—about the abuse from her stepfather. Both times her mother had accused Monica of lying. After that she didn't bring it up again, but she did start drinking and smoking pot daily. Her involvement with a satanic cult began at about that same time.

The connection between parental substance abuse and child abuse grows stronger as substance abuse intensifies and becomes habitual. In Rob's case this connection was clear; in Monica's it was more difficult to establish, though we strongly suspected that one or both of her parents were abusing several substances. Alcohol abuse, which has been studied more extensively than other forms of substance abuse, is associated with physical and sexual abuse of children by parents.[6-9] Opiate and narcotic abuse, particularly in mothers, appears to be more commonly associated with parental neglect than abuse.[10] In general, mothers who abuse alcohol or drugs are more likely to neglect their children than abuse them, while the opposite is true for fathers.[11] There are, however, no hard and fast rules here, and no false assumptions should be made. No form of child abuse should be ruled out solely on the basis of parental sex. As was mentioned earlier, a great deal depends on the parent's level of maturity.

The link between child abuse and neglect and later substance abuse in children is supported by retrospective studies of adults in treatment, as well as by reports from adolescents in treatment. The majority of adults who are in treatment for substance abuse report having been victims of neglect or abuse as children.[7,12] Adolescents, as well as adults in treatment for chemical dependency, describe themselves as having been raised in rejecting (i.e., neglectful) or hostile (i.e., abusive) family environments.[13]

It seems evident, then, that parental substance abuse leads to a vicious cycle. The abusing parent is impaired and may neglect or abuse a child. At the very least this parent's judgment will be impaired, and children may receive less supervision (and protection) than they require. The victimized child or adolescent, in turn, carries emotional wounds that make him or her a prime candidate for compensatory use of substances.

The family assessment should specifically rule out abuse or neglect as factors contributing to adolescent substance abuse. In addition, both parental substance abuse and child abuse or neglect figure significantly into treatment planning and discharge planning. Monica, for instance, could not reasonably be expected to return home directly from six weeks of inpatient care.

The clinician needs to be sensitive to the fact that families are motivated to maintain their integrity—no matter how dysfunctional they may be. They are apt to keep problems of child abuse and neglect a secret, even more so than parental substance abuse. Information about these issues is usually communicated only subtly and is highly understated. In contrast to our style in inquiring directly about parental substance use, therefore, we use an indirect approach to rule out child abuse and neglect. More specific questions can be used to follow up on information gathered from questions such as the following:

- How does your father (mother) punish you when you do something wrong?
- How does your father (mother) reward you when you do something good?
- How do you know when your father (mother) is angry with you? How do you know when he (she) is happy with you?
- Who is home to watch you at night? Do you spend much time at home alone?
- Who cooks the meals in your house? Who cleans up and does the dishes? Who does the laundry and the housekeeping?
- Has your father (mother) ever hit you? What were the circumstances? How often has this happened?
- Has anyone in your family ever touched you in a way that made you uncomfortable?
- Have you ever had a sexual experience, in or outside of your family, that scared or upset you?

As evidence suggestive of abuse or neglect is uncovered, questioning can be directed at eliciting more details, being sensitive, however, to the young person's need to be able to back off if discomfort becomes too intense. He or she can be assured of this and told that the discussion can resume at a later time if necessary. The clinician should be aware of the professional's legal obligation to report suspected child abuse or neglect and must be prepared to take responsibility for this (as opposed to letting the adolescent feel responsible) and to serve as the adolescent's advocate in this regard.

Family Cohesiveness

Abuse and neglect of children tear at the fabric of a family. These are perhaps the most damaging of family dynamics. At the same time, it should not be assumed that a family is cohesive simply because there is no apparent abuse or neglect. Family cohesiveness can play a role in the prevention of adolescent substance abuse; similarly, a cohesive family is a strong asset to recovery. On the other hand, families that lack cohesion are at greater risk for all sorts of problem behavior, including substance abuse.

Family cohesiveness is a function primarily of three factors: the family's ability to work together, its ability to recreate together, and its spirituality. Each of these areas needs to be assessed.

The concept of family cohesiveness is understood intuitively by most people. Imagine your own family of origin. Would you describe it as cohesive or disconnected? In the cohesive family there is a sense of mutual responsibility: of allegiance to and investment in the family unit. There is a feeling of connectedness that is not unlike the intimacy that binds a good, strong marriage. There is a sense of common purpose and trust that contributes to a feeling of belongingness. There is a family identity that is greater than the sum of its individual parts.

In an alienated family, feelings run just the opposite: There is disconnectedness, coolness, and distrust. There are individual but no joint goals, and the atmosphere is more likely to be characterized by jealousy and competition than by cooperation and teamwork. There is no collective identity, only a loose confederation of essentially detached lives.

To assess family cohesiveness, begin by asking how the family as a unit works and recreates together. Have the family members undertaken any family projects in the last year? For that matter, do they ever get together as a group to get something done? Do family members share chores or other collective responsibilities? Do they ask each other favors, and do the favors usually get done? Can they be counted on to help—or teach—one another? Does the family take vacations together?

The ability to work and to play together is one sign of a healthy marriage—and of a healthy family, too. Relationships (and families) that are connected and involved are less vulnerable to disruption or deterioration under stress and are more resilient in the face of crisis.

Family spirituality is also related to family cohesiveness. Family spirituality may or may not have much to do with participation in organized religion. It has a great deal to do with what could be called the "family culture": with personal values, ethics, and priorities, and with traditions, rituals, and roles within the family. Personal beliefs, such as a belief in the importance of social responsibility and commitment, personal priorities, like family life, and a sense of ethics, of the "rights" and "wrongs" of relationships, all play major roles in children's resistance to deviance. Parents are powerful influences when it comes to values, ethics, and priorities. They transmit these things to us through modeling even more so than they do through words.

Families transmit their own unique cultures from generation to generation. A family which is committed to traditions, which invests meaning in rituals, which has clearly articulated values and goals, and which is organized around interdependent roles, is a "spiritual" family.

Family spirituality can be assessed by talking to children and parents together about their religious beliefs, their values and priorities, the traditions they observe, and their ideas about the most important "rules" to follow in relationships. Discussions like this can help parents to appreciate (often for the first time) their importance as spiritual leaders of the family.

Parent Effectiveness

The next area to be assessed concerns parents' effectiveness in setting and keeping reasonable limits for children and adolescents. There is a wide range of acceptable parental behavior in this regard, but the two extremes — excessive rigidity and extra-punitiveness versus laissez-faire permissiveness — represent dysfunctional parenting styles.

Research on families of aggressive children has shown that an extra-punitive parental style — the tendency to use excessive force in disciplining children — leads to increased aggression in children.[14] A related dysfunctional style is seen in the parent who fails to respond initially to misbehavior (thereby allowing it to escalate), but who later reacts with aggression and intense punishment. The damaging factor here is modeling (the parent is literally showing the child how to be aggressive), compounded by the anger and resentment that abusive punishment engenders in the child. By being overly aggressive or by ignoring transgressions early on and responding later with aggression, parents impair their children's ability to develop good judgment and self-control. Instead, they model poor judgment and lack of self-control. They teach their children to use aggression as a way of dealing with others and to build up stores of resentment that invite compensatory substance abuse.

Information about extra-punitive parenting is best obtained from responses to questions listed earlier, particularly questions about how parents punish and how they express anger and disapproval.

At the other extreme are parents who more or less abdicate their responsibilities as limit-setters. These are parents who fail to make expectations clear, who avoid making demands, and who back away from imposing reasonable consequences for misbehavior. Information bearing on this can be elicited using questions like the following:

- Do you have a curfew? What it is? What consequences do your parents give you if you don't keep it?
- What kinds of responsibilities do you have around the house? Do you usually meet them?
- Do your parents review your report cards with you?
- Do your parents ask you to let them know where you're going when you go out?
- When was the last time you were "punished"? What was it for? What was your punishment?
- Do your parents know you use drugs (alcohol)? What's their reaction to it?

Adolescents who are unsupervised and externally uncontrolled can hardly be expected to develop self-control. They can, however, be counted on to be willful and impulsive. Self-control, like good judgment, does not appear out of thin air; these personal qualities develop in response to reasonable external controls coupled with effective parent-child communication. Limits set by parents, moreover, can serve as face-saving excuses for adolescents: How many teens have used a parental limit as an excuse for not doing something they secretly didn't want to do in the first place?

Research has taught us something about effective parenting. We know, for example, that parents who impose reasonable limits, who follow through on their expectations with immediate and appropriate consequences, and who at the same time provide warmth and nurturance, raise children who are self-controlled, who behave in a prosocial manner, and who demonstrate concern for the effects of their behavior on others.[15]

Nurturance

When we talk about child abuse and neglect, we should not assume that the absence of these things implies anything more than that. Effective limit-setting is important in child development; equally important, though, is nurturance and support. As was mentioned earlier, these parental qualities lead to feelings of security in children; their absence produces lasting insecurity. Too many adolescents (and probably an equal number of adults) in treatment for addiction have gotten too little support and nurturance in their lives. They may even have been spoiled, yet still not nurtured.

The need for nurturance in infancy and childhood has already been discussed. What is important to add is that the need for affection, support, and comfort does not end when adolescence begins. In fact, the abrupt withdrawal of these things once puberty begins can be an intensely painful experience, and one that arouses much anxiety. Teens—males and females—need affection, caring, hugs, and comfort. They still need adults to turn to when they feel scared, lonely, or confused.

Assessing nurturance is straightforward: One looks for evidence of comfort and affection, of caretaking and support. Questions like the following can be useful:

- How does your mother (father) take care of you, for example if you're sick?
- How do your parents show their affection and love for you?
- Would you go to one of your parents if you felt depressed, anxious, or confused?
- Which parent can you (do you) turn to for advice? Who do you talk to about your problems?
- Who can you turn to for sympathy—a shoulder to cry on— when you need one?

Communication

Parent-child communication is the final area that needs to be assessed. This in turn relates to parenting style. Excessively rigid, overcontrolling, or uncompromising parents, for example, can add to the risk of substance abuse by cutting off communication with adolescents at a time when that communication could help prevent problems from developing. Adolescents faced with unduly severe, rigid, or intrusive parents will withdraw and stop communicating. They may well express their will through defiance. Ironically, substance abuse therefore sometimes represents a parent's self-fulfilling prophecy.

Lori was a candidate for substance abuse. She found herself caught between a grandmother who was rigid, excessive in her demands, and intrusive in her relationship with her daughter and granddaughter, and a mother who had trouble setting limits and imposing consequences. Watching the three of them interact, I felt that Lori's mother's indecisiveness was probably a reflection of her own mother's tendency to control too much. The older woman did this in the name of love and caring; nonetheless, it came across as smothering and patronizing. It also had the effect of cutting off communication. Whenever Lori (or her mother before her, I assumed) broke a rule—no matter how unreasonable the rule—grandmother would pile on the guilt: "You're doing this to kill me." I imagined she could be relentless in pursuit of remorse.

Lori sat beside her grandmother and across the room from her mother. Though she'd had plenty to say to me when we were alone, with the two women in the room she became a virtual mute. Her mother, meanwhile, sat quietly between the two of them while grandmother complained about Lori's every misdeed—the list seemed endless—and appeared to be incapable of intervening at all. She struck me, though, as decidedly uncomfortable with what was going on. She fidgeted and squirmed while her mother pressed Lori to admit to more and more crimes; but even when I asked her directly what she thought, she avoided giving her opinion.

Both Lori's mother and grandmother had good reason to be concerned. Lori had developed a severe attendance problem at school. Her first boyfriend was currently in a drug rehabilitation program, and her second had just been arrested on drug possession charges. Lori was not yet harmfully involved with substances, but she certainly was at risk for its happening. In a way I sympathized with her grandmother; on the other hand, the alienation and resentment she was causing were painfully apparent.

Lori needed to be able to communicate with her mother, yet feel safe with that communication—that it would not get right to her grandmother, which was the pattern. At the same time, Lori's mother needed to become more effective at parenting and take responsibility for that role rather than abdicating it to her mother. So long as there was this terrible silence between mother and daughter—so long as mother was an absent authority—Lori was going to be making decisions and choices without the benefit of her mother's judgment and in the absence of effective limits.

Despite their grand displays of independence, adolescents want and need parental input into their decision-making processes. Parents are frequently exasperated when they perceive themselves as being ignored; but the truth is that parents who listen to their children and adolescents will in turn be heard, and adolescents who make decisions with the benefit of parental input will develop better judgment in the long run, even if they don't always follow their parents' advice in the short run.

Parent-teenager communication can be observed directly in response to any question the interviewer asks. It can also be helpful to test such communication by posing a problem or raising a conflict and observing how it is discussed. Good parent-child communication improves the prognosis for long-term recovery. If it is absent, it needs to be a treatment goal.

SUBSTANCE ABUSE AND FAMILY DYNAMICS

We have described how family dynamics and parental substance abuse can play a role in determining whether an adolescent will be at risk for compensatory substance use and addiction. At the same time, the counselor must recognize the fact that families, including parents and siblings, respond to a developing substance abuse problem in an adolescent child. A kind of mutual adaptation takes place, which may not be healthy for anyone involved. In addition to assessing the strengths and weaknesses of parents with respect to the role they may play in the problem, it is important also to understand how the family has adapted to (and been affected by) substance abuse.

Codependence

The addict is not the only one who is changed by addiction; family members of an addict are also changed. It is virtually impossible, in fact, to be in a relationship with an individual — adult or adolescent — who is in the throes of addiction and not be affected by it. Often these effects are profound and unhealthy.

As the addict progressively loses control over his or her substance use, so the family too progressively loses control. Talk to the parents or siblings of an adolescent who is a habitual substance abuser and they will tell you about their frustration and anxiety, about how it feels to be in a family that is out of control. The more a substance of choice becomes the center of the addict's life — becomes his or her primary "relationship" — the more other relationships, including family relationships, deteriorate. Resentments build up, leading eventually to alienation and bitterness. Family life becomes an emotional rollercoaster as feelings run the gamut, often daily. Parents and siblings feel alternately scared, helpless, angry, and depressed. As the addict's life unravels, the family loses its cohesiveness. Often other family members' lives become just as narrow as the addict's. Just as the addict becomes preoccupied with substance abuse, for example, so can families become preoccupied with a troubled adolescent. In the process, other children — and marriages, too — may get a lot less attention than they need, which in turn places them at risk.

Addiction does not affect all family members in the same way, any more than addiction affects its victims identically. "Codependence" is the term used to refer to the various ways in which addiction affects family members. It is a concept that is easily understood on an intuitive level, and can be explained using the analogy of living with someone who has a chronic illness.

Imagine that you are living with someone who begins to experience the symptoms of a chronic disease, such as Alzheimer's disease, renal disease, uncontrolled diabetes, or chronic heart disease. Aside from their progressive physical effects, chronic diseases such as these are associated with progressive psychological effects. The personality of the victim of chronic disease changes over time. Generally speaking, the more resilient and effective individuals were before the onset of the disease, the more they are able to resist the regression that typically takes place with chronic illness. On the other hand, the less well adjusted they were before they got ill, the more regressed (child-like and self-centered) they will become as their disease progresses. Issues that were not successfully addressed in infancy, childhood, or adolescence—security, self-esteem, individuation—will reemerge in the course of a chronic illness.

How does the individual in a relationship with someone like this react? How would you react, if your spouse, parent, or child fell victim to a chronic illness? Would you respond in a caring (and caretaking) way? Would your sensitivity to this person (and his or her needs) be heightened? Would you be inclined to think of the ill person first, yourself second? Probably so. Could you imagine your own life, your own personality, changing in over time in response to this person? Can you imagine some of the feelings you might have, at different times, about this person, about your relationship, and about yourself?

The above exercise illustrates the process of codependence. The "symptoms" of codependence parallel those of addiction itself. They include progressive preoccupation, struggles for control, and personality and lifestyle changes. Codependents lose control of their own lives, which accommodate to the addict, just as the addict's life accommodates to substance use. Often, codependents are barely aware of how addiction has affected them, partly because they have been too distracted by the addict's behavior and deterioration, and partly because the changes have taken place slowly. The same is true, of course, for the addict. With the aid of a counselor, however, family members can look back and examine the changes that have taken place over time. A strategy for doing this is to start the family assessment by asking questions about what family life was like before the substance abuse problem started.

The effects of addiction on others can be severe. Families and marriages frequently have to be rebuilt, or at least repaired, and this needs to be part of the recovery process. Ironically, while much help is available to the addict, codependents frequently receive little attention; yet emotional and substance abuse problems in siblings and parents obviously need attention. Almost invariably, resentments need to be addressed and communication needs to be reestablished. Attitudes toward the addict must be identified and aired out; otherwise they will undermine the recovery process. Marriages may need to be repaired or rebuilt. Parents need to reestablish their confidence as parents, and all family members must find a way to trust each other again and build cohesiveness. Finally, the family needs to be prepared for dealing with the recovering addict, including what to do if he or she relapses.

To begin the process of family recovery the counselor needs to communicate an understanding of the fact that addiction affects all members of a family. This will establish the treatment agenda, that is, recovery, as something that extends beyond the addict. The clinician should make every effort to help parents and siblings assess the effects that substance abuse and addiction have had on them. Care should be taken to avoid couching this inquiry in a way that would suggest that the family is being blamed or pathologized. Co-dependence is a natural human phenomenon. Families and marriages naturally adapt when one member becomes dysfunctional. Parents and siblings are victims of addiction just as surely as the addict is. They need support as well as guidance in evaluating their own victimization, and later on in setting recovery goals of their own.

It is naive to assume that all "codependents" are alike. Reactions or adaptations to addiction depend in large part on factors such as self-esteem, social support, spirituality, and stress management abilities. Parents and siblings with weaknesses in one or more of these areas can be expected to experience more severe and dysfunctional reactions to addiction. Innate qualities, such as intelligence, temperament, and creativity, can also play a role. Therefore, while some parents and siblings may react to a substance abuse problem with anger and alienation, others may get depressed. Some may act out in rebellious ways, including substance abuse; others may become detached from the family. Some may fail in their own lives, while others may lose themselves in creativity or achievement as a way of weathering the storm.

In helping family members identify their reactions to substance abuse, a technique that is sometimes useful is to have the various family members identify and characterize their "codependent roles" within the family. This is best done as a group exercise, with all family members helping each other. One word or a short phrase that succinctly captures the essence of individuals' reactions to addiction in their family can be useful later in facilitating communication and change. Below are some examples of family roles and the labels that could be used to describe them.

THE "LEVELER"

This is the sibling or parent who attempts to smooth over conflict, thereby gaining peace and temporary stability. Leveling takes different forms, from distraction, to humor, to obvious efforts at placating. While peace is sometimes achieved, the price of leveling is that issues are avoided, and the long-term consequences may be worse. The leveler is an "enabler" (see below), in that keeping the peace often means protecting the substance abuser from experiencing the natural consequences of his or her problem.

THE "GOOD CHILD"

As a way of attempting to compensate for the family's collective loss of self-esteem (which is one consequence of addiction), one or more siblings may attempt to be model children, high achievers, or both. Ironically, these children often go unrecognized and unappreciated despite their efforts, and end up feeling resentful and depressed. Commonly, comments made by parents and teachers about these children are positive ones: "Never been any trouble"; "Very cooperative," etc. The problem with this role is that it's unnaturally good, and therefore constraining. It doesn't allow for normal development, pressing instead for a precocious (but false) maturity. The individuation process becomes compromised by the desire to not make trouble. These children do not communicate what is really going on inside them. They often do not assert their individuality or take any stands at all against their parents. Inwardly, however, they feel angry and deprived — as indeed they are. Some later surprise everyone by getting into trouble or becoming sick or depressed. This is also an enabling role, since it aims to protect the family from having to deal directly with the substance abuse problem.

THE "RED HERRING"

This is the child or parent whose behavioral and/or emotional problems distract the family from the real issue: the substance abuse that is making the family progressively more dysfunctional. At the same time, these "red herrings" get some attention for themselves. Children may develop bedwetting problems, school phobias, etc. A parent may become depressed or dissatisfied with his or her job or marriage. The message implied in these "problems" is that the child or parent wants more attention but is afraid to ask for it directly. It also helps to avoid having to confront the addicted family member.

The above are only a few examples of codependence roles within a family. Helping family members identify and label their own roles in some convenient way can be very useful in treatment, as we shall see.

Enabling

Enabling, like codependence, is a response to addiction, not a cause of it, though eventually the two become symbiotic. Again, and as with codependence, it is a natural, normal drive that accounts for enabling. That drive is the family's almost instinctual desire to stay intact: to "survive." It motivates families to compensate for dysfunction in one member and to avoid issues that threaten its integrity as a unit (however dysfunctional that may be). This same drive for family survival also accounts for enabling in substance-abusing families. It is, sadly, a normal and otherwise healthy drive gone awry.

Just as families often conspire to keep parental substance abuse a secret, so do parents and siblings often work on many levels to avoid confronting the reality of adolescent substance abuse. Siblings may conspire knowingly to keep parents in the dark. Parents may avoid the subject, even in their private discussions. Explanations of deteriorating behavior and worsening consequences may invoke every possible explanation except the most obvious one.

"Enabling" is the term used to describe the ways in which parents and siblings allow a substance abuse problem to continue. Sadly, the motivation for enabling is exactly the opposite of its real effects. Parents and siblings do not want the adolescent to become addicted, of course; yet in their efforts to avoid confronting the problem head on they unwittingly make it worse. Typically, enabling involves allowing the substance abuser to escape or minimize the negative consequences that he or she would otherwise suffer as a result of substance abuse. Enabling also involves avoidance of the real issue—substance abuse—either by not discussing it or by focusing on something else.

Simon had been smoking pot almost daily for nearly two years. His behavior and personality plainly revealed the amotivational syndrome that is associated with habitual marijuana use. Though extremely bright, his academic performance was dismal. He had progressively lost interest in virtually everything, except smoking pot. When confronted by his parents, Simon acknowledged his use, but responded at the same time with two forms of denial. First, he minimized his own use, while at the same time exaggerating the use of his peers. Second, he attempted (successfully) to divert the discussion away from his habitual marijuana use, his failing grades, and his increasing absenteeism to conflicts he was having with teachers.

Despite my best efforts, Simon's parents took the bait. Convinced that their son was not using marijuana any more than his friends (as if that somehow made it okay!), they "decided" that the intervention needed to be with the school (instead of with him). I later learned that they demanded that one of his teachers be changed. The school administrators gave in, against their better judgment (an example of what could be called "institutional enabling"). When the problem continued, the parents withdrew Simon from the school entirely and sent him to a private one. Then, when Simon was arrested for possession of marijuana, they paid his bail and hired an attorney to try to get him off without mandatory treatment. Their enabling was finally stopped by the judge, who gave Simon the choice of treatment or 60 days in jail.

Given this sequence of events, some might be tempted to offer the interpretation that Simon's parents "unconsciously" wanted him to be an addict. I didn't believe that. On the other hand, their behavior was having exactly that effect. This is the essence of enabling. Simon's parents were reacting to his denial in ways that permitted his substance abuse to continue. If this pattern were not reversed in treatment, Simon's recovery could be seriously threatened.

Enabling can be identified through questions that uncover ways in which negative consequences have been minimized or "cushioned." In the addictions field, the term "bounce" is used to refer to how much enabling from others the active addict can count on. This is contrasted to "hitting bottom", which is what happens when enabling finally stops. Providing money (which is later spent on drugs or alcohol), failing to impose appropriate consequences, avoiding talking about the obvious, and minimizing negative consequences: All are behaviors that should be labeled as enabling. Parents and siblings should be encouraged to own up to these behaviors (which are usually well intentioned), and to label them as enabling, as opposed to helping.

Sibling Substance Use

The last area of inquiry concerns the behavioral contagion that tends to be associated with substance abuse. While the adolescent with the most obvious problem is typically the focus of intervention efforts, concurrent or incipient substance abuse problems in brothers or sisters may be overlooked. Not only does this leave a problem unaddressed, but it also threatens the recovery of the one adolescent who does get into treatment.

Sibling substance use and abuse are best assessed directly, first during interviews with the identified patient and with the parents, and then in interviews with the sibling(s). Do not presume that age precludes use, since with an older brother or sister as a model experimental use can begin as early as age eight or nine. Similarly, do not assume that such information will be volunteered; it is usually uncovered, if at all, through specific questioning. Older siblings may be involved in purchasing, using, and even selling substances. The treatment plan may have to be expanded to provide services appropriate to the level of alcohol or drug involvement of other children.

SUMMARY

This chapter presented a process for conducting a family assessment. The first half of this assessment focuses on some of the most important family dynamics that can contribute to substance abuse. Of particular importance are parental substance abuse, child abuse and neglect, parent effectiveness, nurturance and communication.

It is equally important to assess the effects that adolescent substance abuse has on parents and siblings. No family assessment would be complete without information relative to codependence, enabling, and sibling and parental substance abuse.

The information obtained through diagnostic interviews with the adolescent and the family are ready to be integrated into a comprehensive treatment plan, which is described in the next chapter.

8

Treatment Planning

Jenny was 20. Tall and slender, with eyes the color of irises and dark brown hair, she was nothing less than striking, especially when she smiled. Unfortunately, that was rare. She had come to see me reluctantly, at the insistence of the dean of students of her college. It seemed she had lost her temper on two occasions recently. Once she'd cursed out, and then threatened, a teacher over a disputed test grade. The second time was when she threw a half full can of beer at a dormitory advisor who'd confronted her about breaking the rule that prohibited drinking in the dorm. That got her suspended from school, pending an evaluation. That was where I came in.

Over the past semester — her third — Jenny had missed almost as many classes as she'd attended. She was spending most of her time in her boyfriend's room. He was a daily pot user. In the past, she had always been very involved in school, including co-curricular activities. As a high school student she'd won two statewide swimming competitions. Lately, however, she'd lost interest in all these things; meanwhile, her friends found her increasingly difficult to deal with.

Jenny's father had died suddenly when she was 10, sending her mother into a depression that was only now beginning to show signs of lifting. From the time she started dating — at age 12 — Jenny was described by her mother as "boy crazy." Though her boyfriends seldom lasted more than a few months, she was rarely without one. Her mother, Jenny explained, felt that she was easily influenced by whatever boy she was with at the moment. Jenny told me this, but denied it.

In her freshman year Jenny had tried cocaine, but only a few times, with her boyfriend at the time. With her current boyfriend, however, she'd started smoking marijuana a lot. It sounded to me, I said, that her mother's contention — that Jenny was heavily influenced by her boyfriends — may have been correct, at least as far as

93

substance use went. She frowned, shrugged, and said that maybe her mother (and I) were right, but so what. Then she looked up. "You know," she said, "I don't particularly enjoy the feelings I get from pot—or from alcohol for that matter. Sometimes I pretend to use more than I really do." This struck me as honest, but I found it of little consolation, since she admittedly was smoking pot almost daily now. On the other hand, we seemed to have established a base for honest communication.

Jeff was referred to me for an evaluation after his parents overheard him on the phone arranging to buy $50 worth of cocaine. During our interview he admitted that he'd been using cocaine for about four months. Lately he'd been using about two or three times a week, in relatively small amounts. His total use was less than a gram every couple of weeks. So far he'd experienced only relatively mild withdrawal symptoms: Sometimes, he said, he felt a little depressed and jittery after getting high. This was to have been his first independent buy from a dealer; up until then, he'd been sharing with friends.

Though he'd experimented with alcohol, Jeff didn't enjoy the feeling of intoxication very much—not nearly as much as he enjoyed a cocaine high. He liked the feeling of euphoria that coke gave him, as well as the self-confidence it instilled. It made all of his insecurities disappear, at least for a while. I could tell, from the expression on his face and the tone in his voice, that he was motivated to seek those feelings. Moreover, he'd intended to buy the cocaine and use it alone, not with friends. He wasn't exactly experiencing cravings—yet—but he'd been looking forward with eager anticipation to using the cocaine. From my point of view, I told him, getting caught was the best thing that could have happened.

Jeff's parents had already noticed a change in their son's behavior. Always a shy, quiet, and somewhat timid boy, lately he'd been even more withdrawn. Never particularly moody before, he was now. Once very reliable and inclined to spend a good deal of time at home working on his hobbies, now he was seldom home, and neither parent had seen him at a hobby in months. If they asked him to do something, there was about a fifty-fifty chance of its getting done. Then there was the problem of the missing money: at first five dollars, later on twenty or more. On the other hand, some things hadn't changed, like Jeff's school grades (they were still good), and his part-time job, which he still maintained. They were puzzled and concerned, but until they overheard the phone conversation they figured it was just a "phase" that Jeff was going through.

Dave was a tall, hulking, and handsome young man of 19, a high school graduate who'd played varsity football. His muscular frame took up the greater part of the loveseat he sat on. Throughout our talk he was very cooperative, though his mood was subdued. I noticed that the corner of one of his eyes was blood red.

"What happened to your eye?" I asked.

"I don't remember what happened," Dave replied, his voice heavy. "That's why I asked my parents to bring me here. I've got to do something."

"About what?" I asked.

"About my drinking problem," he answered.

Dave had been drinking almost daily since the winter of his senior year—ever since the football season ended, as a matter of fact. He drank through the summer, too, and had lost a job because of it. Now he was going to college, and in the middle of his first semester was failing all but one of his courses.

Dave's parents knew he drank and had confronted him several times about it. He put them off, minimizing his use and arguing that he didn't drink any more than his friends did. During our talk, though, he admitted that he'd tried a couple of times to stop, but found that he couldn't go more than a couple of days without craving a drink. Once he started drinking, he couldn't stop. He'd already had several blackouts, including one when he was driving. Miraculously, he hadn't had an accident, but it scared him badly when he woke up the next afternoon and realized that he couldn't remember driving home. Then, two days before our interview, he'd woke up again, this time with that red eye. He went to his mother and said he needed to talk to someone.

Jason sat dourly in the chair, his eyes lowered. Occasionally he glanced up at me, his expression clouded. When he spoke, his words were directed at the floor in front of him instead of at me. He had long, dark brown hair that hung past his shoulders. If he'd taken care of it, it probably would have looked good; but he didn't take care of it, and it looked oily and dirty. The same was true for his complexion, and his clothing.

Jason's parents knew he'd been involved with drugs for some time, and he readily admitted it to me, too. His father came to the interview and explained that when Jason had turned 18, four weeks earlier, he'd been asked to leave the house. He did, but then showed up three days later. An argument ensued. The end result was that Jason's father was on the phone with the police when Jason finally realized his parents meant business and left. Now he wanted to come back, and had agreed to see me only because his parents had made it a condition of his coming home.

Jason dropped out of high school in his junior year and had lived at home ever since, doing little else besides playing his electric guitar and going out with friends. His father explained that Jason had been virtually impossible to control during that time. He ignored house rules, and became verbally abusive when confronted about it. He came and went as he pleased. His pattern was set: stay out late, sleep late. He'd threatened his parents more than once, and in general terrorized the entire family with his aggressiveness and belligerence.

Jason had had a few jobs, but none of them had lasted more than a few days. When I asked him if he was interested in a job now, he shrugged. "I guess so," he said, "but I won't cut my hair, and nobody will hire me with it this way." Instead of working, Jason made money by selling cocaine and marijuana.

Four youths; four different situations. Each of them, clearly, needed help. But what kind of help? Did they all need to be in a residential rehabilitation program? How much was substance abuse the "cause" of their trouble, and how much was it a "symptom" of something else?

The object of a good treatment plan is to match the diagnostic formulation to the appropriate level of care. In this chapter we look at how to do that.

RECOVERY VERSUS TREATMENT:
THE CONTINUUM OF CARE

There are many different forms of treatment available today for young persons with alcohol and drug problems. These range from long-term residential care to outpatient groups. They can be thought of as varying on two dimensions: length and intensity. No one of these programs is inherently "better" than any other; the relevant clinical question, rather, is this: What form of treatment is appropriate at a given time? What level of care, in other words, will be sufficient to help an adolescent get away (and then stay away) from substance abuse? Often the answer will involve several levels of care, coordinated so as to engage the youth in treatment of varying intensities over an extended period of time. Together, they form a "continuum" of care for an individual adolescent or young adult. Treatment, therefore, should be conceptualized not as an event, but as a process, extending over time and involving different levels of intensity at different points in recovery.

In general, more "intense" programs involve more extensive removal of the adolescent from his or her normal environment and lifestyle. To the extent that some parts of that environment and lifestyle are functional (for example, Jeff's good grades and his steady job), it is desirable to maintain them. That may mean using a less intensive level of treatment and seeing whether it works.

Some treatment options available in many communities today are discussed below.

Outpatient Treatment

Some clinicians and agencies now offer specialized services for young people who are having problems related to alcohol and drug use. When selecting such services, parents or referring practitioners must verify the clinician's (or agency's) expertise in this area. Training and relevant experience should be openly discussed. Clinicians providing such care should have specific training and experience in this area that can be verified.

A good outpatient program should include group work with the adolescent, plus concurrent family therapy. Twice weekly group counseling for the adolescent, as well as a weekly parent group and/or psychoeducational family program, can form the core of this kind of treatment. Individual therapy and family therapy may be held every other week, or even less often, depending on the dynamics of the individual case. Treatment should be highly structured, with specific expectations and consequences (see Chapter 15). Parent groups should provide education, facilitate mutual support, and focus on basic AlAnon concepts such as detachment and enabling. Periodic random drug testing can provide a helpful external control for the adolescent in the early stages of treatment, but it is not always used in the outpatient setting.

Outpatient treatment may be open-ended, but if it is it should include periodic reviews of progress toward specific goals. Time-limited treatments typically have specific goals and objectives built into them.

After-School Programs

After-school programs are becoming increasingly popular, as are day hospital (sometimes called "partial hospitalization") programs. After-school programs typically involve an adolescent in treatment three to five times a week, for from 10 to 15 weeks. As the name suggests, treatment takes place after school, for example from three to six o'clock. Some programs add weekend activities, such as substance-free parties, movies, outings or family programs that include parents and youths.

After-school programs allow for more varied and flexible programming than standard outpatient treatment, but are consequently also more expensive. They are considerably cheaper than hospitalization, however, since the adolescent lives at home and attends his or her original school while participating an after-school treatment program. After-school programs, like outpatient treatment, should be built around a core of group treatment plus parent education and support. Family therapy, multifamily therapy and, if necessary, individual therapy may be additional components of an after-school treatment program.

Therapeutic Adventure

Any treatment program described here can be enhanced by the addition of a "therapeutic adventure" component. Modeled after Outward Bound programs, therapeutic adventure provides opportunities for nonverbal learning, the development of self-esteem, and the building of group cohesiveness. Based on the concept of experiential learning, therapeutic adventure provides structured group activities intended to touch on specific individual and group issues, such as trust, cooperation, help-seeking, autonomy, communication, etc.

Because of its active, challenging nature, therapeutic adventure has special appeal for adolescents and young adults. It is also easily integrated into the group treatment model presented in Chapter 15, in that it can be ritualized and connected to rites of passage.

Partial Hospitalization

The partial hospitalization (PH) program model includes both educational and clinical components. The teen attends the program five days a week, eight hours a day, for either a school quarter, half a year, or a whole school year. It is an intensive level of care, combining remedial education with alcohol and drug rehabilitation, and the daily program schedule should reflect this, with many structured activities and relatively few idle hours. The adolescent still lives at home, but usually has this time structured as well, through daily "homework" assignments from both academic and clinical staff. For example, a daily journal or a written exercise on self-image might be assigned along with math or language arts homework.

A vital part of a good PH program is a strong family component that goes beyond parent support and education to include regular multifamily and individual family sessions. A family drug education program, covering topics such as the addiction process, signs and symptoms of chemical dependency, effects of substances on behavior, emotions, and health, codependence and enabling, principles of AA and NA, how to find meetings and get a sponsor, etc., should be an integral part of a family program. Individual and multifamily sessions should use material from this educational program as a point of departure for dealing with family-specific issues.

In the PH model the teen is removed from the school environment and in large part from his or her social environment as well. PH programs are in many ways similar to intensive short-term inpatient care. All the basic treatment components are there, including a strong sense of community responsibility and a commitment to 12-step recovery process that is shared by the PH staff and patients alike. The difference is that the young person continues to live at home and will probably have some exposure to the peer group. Depending on the risk factors active in both, and on the youth's own level of substance use, a PH program may or may not be an adequate intervention. Rehabilitation through a PH program therefore fits into the continuum of care either as an alternative to residential treatment or as the next step following residential treatment.

Short-Term Residential Care

Often referred to as "primary" treatment, short-term rehabilitation programs involve four to six weeks of intensive treatment in an inpatient setting. The adolescent is completely removed from his or her normal environment and lifestyle, and is placed in a therapeutic community that includes remedial education and rehabilitation. Again, such programs should be highly structured, with relatively little unstructured time and limited, controlled visitation. Typical program components include community meetings, group therapy, a family program, AA and/or NA meetings (preferably in the community), plus groups focusing on specific issues such as stress management, communication, relationships, sexuality, recreation, and self-esteem. The educational component should include life skills as well as academics, to help remediate both social and academic deficits.

The preferred model for residential (and also PH) treatment is a developmental one, where progress is measured against specific and explicit behavioral expectations that are organized developmentally and are to some extent age-specific. In other words, advancement in the program should be associated not only with compliance with behavioral rules and limits, but also with increasing competence in judgment, social responsibility, and self-control based on values, ethics, and ideals. In order for treatment effects to generalize beyond the treatment center (i.e., after discharge), behavioral change needs to correlate with changes in attitudes and values. If this is not evident, then the risk of relapse into habitual substance use becomes higher.

Long-Term Care

Reserved usually for those who have relapsed into chemical dependency after more than one treatment experience, long-term residential care is less intense than primary treatment; on the other hand, treatment lasts much longer—typically six months to a year or more. The advantage is that the youth who needs it can remain in a "safe" environment that much longer. This level of care is very important to adolescents who make gains in primary care, but whose recovery is not sufficiently consolidated to risk placement back into their original environments or into a PH program.

Group therapy, AA/NA, and sometimes family therapy are parts of long-term treatment. There is also a strong emphasis on the "therapeutic community": on being responsible collectively for the effective operation of the "house" and for mutual recovery.

Halfway Houses

Halfway houses offer transitional living arrangements for a period of time following either short-term or long-term treatment. As the name implies, this is a level of care that is "half way" between supervised residential care and fully independent living. Residents of halfway houses usually work, sometimes inside the house (initially), but more typically in the community. Often, job placements are arranged through networks of friends in recovery. In addition, residents share responsibility for maintenance of the house (cleaning, cooking, etc.). There are therapeutic community meetings (usually run without the aid of professionals), plus a strong emphasis on AA and/or NA. Daily meetings are not unusual. At this level of care, the youth's recovery is supported entirely through AA/NA and the therapeutic community; in other words, through involvement in a 12-step recovery program and a healthy (recovering) peer group.

Drug Testing

After-school, PH, short-term, and long-term treatment programs should incorporate random drug testing into the treatment regimen. While drug screenings for adult patients may be debatable, the issue of developmental arrest in adolescent substance abusers, and particularly their limited willpower, makes an external support such as drug testing a virtual necessity, at least in the earlier stages of treatment. Halfway houses, which offer a level of care at which recovery should be presumed to be firm enough to not require it, may dispense with drug testing except for cause. Similarly, outpatient programs should be aimed at youths whose level of involvement with chemicals has not reached the habitual stage.

Contrary to what many adults expect, adolescents and young adults in treatment do not resent drug testing, especially when it is presented (and used) as an aid to maintaining a safe environment and their own ego development. When testing is conducted in a direct and professional but respectful manner, youths more often accept rather than resist it as a part of their treatment, in the same way that they often accept parental limits despite outward appearances. Naturally, the consequences for failing a drug screening should be made clear to the youth (and to the family) in advance of treatment.

FINDING THE SHOE THAT FITS: MATCHING PATIENTS TO TREATMENTS

The challenge for the clinician is to match the patient to the appropriate level of care. The following guidelines can be helpful.

Experimental/Social Use

Even when involvement with substances is at this level, some form of intervention may be indicated. School-based programs, only beginning to appear on the scene, can be particularly effective with youths who come to the attention of teachers, counselors, or school administrators as a result of incidents related to experimental or social use. A team composed of a professional counselor and one or more trained peer counselors, using a psychoeducational approach, is usually effective. It should be a time-limited program whose goal is to help youths discontinue their use while it is still at the experimental/social level. Topics for discussion should include the physiology and psychology of addiction, stages of use, risk factors, the effects of substance use on development, and alternatives to substance use as a social agenda. Based on personal assessments, some youths may be referred for further treatment, either within the school or through a clinic. Some, for example, may benefit from participation in a group for adolescents who are the children of substance-abusing parents. An organized and active student assistance program (similar to an employee assistance program in the workplace) can coordinate a comprehensive school-based program.

Instrumental Use

Once an adolescent has moved to the active (seeking) level of use, a more intense intervention is indicated. The danger here is that the youth will begin to rely on chemicals as means of recreating and coping, and development will become arrested. If any significant peer group drift has taken place, if the teen has already failed in outpatient treatment, or if the school and/or home environment is judged to be a risk factor (e.g., parental substance abuse), then partial hospitalization or an after-school program is the initial treatment of choice for the instrumental user. If, on the other hand, there has been no outpatient treatment, if the school environment can be reasonably controlled so that the youth can be separated from a peer group of heavy users, and if the home environment contains no significant additional risks, then an outpatient program is the appropriate choice. It is a good idea to establish explicit conditions for remaining in outpatient or after-school treatment and to make these clear to the adolescent and the family in advance. Alternatives associated with failure to meet program expectations should also be discussed in advance. After-school programs, finally, are very useful for adolescents who have done well in residential treatment but need closer supervision than outpatient treatment can provide.

Habitual/Compulsive Use

Once use has become habitual, so that there has been a noticeable accommodation of lifestyle to substance use, there is little choice other than to remove the youth temporarily from the environment. Short-term residential care is indicated for habitual users, as well as for youths who have failed in partial hospitalization or after-school programs. Obviously, compulsive users will also require care away from the environment, but may require long-term care even after a successful stay in a primary treatment program.

In the examples given at the beginning of the chapter, Jenny was referred to outpatient treatment, Jeff was sent to a partial hospitalization program, while Dave was admitted to primary treatment after which he went to a halfway house. Jason, obviously, needed help as well, but in his case help needed to begin with a family intervention aimed at reducing the degree to which the family was unwittingly enabling Jason's problem to continue.

In all of these cases, it's important to keep in mind that recovery is a process, not an event. Recovery is not cure, but growth and vigilance. Treatment may begin at any of the levels described above, but it almost always extends beyond that. Different levels of care along the continuum, from outpatient to long-term residential care, may be the "right shoe" for the same youth at different times.

DEVELOPING TREATMENT PLANS

The treatment plan should take into account each of the following:

1. Level of substance involvement: Experimental, Social, Instrumental, Habitual, or Compulsive.
2. Functional assessment: Personal assets and liabilities such as school performance, emotional stability, work history, etc.
3. Social/family assessment: Risk factors within the social or family environment, such as parental substance use, abuse or neglect, and peer group drift, combined with estimates regarding parent effectiveness, family cohesiveness, etc.

Each of the above areas was the focus of a specific earlier chapter, and each has a specific place in the treatment plan. Essentially, a treatment plan is an outline of goals that the clinician uses to plan out treatment. This treatment plan can (in fact should) be divided into priorities: those goals that require immediate attention and treatment versus those that will be the focus of later treatment efforts. Work with adolescent substance abusers usually goes hand in hand with work with their families, and both need to be planned. An overly ambitious treatment plan—trying to accomplish too many goals in too short a period of time—is just as bad as a treatment plan that is too sparse and limited.

A good, comprehensive treatment plan for an adolescent substance abuser will incorporate several levels along the continuum of care. It may begin, for example, with a six-week stay in a primary treatment program, where work on life skills, educational remediation, self-esteem, communication and 12-step recovery may be initiated, along with family work. Following this, and depending on how much progress is made, secondary treatment may involve a stay in a partial hospital program or after-school program, a referral to long-term residential care or halfway house, or, in the most optimistic case, referral to outpatient treatment. These treatments will continue the work started in primary treatment, and start on goals that may have been deferred earlier.

In working with adolescents, any approach to treatment planning other than the above places the teenager at risk for relapse. Generally speaking, individuation is not so complete that the average adolescent, much less the substance-abusing adolescent with an arrested developmental process, can be reasonably expected to carry on alone following a single intervention of any kind.

In devising treatment plans, the format or approach should be this: What will we focus on first, what second, what third, and so on, and what level of care is appropriate to meet each of these goals? The following outline may be useful to clinicians who need to develop treatment plans for youths with drug or alcohol problems.

Part 1: Substance Involvement

The first part of the treatment plan should include a diagnosis relative to the level of involvement of each substance the adolescent has used. Official diagnoses are limited to substance abuse versus chemical dependency. They should be included; however, a diagnosis that reflects the youth's actual level of involvement, from experimental use to compulsive use, for each substance used is even more relevant to treatment planning.

The treatment goal for substances that are used either habitually or compulsively is total abstinence from those substances. Furthermore, if use of even a single substance has reached the compulsive level or the habitual level with signs of loss of control, then lifelong abstinence from all mood-altering substances is indicated. The middle ground—instrumental use of one or more substances—may require more clinical judgment when setting long-term treatment goals. Even here, however, the short-term goal is still total abstinence.

Whenever substance use has proceeded beyond a social context, into the instrumental or seeking level, the adolescent is at risk. This should be shared in a frank manner with the youth. It can also be effective to educate the experimental or social user about the addiction process and about what lies ahead if use continues.

All treatment goals should be shared directly with the adolescent, and later with the family, as soon as they are formulated. This may engage the teenager's defenses, particularly denial, but it is therapeutic in the long run, since denial must be confronted anyway if recovery is to be achieved.

Part 2: Personal Goals

Personal goals follow from the functional assessment and should reflect answers to questions in each of the following areas:

EDUCATION

- What are the adolescent's academic strengths and weaknesses?
- What is his or her reasonable academic potential?
- Which educational areas require immediate remediation and which can be deferred?
- What are the youth's vocational interests?
- What intellectual, vocational, or creative assets can be used motivationally?

LIFE SKILLS

Communication: Most important in recovery are the abilities to express oneself clearly, to be appropriately assertive, and to say what's on one's mind.

- How effective is the adolescent in each of the above areas?
- What techniques or strategies can be used to enhance communication skills?

Social competence: Social skills are required if the adolescent is to successfully break with a dysfunctional peer group and integrate him or herself into a functional one, as well as into a 12-step recovery program. Even daily attendance at meetings may be of little help to the individual who lacks the skills necessary to get involved in those meetings.

- How does the adolescent relate to peers?
- Does he or she evidence the ability to make friends?
- Is the adolescent accepted by peers, or is he or she a scapegoat, an object of ridicule, or a social isolate?
- What kinds of things can be done in treatment to improve the teen's social competence and acceptance?

Recreation: Substance-abusing youths know little about having fun other than through using drugs. Most habitual users will have done little else since getting involved at that level. Another part of the recovery process, therefore, involves developing an array of ways of recreating — of having fun and experiencing "natural highs."

- What were the teen's favorite activities, before substance abuse? Can any of these be realistically rekindled now, or would they be age-inappropriate?
- What would he or she like to get involved in, and how can this be encouraged?
- What kinds of healthy activities can the youth be exposed to in the course of treatment, and how will this be done?

Stress management: Here again the young person will need to develop a plan and practice new skills, in this case skills in relaxing and coping with stress that do not involve the use of substances. Many of these skills are normally learned in adolescence, primarily through modeling peers and parents. What we call "stress management" is the teaching of these skills to adolescents whose learning has been cut short by (or limited to) substance abuse.

- How had the adolescent coped with stress in the past?
- What role models does the youth have for stress management?
- What are the key trigger emotions for substance use in this youth?
- What alternative means of stress management can the young person be taught, and how?
- Who will model more functional stress management?

SELF-ESTEEM

The cornerstones of recovery are pride (as opposed to either shame or arrogance) and faith (as opposed to either alienation or hopelessness). Low self-esteem and despair are powerful triggers for compensatory substance use. Effective treatment must deal directly with injured self-images and self-esteem.

- What, if anything, is the teenager most proud of about him or herself? What personal attributes or abilities can pride be built on? How can they be recognized and developed?
- How much is the youth burdened by shame, and what kinds of experiences are these rooted in?
- How does the teenager feel about his or her body?
- What concerns does he or she have about how substance abuse has affected his or her health, appearance, or sexuality?
- Does the youth feel attractive; if not, why not? Does he or she feel like "damaged goods"?

SPIRITUALITY

A great strength of 12-step recovery programs lies in their spirituality: in their capacity to replace alienation with involvement, disaffection with hope, resentment with acceptance, and cynicism with faith. This is an essential ingredient in recovery, not only from substance abuse, but also from involvement in antisocial gangs and satanic cults.

- What are the adolescent's personal priorities?
- What, in his or her own words, are qualities in others that he or she most admires? Can the young person point to specific examples of adults whom he or she admires? What values and ideals do these individuals represent?
- What things does the youth feel most guilty about? What role did substance use play in these acts or experiences?
- To what extent are boredom, alienation, and disaffection from spirituality trigger emotions for substance use, either individually or in a group (cult) context?
- How does the young person relate to the concept of a "higher power"? What does this mean to him or her? What kind of God does he or she relate to?
- What prospects does the youth see him or herself as having for personal fulfillment and for a happy adult life? Does the adolescent's own life strike him or her as a "broken dream"? What can be done to rekindle hope?

- What kind of person would this youth like to be, and what would he or she need to change in order to become this person?

In each of the above areas, the clinician should be able to define and write out at least one, and preferably several areas for therapeutic focus, in priority order. Tentative strategies for addressing each of these goals should be noted. As a set they become a "recovery plan." This plan should take into account areas where the teenager has strengths that can be built upon.

Part 3: Family Goals

Family goals follow from the family assessment. Again, the clinician should be able to identify family strengths, plus specific goals for therapeutic intervention in each of the following areas.

PARENTAL/SIBLING SUBSTANCE USE

- Which parent(s) or sibling(s) appear to be harmfully involved with substances and at what level of involvement?
- What implications does parental/sibling use have for the kind of treatment that is recommended for the adolescent? Will the youth be able to maintain recovery in the home environment?
- How will parental or sibling use be addressed in family therapy?

FAMILY COHESIVENESS/SPIRITUALITY

- How cohesive is the family at this point? What are its major sources of cohesiveness?
- Are there any issues of child abuse or neglect that seriously undermine the ability of the family to be cohesive? What, if any, shameful family "secrets" might there be?
- Is this a spiritually sound family? Do family members participate in meaningful traditions and rituals? Do they have shared goals, a common set of ethics and values? Is the family organized into a set of interlocking roles? How can each of these areas be developed?

COMMUNICATION

- How often and how effectively do children and parents communicate?
- Which relationships within the family are characterized by better communication, and which are the ones where communication is either poor or nonexistent?
- Which parent or sibling can be used as a role model for better communication?
- What will the plan be for developing good (clear and honest) communication within the family?

PARENT EFFECTIVENESS

- How effective are the youth's parents at setting and enforcing reasonable limits?
- Are parental expectations and limits clear? Are they consistent over time and the same for each child in the family?
- How appropriate are the parents as role models for their own expectations; in other words, what values and priorities seem to guide their lives? Where are their strengths and their weaknesses as role models?
- How good are the parents at providing support and nurturance? Are there warmth and affection, as well as structure and limits, within this family?

CODEPENDENCE AND ENABLING

- What are some of the dysfunctional family roles and expectations that have evolved in response to substance abuse or addiction?
- Which family members have remained the most functional and can therefore be counted on as resources in the rebuilding process? Who has been most negatively affected, and what treatment goals would you have for them?
- What kinds of behaviors and attitudes, and in whom, have enabled the substance abuse problem to continue?
- How will the counselor work to reverse enabling attitudes and behaviors?

SUMMARY

The treatment plan is not only a comprehensive document, but also a living document that changes over time. It can be thought of as a blueprint for change for the entire family, not just for the troubled adolescent; but it is also a dynamic blueprint that is responsive to events and open to change. It should also be an inventory of individual and family strengths and weaknesses, and as such it should be as balanced as possible. Both the good and the bad should be shared straightforwardly with the family and reflected on periodically throughout treatment. By correlating treatment goals with intervention strategies and by prioritizing goals, the recovery plan provides order and direction to the counselor, the youth, and the family.

9

Counseling and Intervention with Adolescents and Young Adults

The treatment of adolescents can be thought of as a corrective developmental experience. This seems to be true regardless of the primary reason for treatment: substance abuse, delinquency, depression, or some other problem of adjustment or living. Moreover, the therapeutic role vis-à-vis youths is marked by strong parental undertones. Any therapist who refuses to accept the parental aspects inherent in counseling adolescents is pretty much doomed to fail, just as surely as is the therapist who does not understand the developmental processes and needs of adolescents and young adults.

It is important, of course, to be able to engage the adolescent in therapy, but engagement will be fruitless if it is not accompanied by corrective parental interactions. Similarly, acceptance is important, but not at the price of allowing the young person to continue on a self-destructive course. Therapeutic rapport, therefore, needs to be achieved in the context of a quasi-parental relationship—in other words, in a relationship with a therapist whom the adolescent recognizes as an authority and also, at least to some extent, as a surrogate parent.

Effective counseling with adolescents reestablishes a functional individuation process, in which development proceeds along parallel tracks: the development of autonomy, the development of self-control, and moral/spiritual development.

The effective counselor of adolescents conveys his or her understanding of adolescence, but without attempting to relate to the client as a peer. Rather than being a peer, the effective counselor of adolescents is a direct and straightforward individual who readily accepts the responsibility of authority (model and limit-setter). He or she states expectations clearly and will not accept behavior that is not up to those expectations, because to do so implicitly condones that behavior. This kind of counselor believes in the adolescent client's potential to grow, to become more responsible, independent and mature, and expresses that not only through encouragement but also through holding the youth accountable to age-appropriate expectations. In order for a corrective developmental experience to occur, the counselor needs to respect the developmental significance of the peer group, while steering the youth away from dysfunctional peer groups and providing the limits and guidance that healthy individuation requires.

The effective counselor of adolescents is not afraid to challenge the adolescent, to call him or her on misbehavior, and to impose reasonable consequences. At the same time, this counselor provides nurturance, support, and encouragement. This kind of therapeutic relationship facilitates individuation and the development of healthy (i.e., prosocial) willpower.

Finally, effective therapy with adolescents and young adults demands that the counselor accept the role of adviser and model. The counselor must be conscious of the values, priorities, attitudes, and expectations that are represented by his or her own behavior. The best counselors of young people can articulate their values and are prepared to defend and live by them. Such issues as faith and hope, self-respect and personal priorities, and how the therapist stands on them, need to be fair game for open discussion when counseling young people.

Any other style of counseling the adolescent than that described above is likely to lead to problems. The straightforward and direct approach has many advantages. It facilitates the building of trust in adolescents who have survived abuse or neglect and of self-control in those who have not had the benefit of effective limits. Every substance-abusing adolescent is an individual whose life, to a greater or lesser extent, is out of control and chaotic. At the very least these adolescents are slipping out of the social mainstream. Their abuse has already led to negative consequences and to losses of opportunity, of relationships, and of self-esteem. No matter how arrogant a veneer they present, adolescents who are experiencing symptoms of addiction are frightened and angry. On some level they have already begun to give up on themselves. If you look closely at the way they dress and listen closely to the things they say, and if you are able separate the signal from the noise, you can see and hear their despair. The effective counselor recognizes this and communicates hope and encouragement while recognizing and insisting on the need for change.

COUNSELOR ATTITUDES

It was mentioned above that the effective counselor communicates his or her understanding of what it means to be an adolescent. That, in truth, is often easier said than done. The two most common mistakes made by therapists who work with adolescents are, respectively, overidentification and underidentification with their clients. On the one hand, some counselors seem determined to pretend they are still adolescents themselves, even though they are very obviously adults. Perhaps they do this in the belief that it is necessary somehow in order to engage the youth in treatment. In reality, quite the opposite is true: the adolescent who is treated with respect will almost invariably respect the adult who acts like an adult; on the other hand, teens and young adults will ultimately reject an adult's imitation of adolescence. In addition, there is the practical problem of being effective (or even credible) as an authority after attempting to relate as a peer. Some of the most unruly adolescents I've worked with have come not from abusive families, but from families where parents disempower themselves by trying to establish peer relationships with their children.

At the opposite extreme are counselors who act as if they were never teenagers themselves. Typically this is manifested in an intolerant attitude, excessive rigidity, and a basic lack of understanding. Communication with an adolescent from this patronizing perspective is almost impossible.

To break down the barrier that can result from a counselor's inability or unwillingness to empathize, the reader might want to take a few minutes to reflect on his or her own teen years. Find a comfortable chair and relax. Take a deep breath or two, then do the following mental exercise:

Try to remember yourself as a teenager. Conjure up a mental image of yourself if you can. Picture yourself in several different situations: in school, with friends, and with your family. What did you look like? Can you remember the way you combed your hair? What kinds of clothes did you wear? Do you remember the big fads of your day? Tight irridescent pants, thin ties, pointed shoes, and upturned collars are some of the images my own mind uncovers.

Did you ever do anything risky when you were a teenager? Did you ever drink? How old were you when you had your first drink? What other substances did you try? Can you remember the circumstances, and how you felt? Did you ever use any mood-altering chemicals (including alcohol) regularly? For how long? What was going on in your life at the time? Can you remember ever getting drunk? What was that like? Who were you with? What were the circumstances? Did you ever suffer any negative consequence connected to substance use? What kind? Thinking back on it, how does your own chemical history make you feel?

Who were your best friends? Can you picture them? Imagine what they wore, and how they groomed themselves. Which ones did you envy or admire the most? Who (and how) did you try to imitate?

Picture yourself again. Imagine looking at yourself in the mirror. How did you feel about yourself? What did you like, and dislike, about your body? What kinds of things did you do in order to make yourself more attractive?

How did you feel about the opposite sex and about your own sexuality? What were your anxieties about? Recall your first sexual experiences. Who were they with, and how did you feel afterward? Can you get in touch with your innocence? Did you have experiences that made you feel ashamed, damaged, or guilty?

Did you ever break any rules: skip school, cut a class? What was your attitude toward authorities, such as your parents, teachers, neighbors, and the police? Did you have any confrontations with these people? About what? Who were the adults in your life whom you most admired? What about them won your respect or admiration?

How was your relationship with each of your parents? Did you respect and like each of them? Did you feel that they respected you? Whom did you get more affection from? To whom could you talk about whatever was bothering you? Did either of them have problems with alcohol or drugs? How did this affect them? How, in turn, did it affect you?

What were your deepest anxieties and doubts about? What are your saddest memories about?

What were your most memorable moments? When were you happiest? What kinds of "crazy" things did you get away with? Can you remember a time when you felt happy and good about yourself? Hold onto that feeling, and that image of yourself for a moment, before letting it go.

This short exercise might help to loosen up those who are experiencing trouble relating to adolescents and young adults. The capacity to empathize with teens is as vital to being able to guide them effectively as any other factor described here. For the teenager and young adult, a therapist is in many ways a mentor—and the best mentors are those who are capable of providing mature adult advice and reasonable limits, while also being able to appreciate the essense of youth.

EXPECTATIONS FOR ADOLESCENTS

One of the most important aspects of counseling with adolescents has to do with the therapist's expectations. As a surrogate parent, the counselor cannot afford to make the mistake of being either harshly rigid and demanding, or alternatively, lax and indifferent. The first of these tendencies does not allow for individuation of the adolescent and invites needless rebellion, while the latter undermines the development of self-control and morality.

Adolescents are as style-conscious, if not more so, as any adult. The therapist needs to be sensitive to, and reasonably respectful of, current teen and young adult fashion, from pants to jewelry. This is part of respecting the teen's developmental need to identify with a peer group, including its fashions and fads, its language and attitudes. Psychologically, the peer group functions as a transitional object of attachment, marking adolescence as that stage in development where individuation occurs. Through childhood the primary objects of attachment are the parents, with one parent—usually the same-sex parent—being primary. Identification with this parent is strong and often unconscious. The child's sense of individuality is limited. It models every aspect of the parent, from manners of speech to attitudes, as a way of establishing a transitional identity. The mature adult, in contrast, possesses an autonomous sense of self, including values, tastes, interests and attitudes that may differ from those of his or her parent. The successfully individuated adult is capable of having relationships that are founded on an appreciation and respect for the differences, as well as the similarities, among people. Adolescence is that period in development where this growth and change take place. when individuation is stifled, the adult either fails to possess a sense of self or else attempts to substitute a partner for the parent, leading in time to relationships that are built on dependency and a fear of differences.

Individuation is a natural developmental process. A problem develops, however, when the peer group chosen by the adolescent is guided by values that are clearly outside the mainstream of society— for example, satanical cults and street gangs—or when it glorifies antisocial values and behaviors, such as substance abuse. In this case one cannot reasonably support or respect the particular peer group, though one must still recognize the need for the teenager to find a group of peers to identify with.

Respecting the peer group phenomenon does not imply that parents or counselors should accept any and all behavior or attitudes expressed by an adolescent. On the contrary, it is important, developmentally, to hold adolescents accountable for living up to reasonable expectations and for observing reasonable limits. As substance abuse deepens, the teen's ability to comply with expectations gets steadily worse. More and more rules get broken, more and more limits are violated. Attempting to ignore violations of reasonable limits and expectations is counter-therapeutic. It invites further substance abuse. It is interpreted by adolescents as indifference.

Many parents and counselors want to know what exactly are "reasonable" expectations for adolescents. In treatment, it is important for the therapist to have a sense of his or her expectations, and to be prepared to hold the adolescent accountable to them. The message to be given to the adolescent in treatment is that the counselor (and the parent) believe that the teen is capable of living up to expectations such as the following:

At home:

- Get along reasonably well with family members.
- Not have any physical confrontations (aggression) with family members.
- Use appropriate language.
- Complete reasonable chores on time with minimal reminders.
- Account for their money.
- Be willing to say where they will be and who they will be with.
- Keep curfews.
- Be clean.
- Keep their rooms reasonably neat.
- Be honest.
- Follow reasonable house rules.
- Interact with other family members (not spend all their time alone).
- Keep promises.

At school:

- Get there on time.
- Attend all classes.
- Complete assignments.
- Maintain grades consistent with their academic potential.
- Avoid disciplinary problems.
- Be involved in co-curricular activities.

In the community:

- Not get into trouble with the law.
- Be places on time.
- Drive responsibly.
- Be civil and courteous with friends, neighbors, and relatives.
- Participate reasonably in family and community activities.

The reader may want to add to this list or otherwise clarify his or her expectations. Regardless of what the expectations are, what's most important is that the counselor be clear about them. A rule in treatment with adolescents is to confront them each and every time they fail to meet an expectation or violate a limit. Confront them as soon as possible. Consequences may be appropriate at times, but consequences must always follow a direct confrontation of the issue. Do not, however, merely impose consequences in an impartial way, since this is too easily interpreted as indifference. A direct verbal confrontation of the issue is best: "You were supposed to _____, and you didn't. What's happening? When will you do it?"

Confrontation is often more effective in changing behavior than imposing consequences. If confrontation fails to lead to improvement, it can be combined with appropriate consequences. Never stop confronting and/or imposing consequences, no matter how many times the adolescent transgresses.

One could argue that the single most important thing a counselor can do with an adolescent patient is to get him or her to be progressively more responsive to reasonable limits and expectations. As this occurs, dysfunctional peer groups are almost always replaced by functional ones, and the individuation process moves ahead in a healthy way.

INTERVENTION

The term "intervention" has its origins in work with adult alcoholics who are resistant to treatment. These individuals typically have a very obvious (to others) drinking or using problem, which has led to a series of specific negative consequences of a physical, social, or emotional nature. They may have had accidents, been arrested for driving while intoxicated, suffered illnesses, lost jobs, beaten their spouses or children, etc. Yet, despite these objective realities, they continue to deny that a problem exists, shift the blame to someone else, or minimize it. They also refuse to enter treatment of any kind. Faced with this frustrating situation, counselors developed the technique of intervention to help family members pressure the alcoholic into getting help.

Basically, intervention refers to the systematic confrontation of an alcoholic with the negative consequences of his or her drinking, on self and on others. Intervention can work with adolescents and young adults, too. Prior to doing an intervention with a teenager or young adult, however, it is important to establish the sources of leverage available to press the adolescent into getting help. There are three main sources of such leverage: the family, the school, and the legal system. By far, the family and legal system have the greatest leverage, though the school should not be overlooked. If a judge indicates that treatment is necessary, if parents are firm in their resolve that their son or daughter must get help, or if the school refuses to readmit a student unless he or she has gotten help, then the chances of an intervention working effectively are much greater than they are if the legal system, the school, or the family is ambivalent. In that case, the only real leverage is the adolescent's own knowledge that he or she is in trouble and needs help, or the therapist's ability to convince him or her of this. This works at times, but support from some external authority — parents, school or court — is very helpful.

The goals of an intervention are straightforward; it is intended to establish the following:

1. That a problem does exist (as opposed to not existing).
2. That change is necessary; something must be done (as opposed to nothing being done).
3. That help is available (and what the alternatives are).

Interventions are usually led by a counselor, but they can be led by a parent, a school official, or an officer of the court, such as a probation officer. The professional counselor, however, is the one most often called upon to coordinate an intervention. An intervention can be divided into a series of phases. Before getting to this how-to level, however, let's go over a few ground rules for doing an intervention.

Ground Rules

The first and most important ground rule to observe, before attempting an intervention, is to do your homework. Many an intervention has failed simply because the person doing it did not take enough time to prepare: to establish the facts and develop sources of leverage. Faced with denial from the substance abuser, who is motivated after all to avoid the issue altogether (and thereby undermine the intervention), either not having enough facts or not knowing how much the family (or school, or court) can be counted on will most likely lead to frustration and failure. A careful and thorough evaluation is the best insurance against this happening.

Whereas schools and courts usually stand firm, parents sometimes change their minds or weaken in their resolve in the face of denial, anger, and resistance. Some of this can be avoided by outlining the intervention process, by predicting likely forms of denial, and by role-playing problem situations in advance. Ask the parents how they will respond if their son or daughter gets angry. What will they say if the child flatly denies the problem or refuses to go for help? Are they in complete agreement about the basis and goals of the intervention, or would it be possible for the teen to drive a wedge between them? Could they be talked out of it? How would their son or daughter attempt to do this?

This leads to the issue of consequences: the "or else" that backs up the intervention. What will the parents (or the court, or the school) do if the adolescent continues to deny the problem and/or rejects help? This is another area where there needs to be discussion. A hasty commitment made by an uncertain parent is not a commitment to be counted on. Take whatever time is necessary to explore the long-term consequences of not acting. Where will the young person be a year from now, if something isn't done now? Explore the parents' attitudes toward imposing consequences — the so-called "tough love" issue: Is it really helpful (or loving) to allow a child to continue on a self-destructive course? Is it really helpful or loving to not impose consequences, even to the extent of asking the adolescent to leave if he or she won't get help?

Talk also about the basis for the intervention. Are the negative consequences of substance use clear to the parents? Where do they see things leading if decisive action isn't taken? Do they see it as their responsibility to take this action? Do they attribute the consequences you've inventoried to substance abuse, or could they be convinced otherwise? It's better to bring up these difficult issues rather than avoiding them, because you can be sure that, if you don't, the adolescent will! Preparing parents in this way will make an intervention much more likely to succeed.

The second ground rule to follow in doing an intervention is to be sure that it does not end without some clear understanding — a "contract" — among all the parties, as to what has been decided. It's helpful to literally write this out and give copies to everyone at the end of the meeting.

The desired outcome of an intervention is treatment of some form.

The counselor should have a definite idea ahead of time of what sort of treatment is needed. This should be the objective, but it's a mistake to abandon an intervention if this can't be achieved. If necessary, settle for a less intense form of treatment, but follow up with a contract that states what the consequences will be if this level of treatment is not successful. In other words, never end the intervention without an agreement as to treatment or a contract that can be used as leverage later on. An example of such a contract, for a hypothetical youth who refuses a recommendation of residential treatment, is shown in Figure 2.

Don't underestimate the power that an agreement such as the above can have at a later date, if the teen refuses treatment (or the preferred treatment) at the time of the intervention. The specific problems should include all those negative consequences (failing grades, arrests, etc.) that have been associated with progressive involvement with substances.

The final ground rule to follow is simple: stick to the point, and to

Figure 2. Sample Contract

Date:

I, _____, do not agree to enter residential treatment for substance abuse at this time. However, I do agree to see _____ on a weekly basis, and to discontinue all use of the following mood-altering chemicals: _____. I also agree to take the following specific steps to help me maintain sobriety: _____.

I recognize that I must take responsibility for dealing with this problem. Therefore, if the specific problems listed below continue, or if I am not able to stop using, then I agree to take the following steps: _____. Specific problems: _____
_____

_____   _____
Adolescent signature   Parent signature

_____   _____
Therapist signature   Parent signature

the facts. Do not get into arguments with adolescents over whether they are or are not alcoholics or addicts. In fact, it's better not to use these words at all with teens, whose stereotypes of addicts are even more bizarre than adults'. Expect them to deny the link between substance use and negative consequences. Stick to the observable facts and the goals of the intervention: A problem does exist, and something must be done. Do not allow the conversation to get sidetracked onto another problem, your own chemical history, etc.

Conducting an Intervention

Now let's look at the intervention process itself, which can be divided up into a series of steps.

STEP 1: STATING THE FACTS

Before even contemplating an intervention, the counselor will have prepared a thorough inventory of objective facts. This information can be collected from the adolescent directly, and also from collateral sources, such as parents and teachers. If appropriate, probation officers or attorneys should be consulted.

The goal in the first step of an intervention is to confront the adolescent in a respectful yet firm and frank way with the list of problems that has led up to the intervention. A chronological accounting is the most effective approach to take. Begin by citing all accidents, arrests, or school suspensions. Comment on the pattern of school performance, including attendance and grades, over time. Cite patterns of increasing family tensions, fighting, etc.

Next, cite the youth's own accounts of blackouts, embarrassing experiences related to bingeing, and physical reactions (heart palpitations, chest pains, etc.). Share straightforwardly your best estimate of the teen's level of substance use, from experimental to compulsive, citing evidence to support your diagnosis. Finally, point out any and all evidence of accommodation, seeking or chasing behavior, tolerance, preoccupation, and substance substitution. Always let the facts speak for themselves, and let the interview lead to a natural conclusion. To do this, the counselor must have faith in the facts. If the adolescent finally concludes, based on the facts, that he or she has a problem related to substance use, then recovery has begun.

STEP 2: STATING THE CONSEQUENCES

The concept of parents' giving children or adolescents an ultimatum — either do _____ or _____ will happen — has fallen out of favor as a parenting strategy. We have moved toward a more egalitarian approach to childrearing that deemphasizes the overt use of parental power. In fact, what we may be doing is simply avoiding recognizing the reality and necessity of this power. As appealing as the idea of egalitarian parent-child relationships may be (to some parents), it is probably more an illusion than a reality, and a dangerous one at that. Not only are children and adolescents objectively subject to a great deal of external control from parents, schools, and other authorities, but psychologically they need these controls for their own development and, at times, for their own safety. Perhaps there is no area where this is more self-evident than in dealing with a substance-abusing teenager. This is a young person who has impaired self-control and whose very life is ultimately at stake; yet, many parents still balk at insisting that their child do something about it.

The objective of the second step in an intervention is just that: to insist that the adolescent do something. The message is simple and clear: Something must change. This is where the "or else" comes in: some consequence that will occur if something doesn't change — if the adolescent refuses to take some action. The counselor needs to follow the advice given earlier and prepare parents in advance for this eventuality. Role play it until they are comfortable with it and united on it. Be prepared to support them if they appear to lose heart or if the teenager attempts to divide them. Stand with them if they choose, for example, to tell an adolescent that he or she must leave home if he or she does not get help.

STEP 3: STATING THE ALTERNATIVES

Alternatives include all of the forms of treatment or help that are available to the teenager or young adult and that would be acceptable to the parent and the counselor. A helpful hint: Don't even mention alternatives that you are uncomfortable with. For example, if you believe that inpatient treatment is needed, offer a choice of two or three such programs. Don't even discuss, much less offer, weekly outpatient therapy as an alternative. Let the teenager be the one to broach the issue of compromise; then start thinking in terms of a contract.

An intervention that is successfully carried out does not have to be a hostile experience, especially if it is done with respect both for the youth and the facts. When confronted frankly but respectfully, many adolescents and young adults will admit to the reality of their own substance abuse—sometimes more readily than many adults will. Only those who have had too few limits set will tend to be truly rebellious. Accordingly, parents who are unaccustomed to setting limits may need extra support in dealing with their children during an intervention.

What To Do When Things Go Wrong

An effective intervention succeeds on many levels. It gets the young person to admit to having a substance abuse problem. It helps both the adolescent and the parent attribute accumulating negative consequences to their correct cause: deepening involvement with alcohol and/or drugs. Finally, it succeeds in engaging the entire family in a treatment plan.

Of course, things don't always go so smoothly. What happens when carefully prepared parents back off and start doubting that treatment is necessary or that a substance abuse problem exists? What happens when the young person refuses to cooperate or even walks out?

At times like these (and they will happen) it's important to keep in mind the fact that denial—refusing to accept a substance abuse problem—can be contagious. Parents are frequently no more anxious than their children are to admit to the true extent of the problem. They may collude unconsciously with their son or daughter, blaming teachers, "bad influences" (friends), or even illnesses as the causes of the trouble that brought them to your office. Sometimes, parents and teens are not convinced the first time around, or the second. At times, more negative consequences need to accumulate—so-called "bottoming out"—before enabling and denial finally yield to reality.

Whenever an intervention appears to be going awry, remember the ground rule about making a contract. Ask the teen, and the parent, to tell you what would be enough to convince them that a serious substance abuse problem—one requiring treatment—did exist. Write these conditions down. Try to get a commitment from the family that they will contact you again, if and when these conditions occur. Give them a copy of the contract to take along with them. Wish them luck, and don't feel angry or bitter—you may very well see them again.

SUMMARY

This chapter presented a number of ground rules for counseling adolescents. An understanding of the individuation process, plus a recognition of the significant developmental role of the peer group in personality development, must be combined with holding teens accountable for complying with reasonable expectations and limits. The therapist cannot afford to be perceived as indifferent, which is the typical interpretation that teens and young adults place on adults who do not·enforce limits, who appear to have low standards for behavior, and who avoid confrontation.

Intervention with adolescent substance abusers allows the therapist to be perceived as caring and involved, rather than indifferent. Effective intervention has communicative value. It tells adolescents that the counselor will not accept excuses for the negative consequences that substances have led to. It lets teens know that help is available and that the therapist has more positive expectations (and hope) for them than they may have for themselves. It conveys a willingness to get involved rather than give up on the troubled youth. Lastly, it challenges the young person to join with the therapist in working toward improved selfesteem and a better life.

10

Early Phases of Adolescent Recovery: Denial and Compliance

The adolescent's decision to enter treatment, even unwillingly, marks the beginning of the recovery process. For many teens, this represents the first adult expectation they will have complied with in several years. A popular myth has it that teens (or adults) must "want" to recover from substance abuse and addiction in order for it to happen. In reality it is the rare adult or adolescent who seeks out treatment; yet many of those who are pressed into treatment through interventions end up doing very well. To understand why this happens, we have to understand the nature of addiction and of the recovery process.

The recovery process can be divided into four phases, which are the subject of this and the next chapter. Each phase is associated with particular dynamics, and responds best to particular interventions.

PHASE 1: DENIAL

It is part of the nature of addiction that the person who is caught up in it will refuse to admit it. The dynamics underlying denial are not entirely clear, but the phenomenon no doubt has something to do with the ego threat posed by the powerlessness that addiction represents. If we assume that the idea of being out of control is psychologically threatening—a reasonable assumption by most standards—then denial can be regarded as a defense against this threat. This is consistent with the clinical observation that when denial fails the addict is flooded with anxiety, often driving him or her to the point of despair and suicide.

Denial can also be a defense against the shame that the addict typically feels. Loss of personal control is not only anxiety-provoking but also shame-provoking. Historically, addiction was regarded as a personal failure: a failure of willpower. It was not too long ago, for example, that alcoholics were stigmatized for their lack of character rather than treated for their illness. For this reason alone the addict will feel shame. Beyond this, there are practical aspects to the shame associated with addiction, having to do with the harmful and hurtful things that addicts may do as a result of their compulsive need to satisfy their addiction. Overcoming shame is central to recovery, which is why the Twelve Steps speak directly to addicts on this issue. Shame and anxiety, then, are what motivate the addict to avoid confronting and admitting to the reality of addiction. They are the foundation of denial. If not successfully resolved, anxiety and shame pose a decided threat to recovery.

Forms of Denial

Denial can take any of several different forms, and it is important for the clinician to be able to identify them.

STONEWALLING

Stonewalling, the simplest form of denial, is reflected in the flat denial of symptoms of substance abuse or addiction, despite clear and objective evidence to the contrary. Simple examples are the teenager who denies being drunk even after being arrested for driving while intoxicated, or who denies using marijuana even after the substance has been found on him or her.

In addition to denying use per se, stonewalling takes the form of denying an obvious connection between use and symptoms of addiction — for example, tolerance — or clearcut negative consequences. For example, I was told by one teenager that abuse of drugs was in no way related to the progressive changes in her personality that her parents had observed, to her deteriorating school grades, to her abrupt change of peer groups, or to the fact that she had all but stopped going to school. She steadfastly denied any problem with drugs, even though every time she tried to stop using one substance she used more of another one.

It's unclear sometimes whether addicts who stonewall actually believe their own stories. In most cases it appears to be simply a thinly veiled effort to avoid the implications of admitting use — either punishment or treatment — while inwardly the addict knows the truth. At other times, however, it seems that addicts' defense systems literally keep them out of touch with the reality of their own symptomatology and the connection between their deteriorating lives and their substance use.

MINIMIZING/MAXIMIZING

This is a very common technique in which the substance abuser acknowledges use, and perhaps even symptoms of use, but minimizes both use and symptoms, while simultaneously exaggerating (maximizing) the use and problems of others. "I only smoke pot on weekends," the teen might say in self-defense, "but I have friends who get high almost every day." Or, "Yes, I did get arrested for driving while intoxicated, but almost everyone has, and some of my friends have two or three times." Or, "My friends do cocaine and crack; I just smoke pot."

Minimizing/maximizing is an attempt to normalize substance use and the symptoms of abuse by creating an artificial contrast: "I'm not so bad compared to others." The abuser is attempting to convince someone — a parent or a counselor — that his or her use is "statistically" normal, that is, certainly no worse than, and probably not even as bad as, that of his or her peers. This strategy works surprisingly often, since most parents have no idea of what is "normal" use in teens and young adults, and may be reluctant to believe their son or daughter is worse off than his or her peers.

DISTRACTING

The problem is not my drinking, the alcoholic says; the problem is my rotten marriage — or my rotten kids, my rotten job, my rotten health, etc. Variations on this theme are countless. Over the course of time, everything under the sun — except substance abuse — has been cited as the "real" problem for the substance abuser. This, too, works surprisingly often. One adolescent, whose parents knew very well that he was a regular marijuana user, allowed themselves to be convinced that it was poor teachers who were responsible for their son's lack of motivation, as well as his steadily deteriorating grades and attendance record. He was in denial about the amotivational syndrome that marijuana use was clearly causing. Because his parents were successfully distracted, however, he was allowed to transfer schools, thereby enabling the problem to continue (and worsen) for another year.

JUSTIFYING

A close cousin of distraction, justifying follows the generic form represented by the bad joke: If you had my wife, you'd drink too. Among adolescents, parents are most often the scapegoats for substance use, though sibling conflict or academic pressures are also used as justifications. The implication is that the individual can't be expected to control or stop his or her substance use so long as the scapegoat is "driving" it. In defending his use, and the negative consequences it led to, one teen implied that he virtually had no choice but to use: "My parents are always on my case, so what do you expect me to do?" Another complained about how he'd tried hanging around kids who didn't get high: "But they were so boring, I went back to my old friends and started using again." In the first case, conflicts with parents were being used to justify use; in the second case, it was apparently others' "boring" personalities that justified marijuana abuse!

CHALLENGING

Challenging is an attempt to put the accuser on the defensive. It is a counterattack in response to a confrontation. The teen or young adult may question the clinician's or the parent's expertise: "What do you know about addiction?" Or there may be an effort to evoke guilt: "Haven't you ever gotten high?" "Didn't you smoke pot when you were my age?"

Challenging, like justifying and distracting, gets the interaction off the point, which is the teenager's own use, its symptoms, and its observable consequences. Parents are vulnerable to being manipulated through a challenging approach, especially if they ever did abuse alcohol or use drugs. This aggressive form of denial may evoke guilt or embarrassment, it can paralyze parents and cause them to back off from a confrontation or abandon an intervention, if the counselor isn't careful to prepare them in advance.

John was well on his way to being addicted to both alcohol and marijuana. He had a superior mind, however, and he put it to use when it came to denial. Of course, denial always works against the addict's own long-term interests; but the addict doesn't recognize this. John knew that his parents had used marijuana regularly during their college years and that they still enjoyed sharing an occasional joint. He argued with me, with a school counselor, and with his parents during our evaluation interview. He challenged his parents' moral authority, embarrassing them by disclosing what he knew about their own use. In a lawyerly fashion he challenged all of us to "prove" the connection between the problems he was having in school and substance use. He cited his parents' successful careers as evidence that a person could use marijuana "recreationally." I knew that if we attempted to play the game according to these rules, we were certain to fail. Unfortunately, because I hadn't known of his parents' use in advance, I was not able to prepare them for this tactic. As a result, John's attack prevailed, and for the time being he got off the hook. Of course, his substance abuse worsened and he went on to become addicted to cocaine before getting into treatment.

PSEUDO-CHOICE

Perhaps the most transparent form of denial, pseudo-choice takes the form of asserting that substance abuse is a choice, and therefore a behavior that is under control. Again, this form of denial can work, especially if the other person knows relatively little about the process of addiction or its symptoms.

"Yeah, I smoke pot every day," the teen might say, "but it's because I want to." In a similar way, alcoholics can acknowledge getting drunk seven days a week, but again claim that that's what they want (i.e., intend) to do. This defense is a bald attempt to assert that the individual uses alcohol or drugs not out of need, but out of choice.

The young person who uses pseudo-choice in defense of substance abuse is attempting to deny any connection between substance use and its symptoms, in particular negative consequences. It is a form of denial that is easily and effectively challenged, since the substance user is acknowledging use, and perhaps even abuse. It is best challenged by simply repeating signs, symptoms, and negative consequences, over and over again. The clinician can also undermine pseudo-choice by asking the teenager to prove it: by willingly abstaining from all substance use for a period of time, such as one month.

Dealing with Denial

Denial is what the First Step of Alcoholics Anonymous and Narcotics Anonymous is about:

> We admitted that we were powerless over our addiction, that our lives had become unmanageable.

The First Step marks the beginning of the road to recovery; yet it is often the most difficult step of all for the addict to take. Denial—resistance to an admission of powerlessness, of the loss of personal control over use—is a barrier to taking the first step in recovery.

Denial, in any form, represents a barrier to recovery, and it must be dealt with first in treatment. The best approach is a straightforward one. The clinician should take the position that a problem with substance use does exist, based on observable behavior and consequences. Persistence is required, as well as patience and determination, in order to work through denial. The clinician must be convinced of the diagnosis and must be vigilant for further observable evidence—symptoms and consequences—that need to be shared with the teen. Some specific strategies for dealing with denial are described in the following sections.

EDUCATION

Most teens, like most of their parents, are relatively uneducated about substance abuse and addiction. In many cases false beliefs may strengthen denial or undermine treatment. Counselors should begin working on denial by educating the entire family, including the substance abuser, about the nature and stages of addiction. The material presented in earlier chapters can be useful in this regard. However, relying on written materials isn't usually sufficient to break through denial. Reading is appropriate, but it should be supported by discussion and opportunities to ask questions. Check for assimilation of knowledge by asking the family as a whole questions like the following:

- What are some of the key signs and symptoms associated with habitual substance abuse?

- What is "compensatory" substance use?
- What is "seeking behavior"?
- What does "accommodation" mean, and what are its symptoms?
- What does "chasing a high" mean?
- What is "addiction"?

Teens, parents, and even preteenage siblings should all be able to answer questions like these accurately, in their own words. Open discussion of addiction in the family can help reduce some of the shame that the addict feels and make it easier to let go of denial. It can also help to debunk common myths, for example, the ideas that adolescents can't get addicted, that marijuana is not an addictive substance, and that addicts can safely use substances they aren't addicted to, all of which are false.

PEER CONFRONTATION

Because the peer group is so influential with teens and young adults, a group approach is often more effective in dealing with denial than individual counseling, although using the two concurrently is probably even better. Teens in a group should be asked to share their impressions frankly of how each of them denies: What are their own defenses, and what are their peers' defenses? They can be encouraged to "pull each other up" whenever they detect denial—in other words, to call each other on what they observe. The ethic to be promoted is that substance abuse and addiction "bring you down," spiritually, psychologically, and socially, but that recovery and the 12-step program "bring you up." Having had firsthand experience with denial in its various forms, recovering addicts have a credibility in confrontations that a therapist might not enjoy. The group treatment format is helpful for reinforcing a non-use ethic, and for promoting a philosophy of drug-free living and natural fulfillment.

CHEMICAL HISTORY-SHARING

Another strategy that works well at this stage of treatment is to have the adolescent construct and share a personal chemical history. Some of this will have been done by the counselor, but the teen should also construct his or her own chemical history. The format in Table 5 can be used or adapted for this purpose. Once it is completed,

Table 5: Chemical History Instructions

Instructions: The purpose of a chemical history is to help you put your substance use in perspective, and to see how it has affected your life. Begin your chemical history with the first time (at what age) you remember trying any mood-altering chemical (including alcohol). Fill out all of the information asked for before you move on to the next mood-altering substance you've used. It is especially important that you try to recall ALL of the feelings and consequences associated with use, as well as what significant things were happening for you and your family at the time.

For each substance, indicate times when your use significantly increased. Again, list the feelings associated with those changes and what was happening in your life at the time. Here's an example:

AGE	CHEMICAL	HOW OFTEN	WHEN/WHERE	FEELINGS	LIFE EVENTS
12	Alcohol	Weekends	Parties	High Sick	Nothing much
15	"	Daily Daily	Alone Parties	Bombed Angry	My girlfriend got killed
15	Marijuana	Weekdays	Alone In school	Mellow	Nothing

the chemical history should be verbally shared with the counselor, with the family, and if possible with a peer group.

The person who might have filled out this hypothetical (and simple) chemical history was someone who started out drinking, on weekends at parties, at age 12. Alcohol made him feel "high" and occasionally sick. Nothing much was happening in his life, that he can remember, at that time. Starting at age 15, after his girlfriend was killed in a car accident, this person began drinking every day. He also began drinking alone, not just at parties, and also started using marijuana. Sometimes after drinking he'd feel angry; but smoking pot made him feel mellow.

When constructing a chemical history, include experiences with all of the following substances: depressants (alcohol, inhalants, etc.); hallucinogens (marijuana and psychedelics such as LSD, "acid," "shrooms," "angel dust," etc.); stimulants (cocaine, amphetamines and "uppers"); barbiturates ("downers"); tranquilizers; and heroin. Be careful to get information not only on lifetime use, but also on use over the past year and six months, to detect patterns of use and substance substitution.

The feelings uncovered through the chemical history, combined with significant events that coincide with increases in use, provide vital clues to understanding the psychodynamics and progression of substance use. The counselor needs to tie this history into a chrono- logical account of negative consequences that the young person has experienced. Arrests, declining school grades, truancy, behavioral problems (such as aggression or suicide attempts), and emotional problems such as depression can be correlated with the chemical history to present a powerful visual representation of exactly where the youth is in the addictive process, and what role substances are playing in his or her life.

One word of caution when dealing with denial in adolescents: the goal, in the first stage of recovery, is to get the adolescent to acknowl- edge substance abuse and to attribute symptoms and negative conse- quences to that use. This is often sufficient to get the young person into a treatment program, where denial can be dealt with further, under more controlled circumstances. It may be unnecessary (and risky) to press a young person to admit powerlessness at this point. Denial represents not only a barrier to recovery, but a defense against anxiety and shame. Taking away anyone's defenses can be risky busi- ness. If the objective of getting a young person into a treatment program and taking it seriously has been achieved, there is little point in pushing harder unless the situation can be supervised and con- trolled. Step 1 can be taken more fully, psychologically speaking, at a later time.

PHASE 2: COMPLIANCE

Kip was 17, a handsome young man with long, wavy, mahogany- colored hair and a trim, well-proportioned body. He sat on the couch beside his father, a handsome man also, who looked to be in his late forties. Both looked edgy. Kip had recently been discharged from a residential rehabilitation program, where he'd spent six weeks and had ostensibly done very well. A week before our meeting, however, he'd been caught in school with marijuana in his pocket, and was suspend- ed. He admitted to his parents that he'd been using pot, on and off, for several months, and was drinking occasionally as well. His father was understandably upset—and confused, too. His mother was so angry that she wasn't speaking to him at the moment and had refused to come to the interview. The same was true for his older sister.

I asked Kip if he thought he had a substance abuse problem. He said yes. I asked him if he thought he'd learned anything about substance abuse during his treatment, and he replied, quite honestly I thought, that he'd learned a great deal. Then I asked him what his personal, private goal had been during his treatment.

Kip replied straightforwardly: "I wanted to learn how to use without getting into trouble."

"So you believed," I said, "that it was possible for you to learn to use drugs 'safely'?" He nodded.

Kip's attitude toward substance abuse, along with his secret treatment goal, is an example of "compliance." In replacing denial with compliance, persons who have abused substances are on the one hand acknowledging abuse as well as its negative consequences; on the other hand, on a deeper level they have not yet accepted the idea that they must abstain from use. They may be in treatment, but they are not taking it seriously (or as seriously as they should). They may be doing well, objectively speaking, and may be good at "talking the talk" of recovery; but their hearts are not yet in it and they aren't prepared to "walk the walk" of recovery. An attitude of compliance covers up a secret belief in "controlled use," including the idea that some mood-altering chemicals can still be used "safely."

Psychodynamically, compliance, much like denial, is driven by the anxiety and shame associated with loss of control. Much like the early stages of a grief reaction, compliance is characterized by bargaining, i.e., limited acceptance of the loss (of control). Another way to think of compliance is that it is "bargaining with recovery."

Controlled Use

So-called "controlled use" of mood-altering chemicals by persons who are in reality addicted to those substances remains a controversial issue, despite the inherent contradiction in reasoning that it implies. The very idea that an addict can "control" use flies in the face of the concept of addiction. Controlled use may be a viable option for the true social user, but the habitual abuser and the addict are not candidates for controlled use.

Efforts at controlled use lead to failure and further negative consequences when they are attempted by habitual users and those with clear symptoms of loss of control. Common strategies used by these persons include attempts to restrict use to certain times — only after school, only on weekends — to limit the amount of use — no more than a six-pack, no more than three joints — or to confine use to certain substances — no more freebase cocaine, no more hard liquor. Attempts like these to limit use and their subsequent failure are part of the addiction process itself: of the struggle for control. Each successive failure to "control" use engenders increased shame and anxiety, which in turn drives the addict's defenses and motivates him or her to deny the reality of addiction not only to the world, but also to him or herself.

Substance Substitution

Another common form of compliance is the belief that it is safe for an addict to use mood-altering substances other than those which he or she is addicted to. Cocaine addicts, for example, commonly harbor beliefs that they can safely drink, or smoke pot, once they have stopped using cocaine. Alcoholics may think it safe to use marijuana. And so on.

Like "controlled use," substance substitution is actually part of the addiction process, not a solution for it. Addicts will almost invariably attempt to substitute one mood-altering chemical for another one that they are trying to quit. This sort of thinking is symptomatic of addiction. The real issue is not whether the individual is in fact addicted to the substitute substance, but the dependent attitude toward substance use that is revealed in substance substitution. A secondary risk is that while under the influence of the substitute substance — even one to which he or she is not addicted — the recovering addict will revert to use of his or her substance of choice.

Recovery goes beyond simple abstinence from a single substance. The goal in recovery is rejection of substance use as a coping strategy and as a means of recreation; in other words, elimination of both hedonistic and compensatory motivations for substance use. An attitude of compliance, as well as the bargaining it implies, will undermine recovery every time.

Dealing with Compliance

The clinician should suspect compliance whenever a patient admits to substance abuse, or even to addiction, yet seems relatively complacent and unaffected by that admission. This is a tip-off that, psychodynamically, the reality of addiction—and of the need for abstinence—has not "sunk in." Individuals in compliance can talk the talk of recovery very well, but either there is a discernible lack of affect in their talk or else it strikes the clinician as forced and ungenuine.

In working with a client in compliance, the clinician can utilize some of the same techniques that are used to deal with denial. First and foremost among these is repeated confrontation of the client with objective facts: with symptoms of addiction (such as preoccupation, tolerance, and unsuccessful efforts to stop or control use) and with negative consequences associated with use. Confrontation from peers is even more effective than confrontation by an adult counselor. At the same time, it is important to work with the compliant client in three additional areas: self-assessment, ego development, and emotional expression.

SELF-ASSESSMENT

One of the dynamics underlying compliance has to do with the shame associated with addiction. It's already been pointed out that addiction—loss of control over substance use—represents a major threat to self-esteem. To complicate matters, the substance abuser has probably experienced significant losses and failures, and may have committed acts that are either illegal or immoral. The result is that self-esteem is tenuous. From the abuser's point of view, admitting addiction may only make a bad situation worse.

The self-esteem of the substance abuser cannot be rebuilt through any simple technique. Self-esteem is rebuilt slowly but steadily in recovery. The 12-step program, particularly Steps 4, 5, 6, and 7 help get the addict on the road to rebuilding self-esteem through frank acknowledgment of wrongdoing, failure, etc., and through making amends. In working with adolescents, this work can start with a careful and honest self-assessment. This is not the same thing as a "moral inventory," as is referred to in Step 4 of the Twelve Steps. A moral inventory specifically refers to the process of inventorying and acknowledging harm done to self and others as a consequence of addiction. That work is not effectively done by the addict in compliance; a self-assessment, on the other hand, can be done.

The goal of a self-assessment is to identify personal strengths, to explore options available for the future, and to set initial short-term goals that will enhance self-esteem. If this process is successful it can undermine compliance and open the way to recovery.

The self-assessment needs to be thorough; at the same time, the clinician needs to help keep the focus on the positive. The youth who has suffered social, academic, and other consequences of substance abuse can be expected to resist such an approach. Shame and self-hatred are close to the surface in these individuals, and many negative and pessimistic self-statements can be expected. These should not be challenged at this point; a better approach is to simply acknowledge a negative statement and then move ahead with the assessment.

A self-assessment can be started with a "homework" assignment in which the teen rates him or herself along a series of dimensions. This can be done using a questionnaire such as the one in Table 6. It is important for the clinician to follow up on all responses to such an inventory. This should take place in the context of a one-on-one dialogue with the young person. If group treatment is available, personal inventories such as the one in Table 6 should be shared at some point by each member of the group, preferably after the members have shared their chemical histories.

In reviewing the personal inventory, the counselor is looking first and foremost for identified strengths, and secondly for weaknesses that can be remediated. It is important not to overlook "average" responses: inquire further to determine whether they are more negative or positive. Responses in the "average" range but tending more toward the negative represent areas that may be worked on initially, turning them into relative assets as opposed to relative liabilities. Areas that are more negatively charged will tend to need more intense therapeutic work; this may need to be deferred until self-esteem becomes more solid. Often the most negative self-statements point the way to significant traumas, some of which may be related to substance abuse, such as illegal or immoral conduct related to addiction, and others of which may have predated substance abuse, including parental neglect and sexual abuse.

Table 6: Self-Assessment Questionnaire

Attractiveness: I am . . .
---------1---------2---------3---------4---------5---------6---------7---------8---------9---------10
Very attractive　　　　　　　　　　Average　　　　　　　　　　Very unattractive

Self-confidence: I have . . .
---------1---------2---------3---------4---------5---------6---------7---------8---------9---------10
Much self-confidence　　　　　　　　Average　　　　　　　　Little self-confidence

Personality: My personality is . . .
---------1---------2---------3---------4---------5---------6---------7---------8---------9---------10
Pleasant　　　　　　　　　　　　　Average　　　　　　　　　　Unpleasant

Same-sex relationships: I get along with others of my own sex . . .
---------1---------2---------3---------4---------5---------6---------7---------8---------9---------10
Very well　　　　　　　　　　　　Okay　　　　　　　　　　Very badly

Opposite-sex relationships: I get along with members of the opposite sex . . .
---------1---------2---------3---------4---------5---------6---------7---------8---------9---------10
Very well　　　　　　　　　　　　Okay　　　　　　　　　　Very badly

Relationships with adults: I get along with adults . . .
---------1---------2---------3---------4---------5---------6---------7---------8---------9---------10
Very well　　　　　　　　　　　　Okay　　　　　　　　　　Very badly

Appearance: My personal appearance is . . .
---------1---------2---------3---------4---------5---------6---------7---------8---------9---------10
Neat and clean　　　　　　　　　　Average　　　　　　　　Unclean and sloppy

Intelligence: I am . . .
---------1---------2---------3---------4---------5---------6---------7---------8---------9---------10
Intelligent　　　　　　　　　　　Average　　　　　　　　　Unintelligent

Grooming: My personal grooming habits are . . .
---------1---------2---------3---------4---------5---------6---------7---------8---------9---------10
Good　　　　　　　　　　　　　　Average　　　　　　　　　　Bad

Personal character: I am basically a . . .
---------1---------2---------3---------4---------5---------6---------7---------8---------9---------10
Good person　　　　　　　　　Average person　　　　　　　Bad person

Talents: I have . . .
---------1---------2---------3---------4---------5---------6---------7---------8---------9---------10
Many talents　　　　　　　　　Some talents　　　　　　　　No talents

Table 6 (*Continued*)

Coordination: Physically, I am . . .

---------1---------2---------3---------4---------5---------6---------7---------8---------9---------10

Very coordinated   Average   Very uncoordinated

Popularity: Most people . . .

---------1---------2---------3---------4---------5---------6---------7---------8---------9---------10

Like me a lot   Are neutral about me   Dislike me strongly

Self-esteem: If I could make myself over I would be . . .

---------1---------2---------3---------4---------5---------6---------7---------8---------9---------10

Exactly as I am   A little different   Totally different

EGO DEVELOPMENT

Just as improving self-esteem will help to undermine the defenses that support compliance, so will systematic efforts to foster ego development help the young person move on to the next level of recovery. In working with adolescent and young adult substance abusers, the most important consideration to keep in mind is that substance abuse and addiction increasingly deprive the individual of free choice and independent decision-making. As one addicted young woman put it: "Deciding I was an addict was the first real decision I ever made in my life."

Decision-making is a key element in the individuation process: Every true (free) choice that a person makes contributes to his or her sense of self. As ego strength builds—as the will becomes stronger— the healthy individual eventually separates from the peer group, just as he or she once did from the parent. Substance abuse and addiction arrest the individuation process; recovery resumes it.

While providing needed structure, including behavioral limits, explicit expectations, and ethical guidelines, therapy with recovering adolescents and young adults must help whenever possible to facilitate individuation and ego development. These young men and women must be encouraged, under the guidance of the counselor, to begin making decisions. In this regard the therapist serves as a mentor or surrogate parent. By sharing his or her values, opinions, and ideas, and by engaging in a frank dialogue with the teen, the therapist helps the teen clarify values and priorities and to set goals. A corrective group experience, such as that described in Chapter 15, can be equally powerful in this respect.

As ego strength and self-esteem develop, the adolescent's defenses against admitting addiction are weakened. The ego becomes stronger, less paralyzed, and better able to confront the anxiety and shame that motivate denial and compliance, without fear of being overwhelmed. This is the point at which Step 1 can be taken completely, with all of its emotional implications.

EMOTIONAL EXPRESSION

If substance abusers do not learn to suppress emotions prior to getting involved in substance abuse, they most certainly learn to do so afterward. Control of emotions, and specifically the suppression of dysphoric feelings — anxiety, anguish, grief, anger, loneliness, boredom, etc. — is a primary motivation for chronic substance use. These are the key emotions that trigger compensatory use. It's little wonder, then, that the addicted adolescent, even in recovery, is typically an individual who is severely handicapped when it comes to dealing with his or her own emotions.

Compliance itself is simply another defense against emotions. Remember that the individual who is in compliance is a person who lacks emotion, other than on a superficial level. The words may be there, but the gut level feelings are not. Teens in compliance may say they feel angry or sad, but they don't seem angry or sad. They may say they're addicted, but they seem unaffected by that fact.

In working through compliance, it is necessary to help teens to identify and express their emotions. This will be a goal in family therapy as much as it is in individual and group work. The therapeutic objective is to minimize avoidance and acting out, and to maximize getting in touch with and expressing feelings.

Adolescents, like children, are inclined to avoid (deny) dysphoric feelings that they feel incapable of coping with. Typically, however, they will reveal the feelings they are trying to avoid through their actions. For example, the child may act in a way that clearly suggests aggression and hostility but deny actually feeling angry. This pattern, which is called "acting out," is learned within the family and will be carried on into adulthood if there is no opportunity for alternative learning. Similarly, a tendency to suppress feelings rather than expressing them is learned within the family and will be carried on unless some alternative is modeled. Acting out is more than a convenient cover-up; frequently the person acting out is completely detached from (consciously unaware of) the emotions that his or her behavior represents.

Recovery from substance abuse means, in part, moving away from the use of mood-altering chemicals as a means of suppressing feelings, and away from acting out. That, in turn, means that the adolescent must learn to be more comfortable with experiencing emotions and with expressing them.

Expressing emotions — sharing feelings — means revealing ourselves. It is, in a sense, an intimate act. Couples and friends who share a great deal of their feelings with one another tend to feel very intimate and connected. Conversely, people who don't share feelings, or who act them out rather than identifying with them, by and large feel detached and disconnected from others. The loneliness and alienation associated with this can trigger further substance use. A therapeutic goal, therefore, is to encourage identifying feelings and sharing them verbally. This can be done in various ways.

Learning to identify and label feelings in a way that is almost didactic can work well with teens and young adults. In the course of conversation, the counselor should make a point of helping the patient clarify the nature of the feelings he or she has in significant situations. Help the young person learn to attach labels (words) to feeling states; in a group, encourage members to help each other do this. Counselors can also model this by sharing their own emotional reactions in various real-life situations.

The young person in recovery needs to learn over time to articulate what it is he or she is feeling. Naturally, all emotions are important, but especially important are those emotions that trigger substance use. Remember, these may be unconscious, that is, the young person may not be consciously aware of the feelings that motivate him or her to use alcohol or drugs. Key trigger emotions (and their variants) include:

- Anger (frustration, irritation, resentment, annoyance)
- Sadness (sorrow, hurt, grief)
- Shame (embarrassment, humiliation, feeling foolish)
- Guilt (remorse, regret)
- Loneliness (isolation, detachment, emptiness, alienation)
- Fear (anxiety, panic, alarm, nervousness)
- Inadequacy (self-hatred, incompetence, emptiness)

The clinician should be alert for signs of acting out, and be ready to interpret it — to make it "conscious" by helping the youth connect his or her overt behavior with its underlying emotional meaning. The best strategy is a direct one: point out behavior and identify the emotions revealed by it. Some of the most common forms of acting out (and the emotions they suggest) include:

- Self-destructive behavior (inadequacy, shame, guilt)
- Isolation (loneliness)
- Aggression (anger)
- Indecisiveness (anxiety)
- Rebelliousness/oppositionalism (boredom, alienation, anger)

The therapeutic goal is to get the patient to learn to identify with and share feelings, rather than acting them out. Acting out represents a risk for substance use, whereas communicating feelings opens the way to support and problem-solving.

SUMMARY

The first two phases in the recovery process are denial and compliance. The central dynamic underlying both is an avoidance of the realities of addiction. Psychodynamically both denial and compliance are driven by the anxiety associated with powerlessness and the shame and stigma associated with addiction. The individual in compliance may have publicly acknowledged a problem with substance abuse, but privately he or she entertains notions of "controlled use."

Recovery begins with acceptance, on both an intellectual and an emotional level, of the need for abstinence from substance use. Denial and compliance represent barriers to this acceptance. Persistence, along with the consistent use of techniques and strategies such as those described in this chapter, can help erode denial and compliance and move the young person to the next level of recovery.

11

Advanced Phases of Adolescent Recovery: Surrender and Recovery

PHASE 3: SURRENDER

Denial and compliance are associated with a lack of emotion; surrender, in contrast, can be identified by the strong emotions it evokes. Surrender can be likened to another stage of grief: that stage after denial and bargaining break down and yield to reality. Surrender is a pivotal concept within the recovery movement. When denial and compliance fail, the addict is flooded with painful emotions, particularly shame and anxiety. Hopelessness and despair are common; it is rare, in fact, to find an addict who has not entertained suicidal thoughts at this critical moment. Surrender is the antidote to this. It involves not only an acceptance of addiction, of powerlessness over mood-altering chemicals, but also an acceptance of the Twelve Steps as a source of hope and a means of recovery. Surrender represents a leap of faith at the same time that it represents a letting go.

Anxiety, anger, and sadness are the feelings most closely associated with surrender. Recovery itself is not unlike a process of grief and renewal: grief over the loss of personal control, of self-respect, of relationships, etc., and renewal through faith and fellowship. Denial and compliance ("bargaining") are easily understood in this context.

To recover from a loss, one must first confront the reality of it. That is partly what surrender is. It is associated with three related realizations, which are stated in the "Big Book" of Narcotics Anonymous:[1]

1. We are powerless over addiction and our lives are unmanageable;

145

2. Although we are not responsible for our disease, we are responsible for our recovery;
3. We can no longer blame people, places and things for our addiction. We must face our problems and our feelings.

Surrender may occur "spontaneously"; in other words, it may emerge in response to interventions such as those described in the last chapter, which aim at undermining denial and compliance. It can also be facilitated by encouraging a patient to get in touch with the loss that sobriety implies — the loss of the use of mood-altering chemicals as a means of coping and recreating. This can be done by asking the adolescent write a "goodbye letter" to his or her drug(s) of choice.

As a prelude to the goodbye letter, the youth should first make an inventory of all of the reasons why he or she has used alcohol or drugs. Substance use should be framed as a "relationship" between the individual and the substance, one in which the substance has provided for certain emotional needs — pleasure, comfort, relief, avoidance of pain — much the same way that a friend or partner would in a human relationship. Substance use also serves other functions: as a social facilitator, to overcome shyness or insecurity, etc. All such motives that are relevant to the individual's substance use should be listed.

In writing the goodbye letter, the young person should systematically address each of his or her motives (reasons) for using substance, from the point of view of a "relationship": a relationship with substances. The goal of the letter is to end this relationship — in short, to say "goodbye."

Ending a relationship with substances is not very different, emotionally and psychologically, from ending any close relationship. For the addict substance use substantially replaces intimacy and sexuality as sources of love, pleasure, and comfort. It replaces assertiveness, faith, and problem-solving as methods of coping. The loss, therefore, is very real. As with any "breakup," feelings of sadness are to be expected, and sometimes anger and anxiety also. True surrender is an intensely emotional experience. When this affect is missing or appears forced and unnatural, compliance may be suspected. The addict who is truly facing his or her addiction and the need to let go of alcohol or drugs should feel scared, lonely, sad, and angry. Consciously or unconsciously, the addict wonders how he or she can survive without substances. How will he cope? How will she ever experience pleasure again?

The emotions brought on during surrender may drive the addict back toward denial or compliance, and ultimately back into substance use. They must therefore be brought to the surface and worked through. A great deal of support may be necessary, from parents, the counselor, and peers. It is a good idea to encourage increased attendance at AA or NA, to the point of daily meetings.

Hope and Faith

When surrender occurs, the addict can no longer escape into justification, blaming, or any other form of denial. He or she can no longer bargain with substances through fantasies of controlled use. He or she can no longer avoid taking responsibility for achieving the awesome task of recovery. And recovery is indeed an awesome task, involving profound changes in values, attitudes, and lifestyle. It demands that the addict detach from the mainstream culture, with its emphasis on instrumental substance use and immediate gratification, its detraditionalization, and its alienation, and embrace an alternative culture — the recovery movement — along with its values and traditions.

Faced with the tough realities stated above, recovering youths may understandably feel overwhelmed. They are, after all, young and inexperienced in achieving long-term goals. On the contrary, much of their lives so far has probably been characterized by failure and loss. Their ability to assimilate values and delay gratification has been hampered by their distorted relationship with chemicals and the arrested development that relationship causes. At this point two maxims from the recovery movement are especially helpful. The first is the rule which dictates that recovery is a journey that is undertaken "one day at a time." The concept of lifelong abstinence or the vast changes that recovery will demand are too much to contemplate. The young adult or teenager should always be encouraged to take things one day at a time, and to follow the second rule: If you feel bad, don't drink, and go to a meeting.

In the initial stage of recovery — the first six months to one year — long-range planning should be minimized or put off entirely. The addict's primary commitment at this time should be to him or herself; the primary goal of early recovery should be to stay sober, become involved in the program, and to make the AA/NA an integral part of one's lifestyle.

The second issue that surrender raises is that of faith or hope. The Second Step is this:

> We came to believe that a Power greater than
> ourselves could restore us to sanity.

This step is a statement (and test) of faith. The "higher power" spoken of in Alcoholics Anonymous and other 12-step programs does not represent a conventional deity so much as faith itself, in some power that transcends the individual. It is an affirmation of hope: the antithesis of disaffection and alienation. Because of statements like the above, 12-step recovery programs are sometimes thought of as quasi-religions, when in fact they are simply spiritually based societies. The difference is significant. To appreciate 12-step programs, mental health professionals need merely to contemplate the vital role that faith (or hope) plays in accomplishing any major goal, in coping with any major catastrophe, or in overcoming any major loss. Recovery represents that kind of challenge.

The spiritual aspects of recovery begin with the second step. Sanity means having sound judgment, and one goal of recovery is just that: the restoration of sound judgment and clear thinking. According to the 12-step model, addiction is a form of insanity: of clouded judgement and spirituality. It sees the answer as lying in the restoration of clearheadedness, plus a commitment to leading a spiritual lifestyle. In the case of young people, rather than restoration, recovery typically means the development of these things for the first time.

Substance-abusing adolescents are much like the majority of their peers in terms of their alienation and lack of faith. Hopelessness is a common malaise among modern youths, as is disaffection from traditional values, ideals and ethics. What role it plays in the spreading epidemic of substance abuse is uncertain; its role in recovery is not so uncertain. Hopelessness must be confronted head on and challenged. To do this, the counselor must obviously have done this on a personal level first. Perhaps the best way to get in touch with your own spirituality is to think about and then articulate your own beliefs:

- To what extent do you have hope; in other words, positive expectations for being able to overcome obstacles and handicaps and to change yourself and your lifestyle?
- What losses and traumas have you survived, and how did you do it?
- What role have faith and hope played in your own life? Where do they fit in today?

Be prepared to discuss questions like these with teens and young adults in recovery.

Trust

The third step of Narcotics Anonymous is this:

> We made a decision to turn our will and our lives over to the care of God as we understood Him.

This is another statement that many professionals have difficulty with. Even more so than the second step, it may explain why the recovery movement historically has enjoyed close relations with organized religion, while its relations with organized mental health have been tenuous, even competitive. In focusing their skepticism on the quasi-religious content of the third step, however, professionals may miss its real significance, which is that it represents a statement of trust. It is a logical extension of the second step, and one that is no less vital to recovery.

Many substance abusers—adults as well as adolescents—lack sufficient trust to carry them through a recovery program. While admitting to powerlessness over substances (and even grieving the loss of their relationship with alcohol or drugs), they tend to isolate themselves and try to recover alone. In the short run this may work. They are more likely to be successful in the long run, however, if they choose instead to use the help of others to support their recovery.

Trust is what makes the difference between sobriety and recovery: One can stay sober through white-knuckle determination, but true involvement in a 12-step recovery program—much like involvement in therapy—requires trust. Individuals who refuse to trust may attend meetings (usually not too many meetings), but inwardly they resist the philosophy and the spirituality of the 12 steps. They stand more

or less on the outside of recovery, looking in. They are not really "working" the program; they are just along for the ride.

Trust is also a bridge that the counselor and the adolescent client will inevitably have to cross. Many individuals express their distrust indirectly, through skepticism about AA or NA or about counseling. In these cases the counselor needs to learn to "read between the lines": to hear the distrust beneath the skepticism. Once they do hear it, the next step is to bring the issue out into the open, to be able to frankly discuss the patient's level of trust: of others in general, of adults and authorities in general, and of the therapist in particular. This—trust—is where a history of abuse, neglect, or rejection is most telling. These experiences undermine trust and faith.

Recovery from abuse and neglect, which in many ways parallels recovery from substance abuse, begins with a grieving process that acknowledges the loss of affection, support, love, and trust that the victim has endured. In many cases denial will be intense and will take the same forms as are used to deny addiction. Acting out of reactions to abuse—hostility, sexual promiscuity, self-destructiveness—and of distrust—withdrawal and isolation—need to be replaced by getting in touch with and sharing these experiences and their impact. To the extent that this can be done with the therapist, trust is built. To the extent that a therapist models positive values and provides support and guidance, faith can be renewed. Similarly, trust is built when the addict is able to tell his or her story in an AA or NA meeting, or to a group of peers.

PHASE 4: RECOVERY

Recovery begins when the substance abuser acknowledges the connection between substance use and negative consequences, accepts his or her loss of control over use, acknowledges the need to forego substance use as a means of coping and recreating, and "turns over" his or her fate to a recovery program. This is surrender.

Recovery can be conceptualized as an ongoing process of relapse prevention; in other words, one is either actively in recovery or in some phase of relapse. Each is a process, not an event. Recovery requires daily vigilance for any weakening of the will, for any signs of denial, of weakening commitment, or of cloudy thinking. It requires daily efforts to change outlooks and lifestyles. It requires a progressive development of spirituality as it is expressed in the Twelve Steps and Twelve Traditions.

Adults in recovery face a difficult task, to be sure, but adolescents have an even harder one. Adults have some decided advantages over adolescents in this same situation. For one thing, addiction notwithstanding, the average adult is apt to be more mature than the average teenager. The adult, despite the fact that he or she has lost control over substance use, had more opportunity to develop self-control before substance abuse began (unless, of course, his or her own use was already habitual by adolescence). The adult has had more of an opportunity, prior to addiction, to develop personal values. Teenage addicts, on the other hand, have had little chance to develop self-control or a healthy system of values. Instead, they are arrested by virtue of their abuse at that point in development where behavior is controlled primarily by external factors (rewards and punishments) as opposed to internal values. They have had relatively little experience with self-denial (opting not to do something because it violates personal ethics) or even at delaying immediate gratification in the interest of longer-term gains. Assuming that substance abuse began in adulthood, adults are likely to have developed some sense of personal identity: an idea of what they were like before they became addicted. They may even have had achievements and accomplishments to point to as evidence of their potential. Whatever "identity" the teen addict has, in contrast, is as a substance abuser and a failure.

Adolescents who succumb to substance abuse and who suffer negative consequences as a result gradually drift away from the mainstream adolescent subculture. Gravitating more and more toward other substance abusers, they gradually become stigmatized by the majority. They become known first as users, and later on as losers. They're regarded with humor at best, perhaps tolerated but never welcomed. Eventually they give in to the ostracism and become social isolates.

Imagine that you are 16 years old and about to leave a drug rehabilitation program where you've just spent the last six weeks. Daily use of marijuana for nearly two years, plus a fair amount of alcohol use, was what led you here. For the past six months you rarely even showed up for school.

Like all of your peers, the way you choose to dress and groom yourself has always reflected your identity. For the past year or more you've worn your alienation like a banner. It was there for everyone to see: in your jeans and jackets, in your haircut, in the jewelry you wore and the music you listened to incessantly. There was nothing subtle about your disaffection; it was loud and obvious. You became known as a user, and for a time—and for some reason you still don't completely understand—you were even proud of it. You chose to ignore a lot, though, like the looks on your old friends' faces when they passed you on the street or in the mall. Sure, they said hello, with a laugh; but how long has it been since one of them actually stopped to talk to you? When was the last time you were invited to one of their parties?

Now you're leaving the rehab program. At first you hated it here, resenting all the rules and restrictions, inwardly afraid you wouldn't succeed even here. Having lived a chaotic life, you hated all the do's and don'ts, the limits. You didn't like being told when to get up, what you could wear, what music you could listen to. Your parents had given up on getting you to follow any rules; but these people got in your face for the slightest infraction and stayed there until you got in line. They insisted on it; so did the other youths in the program. You didn't like that, either: having peers call you on your behavior, expecting you to be a role model and responsible for others.

Eventually, though, you came to like it here. The truth is, you're nervous about leaving. In sobriety you've come to realize that you've been ill and that to recover you're going to have to make a lot of changes. For one thing, there are your old friends. You heard from your parents that one of them just went into rehab; the rest are probably using just as heavy as ever. You know they'll be there when you get out.

You feel better about yourself today than you have in a long time, maybe ever. You've accomplished some things here. You've contributed something to the community; you've come to be liked, appreciated and respected. You feel affection here. For the first time that you can recall, you've begun to think about your values: what's important to you in life, and where you're headed. You've made a few sober decisions, and you like the way that feels. You look a lot different from the way you did six weeks ago.

What will it be like on the "outside"? Will you be able to maintain your recovery? How will everyone in school look at you when you show up there? Will you ever be able to get out of the pigeonhole you helped get yourself into? Will you be able to make friends? How will you have fun?

This is the situation faced by the recovering adolescent. It represents a challenge of monumental proportions; yet it must be accomplished by individuals who have relatively little life experience.

Recovery rightly begins with surrender, and much of the work the counselor will do with young clients concerns the first three steps of the 12-step program: with identifying resistances and opening the way to the leap of faith that surrender represents. If this work is successful, the balance of this chapter can be safely left to a 12-step program. However, since some of the more "advanced" steps tend to be psychodynamically significant, a few will be discussed here.

The Moral Inventory

Trust also plays an important role in that part of recovery which deals most directly with shame: Steps 4 and 5.

> Step 4: We made a searching and fearless moral inventory of ourselves.
>
> Step 5: We admitted to God, to ourselves, and to another human being the exact nature of our wrongs.

Substance abuse leads its victims to commit many acts that hurt themselves and others. Lying, stealing and cheating, prostitution and burglary: these are but a few of the wrongs commonly committed by addicts. The shame associated with these moral failings helps maintain denial, and it can undermine recovery after denial has broken down. Shame is a powerful emotion, and it can drive an individual to use substances in order to suppress it. Shame that is kept hidden is therefore much more dangerous than is shame that is shared. The fact is, being able to own up to transgressions has a powerful healing effect. Sometimes confession needs to be made many times, and often it needs to be followed by appropriate restitution, but in the end it tends to be a healing process. In contrast, feelings of shame that are kept hidden fester, grow worse, and undermineelf-esteem.

The 12 steps do not specify with whom a personal inventory must be shared; they only say that it must eventually be shared with someone. The development of the inventory can he guided by the counselor over a period of time. Alternatively, it can be done with a sponsor or a clergyman. Similarly, the sharing part can be accomplished over a period of time, with a counselor or with someone else who is trusted.

The recovering person should be encouraged to be fearless in his or her self-examination. At the same time, his or her courage in doing so should be recognized and supported. The end product — a detailed journal that describes the various wrongs the individual has done, to specific others, to society, and to self — is an intimate self-portrait. It must be respected, indeed protected, if necessary, from exposure to anyone who would use it manipulatively.

Because Step 5 is so intimate and emotionally powerful, and because it places the recovering addict in a most vulnerable position, it is understandable that clergy are often sought out by recovering persons for this work. The counselor can also be effective, if a supportive attitude can be maintained. It is important to respect recovering persons' moral view of themselves — it is their moral inventory, after all, not the counselor's — and to acknowledge their perception of wrongdoing. Substance abuse in no way justifies or excuses wrongdoing. Pride can only begin to be built when the ego is no longer the prisoner of shame.

Making Amends

Another very important process within recovery has to do with making amends to those who have been injured as a consequence of substance abuse or addiction. Steps 8 and 9 are as follows:

> Step 8: We made a list of all persons we had harmed, and became willing to make amends to them all.

> Step 9: We made direct amends to such people wherever possible, except when to do so would injure them or others.

Psychologically, Steps 8 and 9 seem to be aimed at resolving guilt, through honest recognition of harm done, along with a sincere effort to make up for it, whenever doing so would be appropriate. Sometimes a simple but honest apology is the appropriate form of amends. At other times something more substantial and tangible may be appropriate, and at other times keeping silent may be the best course.

The counselor can help the recovering teen assess the harm that his or her substance abuse has done, and to whom. Parents and siblings need special attention, but relationships with friends and other relatives, as well as with teachers, boyfriends and girlfriends, should be discussed. What form amends should take can also be discussed, and experiences with these efforts should be worked through.

In making amends the substance abuser is not only acknowledging harm done, but also taking responsibility for that harm, even if it was done while out of control. Rather than adding to shame or guilt, this process has the power to build character and self-respect. Within the family it is a powerful experience that can mark the start of healing, the breaking down alienation, and the beginning of new hope for a better future.

DIMENSIONS OF RECOVERY

Recovery begins with sobriety, but recovery goes beyond sobriety. The person who abstains from substance use but has not dealt with any of the many issues discussed here is said to be a "dry drunk": a person whose body may be free of mood-altering chemicals but whose character is still poisoned by resentment, distrust, shame, guilt, distrust, etc.

Sustained recovery is achieved by "working" the 12 steps of AA and NA. It is marked by increasing commitment to 12-step principles and observance of the various traditions. It is reflected in progressive changes in lifestyle, habits, and values. Some of the areas that are of special importance for adolescents are described in the following sections.

The Recovery Plan

Just as substance abuse and addiction are multidetermined, so must recovery proceed along several paths at once. In working with young adults and teens, the counselor needs to develop a comprehensive treatment plan of the kind described in Chapter 8. Recovery is a process, not an event; similarly, treatment is a process that extends over time and which varies in form and intensity.

When working with a young person in recovery, the counselor may find it helpful to think in terms of dimensions of recovery and to periodically review progress and plans in each of the following areas:

PHYSICAL RECOVERY

How is the young person planning to take care of his or her physical health and development?

- What are his or her eating habits? How is his or her nutrition?
- What, if any, medical conditions does he or have? Are they being taken care of?
- Does he or she exercise regularly?
- What areas relating to physical health would the adolescent like to improve, and what are his or her plans for doing so?
- What body-image issues might threaten self-esteem, and how are these being worked on?

SPIRITUAL RECOVERY

How is the youth working on his or her spirituality?

- What prosocial programs, groups, or religious organizations is the young person involved in?
- What socially meaningful commitments does the youth have?
- How many 12-step meetings is the youth attending, and what is his or her level of commitment to them? Does he or she have a sponsor?

VOCATIONAL/EDUCATIONAL RECOVERY

What is the young person doing about work, training, or at school?

- What is the plan for the next two years, in terms of education or work?
- What kinds of interests and aptitudes does the youth have, and how are they going to be developed?
- What does the young person do for recreation and relaxation? How can these aspects of his or her lifestyle be enhanced?

SOCIAL RECOVERY

How is the recovering youth doing at building a healthy social life?

- What kinds of social skills might the youth need to develop in order to make new friends?

- Who is the youth spending time with, and what kind of people are they?
- What issues does the young person have with respect to sexuality, and how are these being worked on?
- Where is this person with respect to intimate relationships, and how can the counselor help in this area?
- What are the counseling goals in the area of communication skills and assertiveness?
- Are there any problems related to social acceptance that may impede recovery; if so, how can they be corrected?

This brief checklist can be shared with the recovering client and used as a reference for periodic "progress reports," to support positive changes and progress, and to identify new goals and make plans.

People, Places, and Things

Whereas recovering adults primarily face the task of integrating their recovery programs within their families and in their workplaces, recovering teenagers must also contend with a peer group in which drugs and alcohol are readily accessible and substance use is highly prevalent. Dealing with the peer group while preserving a viable recovery program is a major challenge for the recovering adolescent. In the course of becoming more involved in substance use, the teen has probably experienced some degree of peer group drift: a shifting of friends toward those who use more, whose attitudes toward use are more positive than negative, and whose general outlook is characterized by certain attitudes, notably alienation, that promote substance abuse. In recovery, all of that must be reversed.

As part of developing a recovery plan, the adolescent will need to assess people, places, and things that will need to be changed (or avoided) in the interest of recovery. To the teen who has drifted toward a using peer group, it can be more than a little unnerving to contemplate not only making new friends but also avoiding old ones who will most certainly be there, glorifying substance use and offering opportunities to get high. The teen needs to work with the counselor to develop assertive skills that will enable him or her to avoid negative influences and develop new relationships. For the typical teenager who has been using drugs since age 11 or 12, relationships (with the same sex and with the opposite sex) have centered around getting high. Chemicals have become the main social agenda and the great social facilitator. Without substances, many teens have no idea of how to start or maintain a conversation, of how to ask someone for a date, or of what to do for fun and relaxation.

In addition to avoiding certain people, many places and things associated with substance use will also have to be avoided. Clothing, music, and certain places that were an integral part of the addict's lifestyle have the potential to trigger urges to use. Some music, as well as types of clothing, glorifies and promotes substance use. In some cases these have occult overtones, promoting more than substance abuse.

The best recovery plan is a written document, developed collaboratively by the counselor and the adolescent. It should detail the changes that the recovering youth and the counselor agree need to be made in the interest of recovery. The role of the counselor here is to straightforwardly raise issues that he or she sees as relevant to recovery, including all of the people, places, and things that must be avoided. Avoiding this issue, either for fear of burdening the youth or simply out of fear of rejection, does no one any good. The young person deserves to be treated with respect, and this includes being confronted with everything the counselor honestly believes needs to be done.

Another part of the plan should be a list of alternative people, places, and things that should be actively pursued in the interest of recovery. This includes AA and NA meetings (for an alternative peer group), sports and recreational activities, family activities, and so on.

Personal Values

Much of the work that needs to be done in the area of substance abuse prevention and recovery has to do with values. If one looks closely at 12-step recovery programs it becomes clear that certain values are regarded as congruent with recovery. There are three values in particular that need to be stressed in a recovery program.

Naturalness

Instrumental substance use is encouraged in so many ways that it is literally part of the fabric of our society. Faced with a choice between a spiritual and an artificial (i.e., chemical) way of dealing with anxiety, depression, or stress, many Americans today will opt for the chemical solution. This is painfully apparent in substance abuse treatment programs, where patients will frequently argue with staff who suggest a natural remedy for something like a headache.

The connection between the use of chemicals to cope with discomfort and alcohol or drug abuse is this: The inclination to choose a chemical over a natural solution to a problem of minor physical discomfort is not much different, psychologically, from an inclination to use substances over other means of coping with an uncomfortable emotion. Recovery is strengthened by cultivating ethics that emphasize the use of natural over artificial (chemical) solutions for dealing with any form of discomfort, emotional or physical.

Valuing naturalness extends logically to areas such as diet, recreation, and even appearance. Recreation, for example, has become associated with substance abuse to the extent that drunkenness at professional sporting events represents a serious hazard to spectators and players alike. Among high school and college teams, binge drinking after games is a common problem. And as a form of recreation in itself, substance use is an integral part of young adult and adolescent social events. Young people in recovery need to explore the possibilities of socializing without the use of mood-altering chemicals and of promoting the value of the "natural high."

SPIRITUALITY

Spirituality is embodied in the set of values, ideals, and ethics that guide an individual's choices and behavior. Such values as honesty, charity, tolerance, and social responsibility promote healthy lifestyles; a large percentage of substance-abusing adolescents, however, identify with unhealthy, dysfunctional value systems. These range from a general disaffection from mainstream values to involvement in satanic and antisocial cults. They include a selfish belief in personal gain over social interest and a cynical attitude toward charity and honesty. In some cases, such attitudes have their roots in personal experience: in abuse, neglect, victimization and exploitation. In some other cases, negative values are modeled from parents, peers, or even the culture at large.

Recovery is, among other things, a spiritual process. The recovery movement represents nothing less significant than a culture—an alternative to our present detraditionalized society. It is a culture based on spiritual values. Youths in recovery relate to this remarkably well and quickly embrace 12-step programs as an organizing focus for their lives.

SELF-DISCIPLINE

Self-discipline, as a value, appears to have fallen out of favor in recent decades. At the same time, hedonism, self-interest, and impulsiveness have gained in popularity. In the present cultural context self-discipline may be unpopular simply because it does imply some degree of self-denial and delay of gratification. To the extent that we do not promote self-discipline, however, we raise successive generations of unmotivated, uncommitted, immature individuals who are tempted by anything that promises immediate gratification, regardless of the long-term consequences. Recovery, which values abstinence in a society that promotes instrumental substance use, promotes self-discipline.

Values Clarification

Values such as naturalness, self-discipline, and others are influenced most strongly by families and by the larger culture. However, professional counselors, as well teachers, can also influence values and therefore character development. This can be done by engaging the teenager or young adult in an ongoing dialogue regarding the values that are revealed in their choices and their behavior. Values and priorities should be open territory for frank discussion. The counselor should be prepared to share honestly, based on personal experience, values that are relevant to situations and choices that the youthful patient faces. Drug glorification, for example, which is frequently expressed through music and clothing, suggests values that need to be confronted rather than avoided. Silence on the part of the therapist, the teacher, or the parent will only encourage relapse into substance use.

SUMMARY

Recovery is a lifelong endeavor. It goes beyond simple abstinence to involve work on many other levels. The chances of an adolescent's staying free from substance abuse over the long run are dependent on the adolescent's becoming actively involved in (and committed to) a long-term process of behavioral, attitudinal, and lifestyle changes. Recovery begins when the "relationship" with substances and its associated lifestyle is ended and grieved, and when the substance abuser sees hope in an alternative way of living.

12

Individuation
in Recovery

A young psychologist in training spoke about her youth in this way: "As I look back on it, I realize that my adolescence—right through my mid-twenties, actually—was one long search to find my tribe: that group where I felt I belonged."

Adolescence is in many ways just such a search: for identity, for a niche in the world. It begins when the young person actively seeks out a "tribe": a group which he or she can belong to and identify with, and to which he or she can tie his or her future. For the youth who becomes caught in the web of substance abuse this search never effectively begins. No true decisions or choices can be made by an individual whose primary "relationship" is with mood-altering chemicals, whose consciousness is clouded by their influence, and whose life has increasingly accommodated to their use as its focus. The only "search" these young people relate to is the one to satisfy a craving. Any "identity" that addicts have is one that is merely a by-product of their addiction. The so-called "addictive personality" is in fact nothing more than an artifact: the result of chemical dependency and its effects on personality and development. That is why, like addiction itself, the "addictive personality" is so predictable.

For the individual whose substance abuse began at some point after individuation was complete, the pre-addict identity and personality can emerge in sobriety. For the youthful addict, however, there is no "identity" to emerge. It is only in sobriety that young addicts can begin to individuate and develop a true personality of their own. By helping to preserve sobriety one day at a time, 12-step recovery programs make this growth possible.

The primary psychololgical process active during the adolescent and young adult years is called individuation. Prior to adolescence,

162

the child's "identity" is based largely on an awareness of innate characteristics: temperament, abilities and talents, tastes and interests. Beginning in adolescence, and stemming from the child's growing capacity to think abstractly and function autonomously, further development occurs which extends the boundaries of identity. This is individuation. The end product of successful individuation is a psychologically autonomous adult: an individual who is simultaneously unique and representative of his or her culture.

The core elements of the self to emerge through individuation are the following:

- *Willpower:* The ability to make choices and decisions; to know what one wants and likes. The unindividuated (or regressed) person is indecisive and relatively unable to separate personal preferences from those of others.
- *Self-control:* The capacity to delay or deny self-gratification, to persevere in the pursuit of a goal, and to resist the influence of situational factors. The unindividuated self is relatively impulsive, non-persevering, and incapable of resisting situational influences.
- *Morality:* The development of a coherent set of internal standards for behavior (ethics), of ideals, and of values that guide decisions and behavior independently of social or situational factors. The unindividuated person is not immoral, but amoral; he or she makes decisions on the basis of interpersonal influence, hedonism, or simple self-interest.

SOCIAL DETERMINANTS
OF INDIVIDUATION

The individuation process marks the developmental transition separating childhood from adulthood. The adult personality or character is influenced not only by innate abilities and temperament, but by social factors as well. Three factors in particular influence the outcome of individuation heavily: the peer group, the family, and the culture.

The Peer Group

The individuation process starts when the young person selects a peer group. This is an active process: The youth searches for and then chooses a group with which to identify. If this search is unsuccessful, if the youth cannot find and be accepted by a suitable peer group, individuation is seriously compromised. These youths are typically depressed and isolated, and may compensate by forming a symbiotic relationship with a parent.

The adolescent subculture is not unlike a tribal society. Many adolescent "tribes" coexist, more or less peacefully, within any community or school. They are known within the subculture by various names: preppies, jocks, heads, etc. Adolescents never belong to more than one "tribe" and rarely switch tribes once they've achieved acceptance.

Psychologically the peer group functions as a facilitator for the development of willpower. It also provides for certain needs—in particular, security—that in younger years were met by parents. Lastly, it is a vehicle for the development of relationships.

The peer group can be thought of as a source of leverage: a lever that the young person actively seeks out and uses in order to separate from his or her parents. In traditional cultures (as distinct from our contemporary detraditionalized society), adolescence is closely supervised. It is controlled through rites and rituals and defined by traditions. In recovery, and especially through involvement in a 12-step program, young people discover traditions, rituals, and rites that promote the development of self-control as well as prosocial attitudes and behavior.

After successful individuation—a process than cannot even begin so long as the individual's life remains accommodated to substance use—behavior is guided by internal goals and values and personal commitments, more than by peer expectations or fads. At the same time, personal support and validation through intimate relationships gradually replace the peer group as a source of security and support.

Parents

Although the peer group plays an important role in individuation, parental influences continue to be important during adolescence and young adulthood, especially in a society like ours, in which "adolescence" represents a protracted period of life. Parental limits and restrictions, as well as parental values, attitudes, and behaviors, serve as a counterbalancing influence to the peer group. Parental and cultural influences together provide a framework for the development of self-control, spirituality, and ethical morality, which is as important to successful individuation as the development of willpower.

Culture

Culture, as the word is used here, refers to an organized set of traditions, rituals and rites that define the social structure that the individual is being socialized to function within. Culture, to the extent that it informs and supports parental limit-setting, forms one basis for the development of self-control; but its effects go beyond that: Personal ethics, values, and ideals are heavily influenced by the wisdom that is passed down in the form of cultural custom and lore.

In traditional societies, entry into various phases of life — for example, adulthood — is associated with successful completion of one or more rites of passage. Typically, these rites have religious (spiritual) as well as social significance; study and preparation are often required, and they may also be connected to sex-role expectations, being different for males and females. It is partly through such rites of passage that the socio-religious structure of culture becomes a vehicle not only for social control, but also for personality development. Traditions and their associated rituals communicate the culture's spiritual outlook, including its values and ideals, which are reflected in the character of its successfully individuated members.

Contemporary America is largely a detraditionalized society: Most of our religious and social rites and rituals have fallen into disuse; meanwhile, our traditions have lost their meaning, being reduced to little more than pro forma social events. What few societal rites of passage remain — achieving voting status, getting a driver's license, being able to drink, etc. — tend to be more or less devoid of developmental significance. This state of affairs has implications not only on behavioral control, but for personality development in adolescents.

Individuation proceeds optimally when the respective influences of peer group, parents, and culture are balanced. Each is psychologically and developmentally important; each needs to be present; but all need to be present in order to avoid distortions in character development. Generally speaking, adolescents need a lot more parenting and socialization than many of them are receiving today. We have — perhaps out of convenience, but more likely out of necessity — allowed ourselves to become convinced that children of 14, 15, and 16 are "old enough" to be responsible for themselves and to function without parental supervision for long periods of time. If a child happens to be intellectually bright, the temptation may be all the stronger to assume that he or she is socially mature as well, and therefore capable of exercising good judgment and self-control. At the same time, the detraditionalization of our society has seriously eroded the moderating influence of culture.

It is a dangerous illusion to think that any unindividuated youth possesses adult-like self-control or judgment; it is likewise dangerous to believe that individuation is correlated with intelligence, talent, or aptitude. It is a danger, in other words, to think of adolescents as adults.

The latchkey society, however, is a reality, and many 12-, 13-, and 14-year-olds spend a great deal of time outside of parental supervision. Fewer and fewer are involved in organized religion or in anything else that could be described as a culture. They spend a great deal of time interacting with peers; precious little time is spent interacting with adults. School does not make up for the absence of parental supervision or interaction; nor does television, even so-called "educational" television. Similarly, media exposure cannot compensate for a lack of participation in social rites and rituals and in an organized system of meaningful traditions. Under these conditions the individuation process becomes distorted. The influence of the peer group is magnified, with a generally negative impact on self-control and ethical development.

INDIVIDUATION AND
HEALTHY RELATIONSHIPS

Individuation plays a role in determining the kinds of relationships a person will be capable of sustaining. The successfully individuated self is capable of intimacy and commitment: of being able to reveal oneself, to empathize, and to form lasting bonds of friendship and love. The unindividuated person, in contrast, will form dysfunctional relationships that lack intimacy, commitment, or both. They will enter into relationships that are built more on dependency or exploitation than on love, and in which intimacy is compromised by ongoing struggles for control and dominance.

Though the individuation process takes its most dramatic turns during adolescence and young adulthood, some rudimentary aspects of identity exist well before that. The child's own awareness of self, in terms of interests, talents, and abilities, combined with the consistent reactions of others to his or her temperament, plus the relative presence (or absence) of nurturance, support and affection, form a core of identity around which individuation unfolds. Recovery for young people needs to be viewed in this context. In sobriety the young person is faced with the task of individuating at the same time that he or she is likely to be preoccupied with relationships. Such relationships, however, will reflect the arrested development of the youths who form them, as well as any dysfunctional patterns (e.g. abuse) that have been modeled from parental relationships. Given the amount of growth that needs to take place, therefore, the common AA admonition against making interpersonal commitments until at least a year of sobriety has passed makes sense. As individuation progresses, the counselor can expect to see healthier relationships begin to develop. This can be facilitated by frank discussions of issues such as sexuality, intimacy, commitment, and equality in relationships.

FAMILY DYSFUNCTION
AND INDIVIDUATION

In one way or another dysfunctional families undermine individuation. At one extreme are families which impede individuation by violating personal privacy, physical integrity, or both. These are families where, for example, there may be no doors on children's bedrooms, where parents may share beds with children on a regular basis, or where children are sexually molested. Such experiences lead to shame, anger, or anxiety that can trigger compensatory substance use.

A variation on this kind of dysfunctional family is one in which parents punish any and all moves toward independence, including independent thinking. They may stifle disagreement, no matter how slight, or they may insist on blind compliance with any demand or expectation, no matter how unreasonable. In these families, it is parental insecurity that drives their rigidity. Because their own will is so tenuous, their own individuation so incomplete, they can bear no challenge. There is little if any room in their relationships (with adults or with children) for compromise; as a result, there is little if any communication. Adolescents in these families feel smothered and resentful, and are likely to be either angry and rebellious or depressed and self-destructive.

A third type of family dysfunction occurs when one or both parents are active substance abusers. This invariably places children at risk, with effects that vary according to the age of the child. The youngest children will be inclined to develop insecurities, in consequence of having parents whose drug involvement takes precedence over their ability to provide nurturance, comfort, and support. Having one or more parents whose judgement is impaired (for example, by substance abuse) affects self-esteem in a negative way. These parents cannot provide effective guidance or support self-confidence in a way that is credible. During the years when individuation takes place, parents who model substance abuse, who may be ineffectual in setting limits, and who probably lack self-control themselves have a negative impact on the development of self-control and on moral development as well.

When an adolescent is raised in a dysfunctional family, the peer group can assume an inordinately important role in the individuation process. This will certainly happen if a functional extended family is not available, and if cultural supports are lacking. Under these circumstances development is left essentially to chance. If the young person is fortunate enough to identify with a functional peer group, the outcome may be more or less okay; if he or she is not so lucky, the results can be disastrous.

At the opposite extreme from overly rigid families — but no less dysfunctional — are families which fail to provide sufficient limits and reasonable expectations for adolescents. Tony was a good example of this. He was 14, and had been admitted to our program after drinking heavily and steadily for more than a year. With respect to his behavior, the simplest way to describe it was out of control; meanwhile, the best way to describe his parents was "fed up." The last straw had come when he had thrown a party while his parents were away for the weekend. More than 50 teens showed up; by the time the neighbors finally called the police, more than $2,000 worth of damage had been done.

Tony's parents were both intelligent people, who obviously cared about him. During our interview, however, first his mother and then his father admitted that they'd always had trouble controlling their son. "Tony does as he pleases around the house," said his mother. "Always has. We've always had trouble enforcing any rules with him. Lately, he either has friends over or else sleeps at their house, pretty much every night. He comes and goes when he wants. He's very popular, too. In fact, you could say we're more or less his social secretaries. We answer the phone, and then we give the person calling whatever message Tony wants us to give." She laughed — uncomfortably, I thought.

Then Tony's father piped up. "Tony is not very responsible. Frankly, he doesn't seem to see why he should be. Last summer, for instance, he went out and got a job — but only because we told him he'd have to pay half of what it cost for the new drum set he wanted. He went to work for a few days, then missed a couple of days. When I asked him about it he blew me off. He said he could work whatever hours he wanted to — if he wanted to sleep late and not go to work, that was okay with his boss. A week later, when he still wasn't going to work, I confronted him. He admitted that he'd been fired."

"How did he seem to feel about that?" I asked.

His father shrugged. "He acted like it didn't matter to him."

When I asked Tony's parents to tell me what part of our program they expected him to have the hardest time with, his mother responded immediately: "The rules. I don't think he's going to do very well with all the rules you have." Looking at the list, she uttered another uncomfortable laugh. "He never makes his bed at home — never. He never cleans up after himself. He's not gonna like it that he can't play his music, either, or have his friends visit whenever they want. He has lots of free time at home — there doesn't seem to be much of that here, either."

Tony's parents were right: He did have a hard time complying with program rules and observing our limits. That was much more uncomfortable for him, in fact, than giving up drugs. On the other hand, he eventually did very well in primary treatment and graduated to a partial hospital program.

When an adolescent becomes enmeshed in the use of mood-altering chemicals, as a means of socializing or of coping, or both, the individuation process becomes arrested and personality development gets out of balance. The peer group becoming overly influential. In particular, in the areas of the development of self-control and moral development, growth stops.

Once substance abuse itself ends, what one discovers, beneath the addict personality, is a remarkably anxious and immature young person. This is a youth who is vulnerable to peer influence, lacking in self-confidence, impulsive, amoral, and scared. Much work needs to be done, in a short time, if sobriety is to be preserved.

CHOICE-MAKING

Making choices, per se, requires nothing more than willpower; making healthy choices, on the other hand, requires not only willpower but also self-control and a system of values and ideals. In other words, healthy choices are made only by the successfully individuated person whose personality is characterized by a balance among will, self-discipline, and morality. For the substance-abusing adolescent, it is a combination of peers and a clouded mind that makes "decisions," without the benefit of either self-control or ethics. Obviously, this is not a formula for the development of good judgment or autonomy. It is a formula for amorality, self-centeredness, and impulsiveness.

Effective choice-making enhances self-esteem and facilitates individuation. Healthy choice-making, in turn, can be divided into a series of steps.

Step 1: Identifying the Problem

This is the most difficult step of all; too often people get caught up in emotional reactions and fail to define the problem to be solved, the choice to be made. For recovering teens, one problem situation invariably will be what to do when old, using friends invite them to a party or to "hang out" (a euphemism for getting high). There are many other problem situations, however, including situations that demand sexual choice-making, as well as decisions about activities and places to be either avoided or pursued, depending on whether they are consistent or inconsistent with recovery. If for any reason the young person appears stuck in definingroblems or choices, ask him or her to describe times (situations) when he or she has typically gotten high in the past.

Step 2: Values Clarification

Having identified problem situations, young persons must next be challenged to think about and articulate their present values, priorities, and goals:

- Do they value sobriety? If so, why?
- What did they value the most in their using days, and what do they value now?
- What (and who) were their ideals in the past, and what (who) are they now?

Working with youths on this second step requires the counselor to engage them in a dialogue: about values, ideals, and personal ethics. Choices that are made on the basis of external factors — "Because I might go to jail"; "Because my parents would disapprove" — are less mature (and stable) than are choices that are made on the basis of personal values.

Developing healthy choice-making skills is a process of growth for the substance-abusing youth. Like most growth processes, it does not proceed in a neat, linear fashion. Ups and downs, successes and failures, are to be expected. The long-term goals are to build the spirit and the moral self and to replace external with internal control over choices. Choice-making that is not grounded in this way may look good — the youth may appear to be making the right choices — but it is ephemeral: "self-control" that is in reality situational control. It can lead to a dangerous complacency and a false sense of security about recovery. It is vital, therefore, to help the recovering youth clarify and define his or her priorities, ideals, and goals, and why he or she made a particular choice, even if it was objectively the "right" choice.

Step 3: Generating Alternatives

This involves thinking of new ways to act in old situations, of new activities to be pursued and new relationships to be cultivated, consistent with recovery-oriented values and priorities. As a prelude to change, generating alternatives can also generate anxiety. Recovery and healthy choice-making may very well mean ending many old relationships, making new friends, establishing new habits, and cultivating new interests.

The counselor should be careful not to minimize any losses associated with recovery, or the anxiety that goes along with change. For every change made there is anxiety as well as excitement, a loss as well as a gain.

Step 4: Choice-making

This is the proverbial bottom line. The counselor cannot make the choice; the young person must make the choice. Support, guidance, and honest dialogue can help a great deal, but it is the recovering person's ego that must be built, not the counselor's. This prospect may make the counselor nervous at times—just like a parent, in fact—but it is a critical step for successful individuation. At times the counselor should expect the youth to make a choice contrary to what the counselor would have preferred.

Step 5: Evaluation

Maybe the second most important step after defining the problem, evaluation is what builds character and spirituality. Choices that are made and not looked back on leave the youth open to repeating errors and perpetuating bad judgment. Mistakes are inevitable; learning and growth are the goals.

The counselor is in an excellent position to facilitate ego development and individuation through a dialogue about choices that have been made in the past and how they've worked out. Have they led to trouble; if so, how? Have they been consistent with personal values; if not, why? Evaluation completes the loop in the choice-making process, and essentially brings us back to its beginning, for a choice that led to trouble defines a new problem situation.

Obviously, a caring and involved but nonjudgmental stance is called for in this work with young people. Keep in mind that if a youth's choices lead to trouble, it's the youth who is the victim, not the counselor. Scolding and moralizing are good ways to undermine the therapeutic relationship and discourage honest communication. When things don't work out, the counselor's wisdom and guidance are what the youth needs.

Exercising the ego—choice-making—is not unlike exercising the body: Regular practice, under the guidance of a good coach, builds strength and resilience.

SELF-ESTEEM

If adolescence is a quest, then self-esteem represents the staff that we lean on throughout that journey. Self-esteem plays a decisive role in determining the outcome of the individuation process. This one theme is repeated time and time again in stories of youth moving into adulthood: that adult life often turns out to be a self-fulfilling prophecy: a reflection of each adolescent's self-image.

Teens are intensely preoccupied, first with themselves, and secondly with each other, and while adolescence is frequently romanticized by nostalgic adults, for those who are in them the teen and young adult years are filled with as much anxiety as joy. Despite this reality of youth, healthy adolescents are blessed with an inordinate capacity for having fun, for being silly and outrageous, and even for being able to laugh at themselves. Watching a group of healthy adolescents at play (including adolescents in treatment) should be enough to convince anyone of this.

In contrast, psychologically unhealthy teenagers experience all of the stresses but few of the joys of these years. The stone on which this turns—and which determines not only how youth will be experienced, but also the sort of adulthood that will follow it—is self-esteem. Simply put, self-esteem leads to self-confidence, to a willingness to accept life's challenges, and to an attitude of hopefulness. Low self-esteem, on the other hand, leads to pessimism and cynicism, to avoidance of challenge, and to self-hatred.

Low self-esteem not only invites substance abuse but also threatens recovery once sobriety has been achieved. High self-esteem supports the development of willpower and self-control; low self-esteem weakens both.

Self-esteem does not necessarily improve spontaneously along with recovery from substance abuse or addiction. Sobriety is a good foundation for self-respect, but staying sober, in and of itself, cannot heal wounds whose roots go deeper than the years when substance abuse began. The counselor therefore needs to help the young person understand the origins of low self-esteem and to be vigilant for opportunities to enhance self-esteem.

Living according to healthy values, while making healthy choices, is one route to building a healthy spirituality. This is another way to view self-esteem. After all, when a person is depressed, we usually say that his or her "spirits are low." A person who is on a natural high, on the other hand, is said to be in "high spirits." Young people often relate to the concept of spirituality—to the idea of their "spirit"—better than they relate to the psychological concept of self-esteem.

The development of self-esteem is a process that begins with the child's first attempts at mastery. Depending primarily on experiences of mastery and the parents' attitudes (accepting versus rejecting), the adolescent enters the stage of individuation with either positive self-esteem (which will help him or her to face the challenge of autonomy) or low self-esteem (which will motivate avoidance of this challenge and excessive dependency on peers).

Recovery itself is a forum for building self-esteem. It represents a significant personal achievement, in which each day of success deserves recognition. At the same time, slips and setbacks need to be put in perspective. They warrant attention, of course; but they are not grounds for despair; neither do they negate the successes that preceded them.

The counselor's attitude toward a recovering young person has the power to be therapeutic with respect to self-esteem. Particularly after a therapeutic alliance has been developed, a counselor's positive regard can gradually heal the effects of rejection, abuse, or neglect. A supportive peer group helps even more.

Additional ways to work on self-esteem are described in the following sections.

Educational/Vocational Remediation

Opportunities to develop intellectual and vocational competencies, that is, to experience mastery, are as important to recovery from substance abuse as any other factor discussed in this book. To the extent that circumstances deprive youths of access to educational and vocational resources, they are relegated to a condition of hopelessness that is based in reality and difficult to change, and which promotes alienation and compensatory substance use. Some youths in this situation see drugs not only as a viable way of coping and enjoying themselves but also as one of the only viable "careers" open to them. Their idols may be the "high rollers"—dealers who make thousands of dollars every week selling drugs and who live life in high style (so long as they are alive).

Substance-abusing youths typically have lost a great deal of ground academically, and therefore need remedial educational and/or vocational services. If they cannot (or will not) return to school, then equivalency diplomas can be pursued. Treatment should include vocational assessment, as well as achievement testing, to help the young person develop a plan that will lead to social functionality and improved self-esteem.

Goal Setting and Planning

Carl was putting in time in a residential facility for adjudicated youths, after having been arrested for selling cocaine. A meeting was being held because he had been sent back to his cottage by one of his teachers, who said that he was having attitude problems in the classroom. The group of 15 — all boys — sat in a circle. All eyes were on Carl, who slouched in his straight-backed wooden chair until the counselor asked him to sit up. He did so, slowly, bringing his long sinewy limbs into something resembling attention. His skin was a deep, rich brown, almost black; his eyes were large and round, and suggested a sensitivity that starkly contradicted the reality of his life so far.

From my seat outside the circle, I watched Carl's face. His expression was remarkably fluid, changing more or less constantly, moving from boredom to sadness to anger so fast that I was transfixed.

The meeting was called to order by the counselor. Carl stared down at his sneakers while a peer spoke to him. "Carl, you got to get serious, man. There's no more time for foolin' around, man. You know what I mean?"

Carl nodded in a placating way; the peer frowned and continued: "I know you don't wanna hear this Carl, but you gotta hear it. You gotta stop this bullshit, man. Like this bullshit at school today. You gotta cut that out — get control of yourself. You're a father now, man. You gotta family to support when you get outa here. You need to get serious, Carl."

The youth who was speaking was 17 years old; Carl had just turned 15. He glanced up, and for a brief moment our eyes met. I found it hard to accept the idea that this boy was a father, much less to imagine him "supporting" a family. Then he looked away, and I sighed.

This brief incident brought home, for me at least, the scope of the problems that young people sometimes face. Needless to say, being still a child himself, Carl had nothing even remotely resembling a "plan" for what he would do once he left the institution. He hadn't gone to school for two years and had stopped learning long before that. He talked a good game, claiming that he was going to get a job and support his family. I found it sad, listening to him talk about how he was going to see to it that his son had a better life than he had. How, I wondered, was he going to do that? How could his peers — and the counselors, for that matter — sit there and nod while he spoke? Who were we kidding? Weren't we all, in our silence, allowing Carl to set himself up for yet another failure?

Effective planning and meaningful goal-setting can enhance self-esteem, but both must be rooted firmly in reality, beginning with an accurate assessment of resources and options. Unrealistic goals, or goals that are not supported by realistic plans and resources, lead only to failure and lower self-esteem.

In helping youths learn to set goals and develop plans, the counselor is once again functioning as a surrogate parent. The counselor provides the external ego controls — assessment and planning — that the youth in time will hopefully develop for him or herself through individuation. Guiding youths through this process helps them build self-control, the ability to persevere, and the capacity to see beyond the immediate moment. To help this along, it is useful to set goals frequently, to make plans, and to guide youths to their successful completion. Examples of realistic goals can be to get a part-time job, to get a high school equivalency diploma, to make new friends, or to build a healthier body. These should be supported by concrete plans that are worked out with the assistance of the counselor. Resources need to be identified. Finally, progress should be assessed periodically and moved along as necessary through support, prodding, or problem-solving.

Life Skills

How, exactly, does one go about applying for a job? What do you wear? What do you say? How do you "sell" yourself to a prospective employer?

How do you make a new friend? How do you start a conversation with someone you're attracted to? How do you avoid "dangerous" situations without making a fool of yourself?

How do you open a checking account? How do you balance a checkbook? Make a budget?

These and other related skills are central to effective planning. The most admirable goals, supported by the neatest plans, will fail if the youth does not possess "life skills" like the above. This sort of practical knowledge and social skill makes the difference between success and failure. The counselor can be a useful teacher and coach here. The best approach is a direct, pragmatic one: Help the youth decide how to go about getting a job, how to fill out an application, how to interview, etc. Role-playing is a good way to teach life skills, along with practice.

Body-Image

Tell an adolescent or young adult that he or she looks good; then watch his or her reaction. The healthy ones will glow; the unhealthy ones will frown or look away. The ones with healthy body-images will soak up the compliment; the ones lacking this will shrug it off or look decidedly uncomfortable.

Think back for a moment on your own teen and young adult years — roughly from age 13 through 20 or so. How did you feel about your body? What did you like — feel good about — and what did you dislike? Were you pleased with the way your body developed and the rate at which it did? What were your best features, and what would you have changed if you could have? Who did you most admire in terms of physical appearance, and why? What did they have that you didn't, but wished you did?

How did you feel about sex? Did you think about it a lot? Did the prospect of making love make you feel excited or anxious, interested or repulsed? Was there anything that you felt guilty over or ashamed about, sexually speaking? Were you ever sexually abused, assaulted, or exploited? Did you ever trade sex for drugs, directly or indirectly?

Adolescence is virtually synonymous with self-consciousness: that painfully acute awareness of every hair, every pimple and blemish, every muscle and millimeter of fat, every word spoken. Validation is what the young person seeks: validation that he or she is in fact attractive, acceptable, competent. As frustrated parents are often only too aware, the most important — in some sense the only — source of acceptable validation for teens is the peer group.

Not only do teens who abuse substances become cut off from mainstream peers (who are important "validators"), but, when use becomes habitual (and life accommodates more and more to it), personal appearance begins to deteriorate, increasing the likelihood of rejection, with consequent effects on body-image and self-esteem.

In some cases a poor body-image precedes substance abuse. This is true, for example, when a youth has been the victim of physical or sexual abuse. These experiences generate feelings of shame and guilt; they create disgust, as opposed to feelings of pride, about one's sexuality. These emotions are among the strongest triggers for compensatory substance use. They will also persevere in sobriety, thereby threatening recovery. If they are not uncovered and worked through, these feelings will undermine relationships, cause sexual dysfunctions, and trigger substance abuse. Working on and improving one's body-image is therefore very important for a recovering teen.

Body-image can be explored by asking youths to list ten things that they like and ten things that they dislike about themselves, physically. Initially this may strike the youth as an overwhelming task; however, if it is pursued, it can be a powerful therapeutic exercise. (A word of warning: Opposite-sex counselors should approach this work cautiously and are well advised either to defer to same-sex colleagues or to work on this issue in the context of group treatment with an opposite-sex colleague.)

Children and teens who have been sexually molested, assaulted, or exploited will tend to react to these traumas and humiliations in one of two ways. On the one hand, they may withdraw and develop an aversion to sexuality—their own as much as others'. They develop phobias about sex, hate their own bodies, become overweight, etc. These youths need to be desensitized to their anxiety and disgust and to learn to feel comfortable again about their sexual selves.

The other common response to sexual victimization is represented by the sexualized child or adolescent: the youth who is overly sexual, provocative, seductive, and perhaps promiscuous. Though most young people can be accused of being "oversexed," the sexualized youth stands out even among his or her peers. The treatment issues here are complex. These youths must be helped to learn to relate to others in ways other than sexually. To do this, their seductiveness needs to be toned down, without invalidating their sexuality per se. It is not, after all, their sexuality itself that's the problem for them (and others), but the fact that they relate only through sex. This often leads to further victimization or exploitation (repeated rapes, pornographic involvement, sadomasochistic relationships, etc.).

Body-images can be improved in two ways, starting with perceived "liabilities." These may be more imagined than real: the result of parental rejection or indifference. One young woman, for example, had a jealous father who criticized her crudely whenever she wore anything that revealed her feminine figure. His lewd and derogatory comments caused her to feel anxious and shameful about being sexual. It caused her to conclude that her breasts were too large and that she was "oversexed." Feedback from other young women eventually persuaded her otherwise — that the problem was in her father's personality, not in her body.

A second way to build better body-images is through nutrition and exercise. A counselor need not be an expert in these areas in order to encourage both. Recovery, remember, goes beyond sobriety; it includes spiritual, social, and physical dimensions. Young people naturally possess a great deal of energy, which becomes available to them in recovery. They should be encouraged to treat their bodies with respect (even if others have not), and to take care of them through exercise and healthy eating.

RELATIONSHIPS

Nowhere are problems of individuation more apparent (or telling) than in the relationships formed by teens and young adults. The arrested development caused by substance abuse invariably leads to dysfunctional relationships: relationships in which sex, dependency, or aggression can be confused with love and intimacy.

Jane was 18, and though she'd been doing well with respect to many aspects of treatment, she continued to have one obvious problem: boys. Within the program she was an outrageous flirt. She was very manipulative with the boys, causing a great deal of conflict among them. With the girls she was even more competitive than normal, and quite vicious to boot. Her "boyfriend," in his early thirties, was a drug dealer who was caught trying to sneak into the house and had to be escorted off grounds by security personnel.

At one point Jane's behavior was so problematic, and was causing such a stir, that the entire community confronted her and voted to put her on a "10-foot restriction." That meant that she was not allowed to be closer than 10 feet to any male in the program. In addition, she was required to spend a minimum of half an hour every day talking to other females, including peers and staff. Since these demands had the consensual support of the entire house, Jane's only choices were to comply or leave.

At the same time that Jane's behavior was being subjected to limits imposed by the community, she was working with a female counselor on her experiences of sexual victimization and exploitation. This work continued after she left our program, but during her six weeks with us she made significant progress on understanding her sexualization and how it was affecting her relationships. Despite her initial protestations (and threats to leave), Jane stayed and ended up feeling very close to at least two female peers and one woman staff member. Eventually she was even able to laugh about having to be put on a 10-foot restriction.

It is not unusual to ask teens to talk about relationships, in particular what they are looking for, and how they view intimacy and sexuality. What do these words mean to them? What kinds of emotional reactions do they evoke? Is there any justification for violence in a "loving" relationship? How does sex relate to love? Were they ever in a relationship where their love was exploited; where sexual exploitation, or violence, was justified in the name of love? What qualities do they value the most in a partner, and what are they looking for in a relationship? These and other issues can be explored in individual counseling, as well as in group therapy.

MORAL DEVELOPMENT

No discussion of individuation would be complete without mention of moral development: of ideals, values, and ethics. This is the spiritual part of recovery, and it is also the part of the personality that is most negatively affected by addiction.

Pete was just 12 years old. He was serving time after having been arrested (for the third time) for selling crack. Unfortunately for him, the third time he was caught he had enough crack on him so that he couldn't get off. In a group session his peers were confronting him. I

could see that at least some of them were put off by his cocky attitude, and also by his stated goal of becoming a big-time dealer: a
"high roller."

"Pete," asked one of the peers, "I know two guys who died from
crack, man. Doesn't it ever bother you that you're out there killing
people?"

Pete looked aggrieved. "I'm not killing nobody," he said defensive-
ly. "I'm just selling them what they want to have. It's their business
what they do with it. If they kill themselves, that's not my fault. I
mean, if I don't sell them, somebody else will. So what difference
does it make?"

Another peer chimed in: "Don't you worry about gettin' killed,
man? I know somebody got killed just because he was selling one
block out of his dealer's territory."

Pete stared back impassively, then shrugged. "That was his own
fault," he said. "I mean, that's part of it. If you're stupid enough to
go out of your territory, that's what happens."

Listening to this interchange left me feeling cold. Sadly, I've come
to learn that Pete is not so unusual. A product of generations of
inner-city poverty and desperation, his "values" and "ethics" were
those of survival on the street. His life was devoid of any viable
culture; therefore, he was amoral.

The issue of morality has been raised before in this book, and it
will be again. The important point to remember is this: Any treatment for youths that relies too heavily on external "structure" and
behavioral control, to the exclusion of moral development, will tend
to produce only transient results. So-called "improvement" under
such conditions is suspect. It may prove to be quite ephemeral, and
may merely represent the youth's capacity to respond to a situation,
rather than anything that has been internalized as a result of the
therapeutic experience. Limits and structure are important, to be
sure, but rewards and punishments, points and tokens, have their
limitations. When dealing with problems of developmental arrest, a
developmental treatment approach is required. Reliance on behavioral treatments, and too much faith in control through external consequences, is ultimately a self-defeating strategy. Sooner or later the
young person will perceive it as "safe" to use (or to act out, steal,
etc.). The only viable alternative is to adopt a corrective developmental perspective.

Higher levels of moral development and self-control are associated with internal as opposed to external control: to self-control based on ethics, values and ideals, rather than on perceived consequences in the moment. At this developmental level "rewards" are largely internal. Self-respect replaces tokens, points, or even the approval of authorities, as a motivator of behavior. Personal values transcend the immediate situation and play a key role in personal choices. If treatment programs fail to appreciate and plan interventions so as to promote moral development—for example, by creating a therapeutic culture as described in Chapter 15, and engaging youths in open dialogue about values and ethics and their relation to choice-making and behavior—they set the stage for quick relapse following treatment.

Ethics have to do with the individual's rules for conducting relationships. In the above example, Pete's ethics allowed him to sell crack without regard for the social implications; others in the group were questioning those ethics. His ideals were tied up with making money, regardless of how it was made. The only thing he valued was power; even if it had to come through the drug culture, he'd pursue it. Interestingly enough, within the confines of a custodial institution, Pete's behavior was reasonably good, but that was only because he was intelligent and able to read the system well. I had little doubt that he would resume his dealing career as soon as his first weekend visit home was approved.

SUMMARY

Values are developed (and changed) not so much in response to didactic intervention, as in response to modeling respected adults, plus involvement in culture. We need to systematically expose young people to adults whose lives are grounded in sound values, and who will engage them in a dialogue about choices, values, ideals, and ethics. Similarly, treatment programs need to be viable cultures.

For adolescents in recovery, developmental issues are central. To be truly effective, rehabilitation programs need to think not just in terms of situational control of behavior (which is important), but also in terms of extending their impact through interventions that aim at accelerating individuation. Any other approach invites disaster. Teens and young adults face unique issues in recovery, such as self-esteem and body-image. Actively working a 12-step program makes it possible for individuation to proceed.

13

Family Recovery

We sat at a large round table, Jimmy across from me, his parents on either side of him, across from each other. The expressions on their faces alternated between frustrated anger and helpless exasperation. In a long session with the three of them, Jimmy had been confronted with the fact that he was currently failing three out of four subjects, that his grades had declined dramatically in this, his senior year, that his parents had found cocaine in his bedroom, and finally, that his school had gotten an anonymous call claiming that Jimmy was dealing in cocaine.

Through all of this Jimmy steadfastly denied any drug problem. He maintained that the phone call had been an act of harassment (though he had no idea who would have a motive to harass him). Grudgingly he owned up to having tried cocaine, but claimed it was only a couple of times. On the other hand, he readily admitted that he enjoyed smoking marijuana, which he defended as a "benign" drug. Furthermore, he declared his intention to keep on using pot on a "recreational" basis. His problems in school he dismissed altogether, saying he just didn't like school, period.

"Well," I said to Jimmy's parents after listening to this for nearly an hour, "what's it been like living with Jimmy this past year?" His father looked at me and after a pause heaved a huge sigh; Meanwhile I saw tears well in his mother's eyes. I nodded sympathetically. I could well imagine what it must be like for them. "It's tough," I said after a moment of silence. "Having a kid who's into drugs can be hard on families—hard on marriages, too." Jimmy's mother looked away; her husband stared at me anxiously.

"Anyway," I continued, "since Jimmy is being pretty clear about what he intends to do, the only choice you two seem to have is to get together and be as clear as you can about what the terms will be for living in your house. I might be of help to you with that. Then you'll need to let all three kids know what those terms are—not just Jimmy—and then stick to them. I can help you there, too. One condition I'd suggest is that your children can only live with you so long as they don't bring drugs into the house, use them there, or advocate their use. You may not be able to stop Jimmy from using, since he's 18 now; on the other hand, you might be able to minimize his influence on his siblings."

Next, I turned to Jimmy and looked him in the eye. "Jim," I said, "We've talked about your situation, and you know how I feel. I think you're in trouble with drugs—marijuana for sure, and maybe cocaine too. No one can change your behavior or your attitudes, though, but you. I can only hope that you'll decide to get some help. In the meantime I can't let your behavior and your attitudes put your younger brother and your sister at risk. So I have to help your parents be clearer with you about your options. The rest will be up to you."

LIVING WITH ADDICTION

The example of Jimmy and his parents illustrates the point that it is impossible to be in a relationship—or live in a family—with someone who has a substance abuse problem and not be affected by it. The way people are affected varies a lot, and depends on a number of factors, including their innate abilities and talents, their temperament, and how mature and well-adjusted they were before the substance abuse began. Some people are all but devastated as a result of living with substance abuse; others come out more or less okay. Still, everyone is affected in some way. Substance abuse changes not only the abuser but also those who are close to him or her, including friends and family.

The following exercise is useful in helping families get in touch with how substance abuse affects them:

Begin by asking the family members to line up shoulder to shoulder. Now, ask them to walk across a room together, while being careful to maintain shoulder contact at all times. This is what it feels like to be part of a family: getting through life together, having to take each other into account, but moving along as a group. Ask the family this: Are you aware of this feeling of getting through life together, or do you feel detached and separate from each other? Are you used to moving together and being "connected" as a family in this way? Does it feel comfortable — supportive — or does it feel uncomfortable? Why?

Now, have the family members line up shoulder to shoulder again, but this time tie one person's shoes together, so that he or she is able to take only short steps. Ask the family members to walk across the room together again, maintaining shoulder contact as before. Ask for their reactions again, especially how the two different variations of this exercise made them feel.

In processing this exercise with the family, make the point that the person whose development is "slowed down" by substance abuse has a "ripple effect" on other family members, who must also slow down. Also, point out how families are motivated to stay together when one member becomes dysfunctional, even though it affects them all.

If family members have a hard time identifying feelings evoked by these exercises, have them walk across the room a few more times — until the strain begins to show in their faces. Search their faces for expressions that reveal emotions like frustration, anger, or boredom. Suggest that feelings like these are normal and that suppressing them causes damage to the person who suppresses them, as well as to the family as a unit.

Codependence

The exercise above illustrates "codependence": the process by which the family adapts to a substance abuse problem. Codependence is what we are referring to when we say that substance abuse is a "family illness." Addiction affects everyone, not just the addict, and not just those family members who are "closest" to the problem, like parents, but also those who are more "peripheral," such as siblings and cousins. Even family members who have left home can be deeply affected by addiction in another family member. The growing popularity of 12-step programs for adult children of alcoholics, for young children of substance abusing parents, and for parents of addicted youths attests to the reality and depth of codependence.

The counselor should engage family members in an ongoing dialogue about codependence: about the many ways in which substance abuse has affected them as a unit. Exercises like the above can facilitate this dialogue. It can help family members to feel freer to express how it has "slowed them down."

Though discussions of codependence may evoke guilt in the addict, it is nevertheless a reality that must be faced. It will be part of the addict's 12-step work to confront the harm that addiction has done to others and to attempt to make amends for it. In the meantime, it is helpful to all concerned to realize that addiction causes not only the addict, but eventually the whole family, to lose control.

Codependence is a natural phenomenon and should not be pathologized. It is a normal outcome of living with someone who has a chronic illness. In terms of its effects on others, substance abuse is not very different from chronic illnesses like renal disease, heart disease, Alzheimer's disease, or diabetes. All of these illnesses have effects on others besides the one with the illness. Much like the substance abuser, the person with a chronic illness, especially a deteriorating one, is apt to become more dependent, more "regressed" (infantile and self-centered, demanding and immature) over time. Of course the extent of regression varies from one individual to another; but it is difficult to avoid altogether. This progressive regression in turn creates more and more stress on others; even though some persons living with someone with a chronic illness cope better than others do, again it seems impossible to be unaffected by it. Therefore, family members who deny codependence should be thought of as being in denial. Much like the addict, they will use a variety of strategies (minimizing, distracting, etc.) to avoid facing up to how addiction has affected them.

A variation on the above exercise is useful in getting families in touch with the progression that codependence usually takes:

Tie up another person's shoes, this time much more tightly than before, so that he or she can only hop forward. Now, have the family walk arm in arm back and forth across the room several times.

Codependence follows a course that is predictable. It starts out with concern and helpfulness, progresses into resentment and guilt, and ends up in alienation and bitterness. Most family members will report something akin to the first reaction — helpful concern — early on in this exercise. As the exercise continues, however, at least some of them will begin to show — and hopefully report — feelings of frustration, annoyance, or impatience. If no one does, chances are they are suppressing those feelings, either intentionally or unconsciously, perhaps out of a desire to show their cooperativeness. Suggest this to them. In families troubled by substance abuse, negative reactions are rarely expressed directly. Rather than continuing that pattern, the family should be encouraged to take a risk—to communicate feelings—and to use this kind of exercise as a laboratory for change. Caring and concern are certainly legitimate, and a willingness to help is admirable; but feelings of resentment, impatience, and frustration are also legitimate, and a desire to "bail out" is understandable.

If it remains unexpressed, the resentment generated by a substance abuse problem ultimately leads to alienation from the dysfunctional family member. In time, this alienation will spread; it will poison all relationships within the family, rendering it a mere shell, devoid of love, cohesiveness, and meaning. In this psychological environment others in the family will become less functional over time.

Codependence is associated with a gamut of emotions, including fear, guilt, and shame. Parents and siblings alike will experience anxiety over the possible loss of a sibling or child to substance abuse. Anxiety is also generated by growing alienation and the steady erosion of the family as a cohesive and functional unit. Most family members will experience guilt at one time or another, caused by thoughts that they have somehow caused the problem, are contributing to it, or at the very least don't care about it as much as they should. Shame will attach to the "problem child." This will spread to shame about the family as a whole, and undermine the self-esteem of all family members. Finally, there will be a good deal of confusion and self-doubt as family members struggle privately with the progressive loss of control that threatens their lives.

Communication in the substance-abusing family gets worse over time. It starts with not wanting to talk about "the problem." Eventually, no one talks about anything substantial at all or dares to confront real issues. As the family "secret" continues to breed resentment, dishonesty, and detachment, positive feelings (love) give way to negative ones (resentment). Children spend more and more time out of the home, and spouses drift apart.

Family members who are most unable to express negative feelings can be expected to be the most alienated, angry, and withdrawn of all. Often they resist getting involved in treatment. This is one way for them to act out their unexpressed resentment and anger. It usually works, causing further stress within the family, while drawing attention to the resistant family member. Siblings who are most angry may begin failing in school or get into trouble for any number of reasons. Disaffected parents may lose themselves in work or hobbies or become dissatisfied with their jobs or their marriages.

Uncovering the various facets of codependence and working toward undoing alienation are vital to family recovery. The counselor should consistently work to replace silence with communication, avoidance or acting out with direct and honest expression of emotions, validating those emotions and supporting the right of family members to express them. Do not expect these feelings to be forthcoming. Typically, the family has lived with its "secret" for so long, and so much resentment has built up, that communication itself becomes threatening. Every step in the direction of openness is a significant one.

Enabling

One goal in family recovery is to get family members to appreciate how substance abuse had affected them all, and to work through those effects. Another goal is to help them get in touch with the concept of "enabling." To do this, have them start with the following exercise:

Have one family member stand in the middle, surrounded by all the others. If there is only one child, have him or her stand between the parents. Have the others place their hands firmly on the one in the middle, getting a good grip. Instruct the family member in the middle to keep his or her legs stiff, but to begin leaning one way or another. The other members of the family are told to literally hold the person in the middle up. If the exercise is done correctly, the individual in the middle would fall over, were it not for the support of the rest of the family.

Let the family members experience this for a minute. Then instruct them that, at the count of three, the person in the middle will slowly let his or her legs go limp; in other words, he or she will stop supporting him or herself completely, and will not merely lean on the others, but will need to be totally supported by them. Ask the others to help support the person in the middle for as long as they can. Count to three, and see how the family handles the challenge.

This exercise illustrates enabling and its effects. Though family members often don't realize it consciously, without their implicit "support" the substance abuser would probably "fall down" much sooner than he or she actually does. Enabling is a generic term that encompasses the many ways in which family members allow a substance abuse problem to continue by unwittingly supporting it. Like codependence, enabling is common, and it is not motivated out of any pathological desires or needs. On the contrary, enabling is motivated out of the same desire that motivates the family to support the person in the middle in the above exercise. Few family members — especially at first — are inclined to let the one in the middle "fall down." Most would consider that unloving or disloyal. Ask them if this is true, and how each one of them would feel being the first to stop supporting the "dysfunctional" one in the middle.

The second part of the exercise illustrates what enabling leads to in the long run. Instead of becoming more functional — "learning to stand on their own two feet" — those who become entangled in substance abuse become progressively less functional — more dependent not only on substances, but also on others. Within the family they need more and more support. Even when it is motivated out of genuine concern and love, enabling becomes more and more burdensome. As things get worse and worse (instead of better as the enabler hopes they will), feelings change: Concern becomes resentment, and anxiety sets in, often along with guilt and shame.

This exercise is a good icebreaker when working with families. It can facilitate a frank discussion of enabling. Often this is the first time family members have openly discussed this issue. Family members can be asked to describe the ways in which they feel they have enabled the substance abuse problem to continue: how they've personally "supported" the substance abuser, from turning the other way, to covering up, to bailing him or her out of jams. So long as the session isn't allowed to deteriorate into fault-finding, family members can also share their impressions of how others enable. Finally, the substance abuser can be asked to talk about the ways in which his or her substance abuse has been enabled by each member of the family.

Common forms of enabling that should be explored are discussed below.

AVOIDANCE

This is denial in its purest form: Ignore a problem and hope it will go away. Parents (or siblings, or friends) may choose to keep quiet, instead of saying what's on their mind. They may smell alcohol, but turn the other way; see a life on the skids, but bite their tongues.

Avoidance is sometimes based on blind hope; but hoping that a teen who is using mood-altering chemicals on a habitual basis will somehow "outgrow" it is a risky bet at best. It's true that some people give up substance abuse after a period of (sometimes reckless) experimentation. On the other hand, there is scarcely a teenager or young adult alive today who has not had at least one friend enter an alcohol or drug rehabilitation program, known others who dropped out of school because of involvement with alcohol or drugs, or lost at least one friend to a fatal car accident that involved drinking or drugging. Waiting (and hoping) for a problem to pass may be waiting for tragedy.

RATIONALIZING

This means explaining away negative consequences of substance abuse by attributing them to something else. School failure can be blamed on poor teaching, a faulty curriculum, or lack of innate interest. Car accidents can be justified by mythical weather conditions. Arrests can be blamed on bad company. Usually the substance abuser can be counted on to actively promote rationalizing as a way of avoiding the correct attribution. Parents sometimes enable substance abuse by convincing themselves that it is somehow less harmful if it takes place under their own roof. They do this in the belief that this is safer than having a child "hide" his or her use.

COVERING UP

Parents or siblings may know of or strongly suspect substance use, yet actively conspire with the abuser to avoid (or minimize) negative consequences. Sibs may lie about where one of them has really been, back up alibis, or help to hide incriminating evidence from parents. Parents may provide excuses for school absences, lie for children in order to "protect" them, or hire attorneys to help avoid or minimize the consequences of alcohol or drug-related legal problems.

CAPITULATING

In the case example given at the outset of this chapter, Jimmy's parents were exasperated as a result of their inability to get their son to acknowledge, much less do something about, his substance abuse problem. Each time something would happen, they confronted him. Often they made threats of one kind or another. Never, however, had they felt confident enough to follow through on any threat they made. They enabled the problem to continue, by virtue of not imposing limits, conditions, or consequences.

Throughout recovery families need to be vigilant for tendencies to enable a substance abuse problem. Families can "relapse" into enabling, just as an addict can relapse into substance use. This is not to say that an adolescent should be permitted to be totally responsible for his or her own recovery program. Unlike adults in recovery, adolescents have parents who have both moral and legal responsibilities for their welfare and development. Parents need to play a role in adolescent recovery. The line between responsible parenting and enabling is not always clear or sharp. The counselor needs to engage parents in an ongoing dialogue, to help them maintain some perspective regarding responsible parenting, and where responsible parenting ends and the teen's responsibility for his or her own behavior (and its consequences) begins.

Enabling is most often motivated by caring and loyalty, and these benign intentions should be recognized. The term "enabler" should not be used pejoratively, to criticize or incriminate individual family members or the family as a whole. Recovery from substance abuse involves reeducating family members about the reality of what they do: about the real effects of their behavior on the substance abuse problem, as opposed to their intentions.

SUPPORTING FAMILIES IN RECOVERY

The recovery movement dates from the founding of Alcoholics Anonymous in 1935.[1] In the succeeding decades AA has grown from an essentially secret society of the stigmatized and hopeless to a worldwide movement which counts its members in the millions, many of whom are openly proud of their association with it. AA has, in turn, spawned a number of related 12-step programs: Narcotics

Anonymous (NA), Cocaine Anonymous (CA), Overeaters Anonymous (OA), Sex and Love Addicts Anonymous (SLAA), and Emotions Anonymous (EA), to name a few.

Al-Anon began as a movement, also based on 12-step principles, for persons who were in relationships with addicts. In this case it is another person's addiction that one is powerless over. Using 12-step principles, Al-Anon, Al-Atot, Families Anonymous, and Al-Ateen all provide support for children, teens, parents and partners of persons who are recovering from (or not recovering from) addictions.

All 12-step programs share some common characteristics. They all emphasize anonymity, using first names only during meetings. They are all supported by voluntary contributions from members, whose participation is also voluntary. They are groups of peers, who share common problems, and which function without professional supervision or guidance. Some meetings are "closed," meaning that attendance is limited to persons who acknowledge being addicted, while others are "open" to non-addicts.

The agenda for a 12-step meeting may vary. Some meetings are "step" meetings, in which the agenda is to focus on a particular step in the program, what it means to each individual, and how he or she is "working" it. Other meetings are open to individuals' "telling their stories": their personal histories of substance abuse, and the consequences of that abuse.

Twelve-step programs benefit from many of the advantages traditionally associated with group therapy. There are, first of all, opportunities for support and encouragement. Social support is an important form of stress management, and persons in recovery must be able to cope with stress without the use of mood-altering chemicals. Encouragement and practical advice, from sympathetic and nonjudgmental peers, are also important parts of 12-step programs.

Finding 12-Step Programs

Twelve-step programs, and in particular AA and Al-Anon, list information and hotline numbers in the white pages of the telephone directory in most towns. Information about meeting locations and schedules can be obtained from the information bureau; hotlines should be used for crisis intervention. Often, information about other 12-step programs can be obtained through AA and Al-Anon, especially at meetings.

The hardest part of getting involved in a 12-step program is breaking the ice—in other words, going to those first three or four meetings. For some people, open meetings may be less threatening at first than closed ones, while others prefer the "confidentiality" of closed meetings. It is a good idea to try several different meetings (groups), instead of only one. Counselors should become familiar with meetings in their areas and should be prepared to go with a teenager the first couple of times. They are also well advised to attend meetings themselves on a regular basis.

Getting a Sponsor

Getting a sponsor requires two steps: first, go to a meeting and wait until it is time for announcements; second, say "I need a sponsor."

Sponsorship is central to the recovery movement. Generally speaking, sponsors should be individuals who have achieved several years of sobriety and who attend meetings regularly. They should be of the same sex as the person seeking a sponsor; in addition, the new member should feel comfortable talking frankly to his or her sponsor. If any of these conditions is not met, the new member should be encouraged to seek a different sponsor.

The sponsor is a source of information about the program, as well as sensible advice born of personal and collective experience. There is much wisdom embedded in the lore of 12-step programs, and the sponsor is a source of this wisdom.

While he or she is an important resource, the sponsor is fundamentally a peer, and a nonprofessional. Sponsorship is not psychotherapy, family therapy, or marital therapy. Although more experienced in recovery, the sponsor who ventures into counseling on issues outside of recovery is likely to do as much harm as good. These issues, which are important, are better addressed with someone trained to deal with them. There is no reason not to have both a therapist and a sponsor.

Adolescents in recovery should be strongly encouraged to attend several meetings a week and to get a sponsor as soon as possible, in addition to meeting with a counselor regularly. In some areas "young people's meetings" are available. These are helpful in providing access to other adolescents and young adults in recovery, who are facing similar kinds of stresses (peer pressure, individuation, sexuality, etc.). At the same time, the recovering teen can benefit from exposure to adults in recovery, and regular adult meetings should be part of their recovery program. Family members, meanwhile, should be encouraged to explore Al-Anon, Families Anonymous, or Al-Ateen as sources of support and information. Weekly individual or family therapy does not constitute a recovery program, and the counselor should work steadily toward broadening the youth's (and the family's) involvement in 12-step programs.

THE FAMILY RECOVERY PLAN

Recovery from substance abuse and addiction is a task for families, not just for addicts. The realities of codependence and enabling leave little doubt that everyone in the family is affected by substance abuse, and therefore that everyone stands to gain through recovery. Resistance to becoming involved in treatment or to participating in the construction of a family recovery plan can be safely interpreted as a reflection of unexpressed and/or unresolved resentments on the part of the individual(s) involved. They have most likely reached that stage in codependence where they are alienated from the substance abuser, and perhaps from the family as a whole. They need to be drawn in, but to do this they will first need to be able to express their feelings. It may be that they have done this at some time in the past, but have given up since it didn't seem to have much effect, to make much difference for them or for anyone else. Siblings are especially likely to react this way, and their alienation and anger are usually obvious. The most common way they are expressed is through resistance and negativity. They don't want to talk to anyone, least of all a counselor, about the problem. They steadfastly maintain that it isn't their problem, therefore they don't want to be bothered about it. They have other things to do, other people to see.

Rather than responding to negativity with rejection or coercion, the counselor should take pains to reach out to resistant family members, to validate their resistant attitude, and to invite their participation. A genuine effort at making amends on the part of the substance abuser can also help. Meanwhile, even if this doesn't succeed in engaging everyone, work with the rest of the family should continue. Part of this work involves the construction of a family recovery plan.

The plan should be a written document that is developed collaboratively by the counselor and all family members. It should start, however, with the individual recovery plan made up by the substance abuser. This needs to be a document that is public within the family. Everyone should know the following:

- Which people, places, and things the substance abuser intends to avoid in recovery.
- How the recovering teen plans to schedule his or her daily and weekend activities.
- What kinds of alternative recreational activities (alternative to substance abuse) he or she plans to get involved in.
- Which AA or NA meetings the recovering teen plans to attend each week.
- What kind of counseling the young person will be involved in.

Using this as a model, other family members can be encouraged to develop recovery plans that are eventually shared with others. Begin with the parents and what 12-step programs they could get involved in. Help them to make a commitment and follow it up. If necessary, go with them to a first meeting. Follow this up with problem-solving sessions about daily and weekend schedules, and how these can be changed so as to allow for family activities and time together. Equally important is planned time for spouses to spend together. A cohesive marriage is a powerful tool for substance abuse prevention within the family. Codependence and enabling erode the fabric of a marriage, and much mending often needs to be done. Making a commitment to a better, happier, and more fulfilling marriage is an excellent addition to a recovery plan.

Next, help siblings identify personal goals they might have. This may involve wanting to spend more time with one or both parents, doing things as a family, or pursuing some recreational activity. Siblings who may be experimenting with substances can be prevented from getting more deeply involved through the family recovery plan.

The family recovery plan should become a focus for counseling. Being of the family's making, it is a living document that becomes a vehicle for building a healthier family and more confident parents.

SUMMARY

Understanding key concepts like codependence and enabling early on in the recovery process is important. Family members need to understand how substance abuse has affected them as a family and as individuals. They need to be encouraged to express their true feelings, and they need to have those feelings validated as reasonable and understandable. This opens the way to communication, which usually has broken down, and to constructive involvement instead of alienation and detachment. Twelve-step programs provide a vital source of support and practical advice from others who have struggled (and are struggling) with similar issues. Opening the family up, and getting family members in touch with the resources of the recovery movement, marks the start of family recovery.

14

Working with Families: Structure and Communication

Family recovery from substance abuse can be likened to changing a lot of old habits — especially the dysfunctional roles that family members have drifted into over time. In this chapter we look at some of the key areas where habits and roles need to change, not only to help young persons maintain their recovery, but also to prevent others from falling victim to substance abuse.

STRUCTURAL ISSUES

Limits

It was said earlier that teens need more parenting than they often get, and this is worth repeating. They also need more parental involvement in their lives in general than many of them receive. Adolescents are not small adults, so much as large children. Adolescence itself can be likened to an apprenticeship. In this apprenticeship, the object of learning is to develop the skills necessary to function effectively as an adult. These skills do not emerge "naturally"; they are not in the genes. The need to develop effective "adulthood skills" must be recognized, and opportunities for learning them must be provided. In this regard, supervision and guidance are vital, Would you teach someone to become a skilled carpenter by providing him or her with wood, nails, and saws, but no supervision? Would you expect a group of apprentices to teach each other how to become skilled carpenters?

When we speak of structure we are talking about three things: limits, support, and direction. Parents are family leaders, and effective leaders provide all of these things to the groups they lead. First, they provide limits: expectations, rules, and consequences. These are explicit and clear. Everyone knows pretty well what the rules of the house are, what they are expected to do and how they are expected to act, and what the consequences are for violating the limits. Limits and expectations define the parameters of the quality of life that parents establish — much the same way that the master sets standards of quality for the apprentice.

Limits facilitate the development of self-control. Children deprived of adequate limit-setting invariably develop impulse-control problems. They tend to be willful, impulsive, and unrealistic. Limits also have a relation to moral development, since they reflect the values and priorities of those who set them.

In working with families in recovery, the issue of limits is a crucial one. Limits are defined more easily when parents think about their expectations for their teenage children: about what they expect from them at home, at school, and in the community. The subject of "reasonable expectations" for teens was discussed in Chapter 9. This set of expectations can be used as a starting point, to help parents define their own expectations.

In working with parents it may be useful to talk about how expectations relate to limits. In reality, limits follow naturally from parental expectations. If, for example, a parent expects adolescents to dress neatly and to be clean, what follows naturally is some limit that separates acceptable from unacceptable appearance. The parent has both the right and the responsibility to define limits, in other words, to set expectations. Parents also have the right and the responsibility to enforce standards through appropriate rewards and punishments. To do this effectively, they need the flexibility to evaluate situations individually. What may be acceptable in one situation may not be so in another.

Sometimes parents can be excessive in their standards and fail to allow room for individuation. The counselor can help the rigid parent to recognize the teen's need for individuation, to appreciate the role of the peer group in development, and to establish reasonable standards. Much more common, however, are parents who agonize over whether they have the right to establish any limits or enforce any standards at all, even on matters as mundane as clothing. They need to be supported in having not only the right, but also the responsibility, to do this.

Table 7: Parent Inventory: Part I

How do you see your role in the family?
- What responsibilities do you have as a parent?
- How much authority do you think a parent should have? How much authority do you feel that you have with your child?
- Do you think a parent has the right to stop a child, particularly a teenage child, from doing something he or she wants to do? When is it appropriate for a parent to exercise this kind of 'veto power'?

In what ways is a parent a leader in the family?
- How important is it for a parent to set standards for behavior?
- How important is it for a parent to model behavior he or she wants to set as a standard?
- In what areas have you not set standards?
- In what ways could you be a more effective model?

List your standards for your teenage child in the following areas:
- Curfews:
- Clothing: Acceptable:
          Unacceptable:
- Personal appearance: Acceptable:
                      Unacceptable:
- Social activities: Acceptable:
                    Unacceptable:
- Manners: Courtesy:
          Respect:
- Work habits:
- Household responsibilities:
- Family involvement:

They should be encouraged to establish standards in areas such as curfews, dating, social behavior (manners), and work habits.

If parents appear to be stuck with respect to setting limits, the counselor can help by asking them to think about their own roles. Questions like those in the Parent Inventory, Part I, shown in Table 7, can be useful food for thought. These can be used to help parents become explicit about their expectations. Once this is done, the work shifts to supporting parents in enforcing their standards: in making them known, in confronting teens when they violate limits, in imposing reasonable consequences, and in learning to reward compliance appropriately.

Parent support groups are very useful when it comes to expectations and limits. Some sessions can be structured or guided by the counselor so as to deal with issues like limits, confrontation, rewards and consequences; alternatively, some may be more free-ranging, with the parents themselves setting the agenda. Parents today are frequently isolated, deprived of the guidance once provided by extended families. They have to go it, as it were, "one-on-one" with their children, without the added moral support, hands-on help, and practical advice once provided by grandparents. Opportunities to talk to other parents and to tap into the support and guidance that come from shared struggles are rare today, according to many parents.

Support

The second critical component of a functional family is support. Families that lack support for children and teens will also typically lack support for adults as well; in other words, parents who can't provide emotional support for their children usually can't provide it for each other. As a consequence, the family is detached instead of cohesive. Each member of the family feels that he or she is basically "going it alone" in life. Trust levels are low. This family environment is ripe for substance abuse.

To prevent substance abuse it is necessary to build families that are cohesive and which provide emotional support. Included under "support" are things like affection, sympathy, encouragement, and comfort. A questionnaire like that in Table 8 can be used to generate a productive discussion.

Family dysfunction is transmitted across generations largely through modeling of dysfunctional family structures. Support is one

Table 8: Parent Inventory: Part II

- When you were young, who were your sources of comfort when you felt sad, scared, or hurt?
- Think of two or three adults who provided you with encouragement in your formative years. Who were these people? What did they say? How did you feel about them?
- Was your own family, your "family of origin," affectionate? How was love and caring expressed?
- How do you express each of the following: affection, love, sympathy, encouragement.

of the cornerstones of healthy families; conversely, an absence of support sets a family up for stress and alienation. Helping a detached family break the ice of alienation is not always easy. Distrust may be so thick that it needs to chipped at over a period of months. Parent support can play a decisive role in helping the divided family find common ground.

Direction

The final structural issue that the counselor can address with families in recovery has to do with another aspect of the parental role as a leader. This is the issue of direction. Too much has been written about the so-called "downward mobility," apathy, and alienation of today's youths, with surprisingly little consideration of the role that parents play in these issues. To what extent, for example, is the problem of alienation among youths merely a reflection of a similar problem in their parents' generation? How much do adults today suffer from apathy and hopelessness, distrust, cynicism, and other symptoms of aspirituality?

The solution to problems of direction is not an easy one. Spiritual issues can be both subtle and complex, and many counselors understandably shy away from them. Perhaps the best a counselor can do is to engage parents in a dialogue about their own goals in life: individually, as a couple (if they are married), and as a family.

A family without direction is not unlike a ship without a rudder. There is little to bind its crew together, to give them a goal to work toward as a team; yet historically, families have been teams. How many families today think of themselves in these terms? How many tasks and challenges have they tackled as a group in the past year? How many recreational activities have they participated in as a family? Cohesive families are interdependent, with each member playing an important role, each being responsible to the whole. In how many families today are members aware of their individual responsibilities to the group? How many feel accountable to each other for what they do?

Goals bind all groups together, and families are no exception. Goals, especially for families, relate in turn to values and priorities. Cohesiveness and spirituality go hand in hand in families. A family is more than a collection of individuals pursuing separate lives. A family is a living entity. It grows, changes, and adapts, and it is defined by its values, its ideals, and its goals.

COMMUNICATION

In considering the need for changing roles and old habits within the family, we must look closely at communication. Substance abuse itself represents an attempt to cope with issues and emotions without communicating about them; therefore, communication becomes vital to recovery. So much of substance abuse—for adults no less so than for adolescents—boils down to an attempt to manipulate feelings: to create pleasure and to avoid pain. The more "involved" the user becomes with his or her "relationship" with chemicals, the less involved he or she is with human relationships—and communication gets worse and worse.

In families where one or more members are abusing substances, communication progressively breaks down as the relationship with chemicals grows stronger, and as more and more real issues and feelings are avoided. The therapeutic goal is to open channels of communication in these families. By opening communication, we mean helping family members learn to express emotions and to deal effectively with conflict.

Feelings

Two exercises that can be used to break the ice within families have to do with grief and gratitude: two emotions that figure prominently in recovery.

GRIEF

Grief is the natural human emotional response to loss—any loss. So long as something has emotional significance to us, so long as it is something we've become "attached" to, we will react to its loss. Grief, because it is perhaps the most painful of human emotions, has the capacity to trigger substance use as a way of coping. Alcohol, in particular, has long been used to "drown" grief.

Anger, sadness, and the pain of emptiness are emotions that lie at the core of grief. And, although it is often overwhelmingly painful, grief is one emotion that can't be avoided if we are to grow in character.

People can grieve the loss of many things, including people, places, and things. We grieve the loss of a pet, the loss of a neighborhood (or a country) when we must leave it, the loss of someone we love, and the loss of children who grow up. We grieve the loss of relationships, the loss of goals that cannot be attained and dreams that must be forsaken. We grieve the loss of self-esteem. What we grieve sometimes is the loss of a part of our past; at other times it is a part of our present or our future that we must part with.

Substance abusers often have much to grieve. They have suffered negative consequences and have lost many things en route to addiction. This is partly addressed in the 12 steps, but to a larger extent it is dealt with through involvement in the recovery movement, where one finds an acceptance of grief, as well as support for those who feel it.

The expression of grief is most frequently blocked by anger (sometimes in the form of resentment), by shame, or by guilt. Parents and siblings may feel resentful, for example, over the stress and disruption that substance abuse has caused them. If they do not express this resentment, they may not experience their grief at having "lost" a relationship with a brother, sister, son, or daughter. Similarly, the substance abuser may be so filled with shame or guilt that he or she does not feel free to express grief over what has been lost.

The longer the list of emotions that are not expressed within a family, the greater the degree of alienation. At the same time, a family is more likely to enable substance abuse as a result of its avoidance of feelings. This creates a vicious cycle, in which poor communication and substance abuse perpetuate one another. The exercise outlined in Table 9 can be used with families to open communication by facilitating the expression of grief.

In helping the family members express and deal with grief, the counselor should be prepared to confront this issue in his or her own life. Emotional catharsis, combined with comfort and solace, is the best treatment for grief. Do not be surprised to discover people carrying unresolved (unexpressed and unconsoled) grief whose roots lie in the distant past. Keep in mind that the loss of love, as well as of self-esteem, comes up very often in work with substance abusers.

Table 9: Grieving Exercise

Step 1. Think of something you have lost in your life. It may be a person, a thing, a place, an opportunity, or even a dream. Describe it.

Step 2. Tell the other members of your family about this loss you've experienced: about what it was, and what it meant to you. Why were you attached to this thing (or person, or idea)? What role did it play in your life?

Step 3. Describe how you felt about this loss. What emotions did you experience? Did you feel angry, sad, empty, scared? If not, why do you suppose you may not have experienced these emotions? What other feelings, like anger, guilt, or shame, might be standing in the way of your experiencing grief?

Step 4. Describe how you coped with the loss. What consoled you? Did you talk to anyone about it? Did anyone comfort you? Did you ever attempt to deal with a loss through substance abuse? What would be a better way?

Step 5. How can the members of this family help each other cope with loss, and express grief?

GRATITUDE

Though it is a very different emotion, gratitude, like grief, is also often hidden behind unexpressed resentment, guilt, or shame; yet gratitude can play a pivotal role in healing wounds and building cohesiveness in the family. Next to making amends, nothing seems so powerful as gratitude in bringing divided families back together. The exercise in Table 10 has been used with families who are trying to come back together after being driven apart by substance abuse:

Table 10: Exercise for Expressing Gratitude

Step 1. Think of three things in your life that you are grateful for: things that make your life better and that you'd miss if they weren't there. Write them down.

Step 2. Share with each other some of the things you are grateful for.

Step 3. Think of a relationship you have that you are grateful for: a relationship that makes your life better, and that you would miss if you were to lose it.

Step 4. Share with each other one relationship you are grateful for having.

Step 5. Think of one or two things that someone in your family has done for you for which you have been grateful. Have you ever expressed your gratitude to that person for this? If not, what has stopped you? Resentment? Over what? How would you express your gratitude?

Step 6. Express your gratitude to someone in your family for something he or she has done for you, in a simple and direct way. Say "Thank you for . . . "

If family members have trouble either identifying or expressing their gratitude, the counselor can shift the focus of the exercise to why: What is blocking the expression of gratitude? Resentments, for example, may need to be aired before they can be buried. This exercise is "diagnostic" in a sense, since it quickly identifies families (or family members) who are having problems being supportive and loving with each other. Along with grief work, the expression of gratitude can mark the end of a long emotional drought.

Conflict

Nothing seems to undermine relationships, including family relationships, more surely than the avoidance of conflict. Avoidance plays a major role in problems of intimacy in marriage, and it plays a similar role in destroying cohesiveness in families. When conflicts are avoided, resentments build — it's that simple. Feelings of resentment in time turn into a bitterness that descends like a freezing rain over a family.

As substance abuse erodes the fabric of a family, communication and conflict resolution give way to alienation and avoidance. Family members become cold and detached, whereas what they need is to be engaged. Violence may threaten families, but conflict itself does not; on the contrary, successful engagement and conflict resolution strengthen the bonds within a family.

Conflict resolution, like assertiveness, is very much a skill, which can be developed with practice. As with assertiveness, following a few simple rules can help a great deal; however, before conflict resolution can even begin, some of the alienation within the family may need to be addressed. Chronic frustration leads to a pervasive sense of hopelessness that drives avoidance. This is a normal part of co-dependence, and the counselor needs to validate this process — and the emotions it arouses — while at the same time working to bring the family out from under it.

Below are some of the basic rules of conflict resolution for families.

RULE 1: CONFRONTATION

Confrontation does not mean aggression. It does not mean fighting. Confrontation means, simply, saying what bothers you rather than keeping it in. Confrontation is the opposite of avoidance.

Whereas avoidance breeds resentment and alienation, confrontation leads to engagement and involvement. The family that's engaged and involved is resilient to stress.

RULE 2: LISTENING

Conflicts cannot be resolved if family members don't listen to each other. The counselor must be vigilant for family members who don't listen. This should be pointed out, since it frustrates and discourages communication. A useful intervention is to ask family members to paraphrase each others' comments. The counselor can ask: "What did _____ just say?" This simple intervention helps keep family members alert to the need to listen to each other. This includes parents listening to their children and children to their parents. This simple intervention, if practiced consistently, can build bridges and heal resentments.

RULE 3: NEGOTIATION

Conflict resolution is the art of compromise and negotiation. Parents need not abdicate their parental responsibilities — or compromise their integrity or authority — in order to compromise now and then; on the contrary, appropriate compromise helps build judgment in teens and promotes healthy individuation. Excessive rigidity is no more a virtue in parents than is the inability to set limits. The counselor can be a resource to parents in this regard, almost like a member of the extended family. He or she can help parents to evaluate their son or daughter's position on a matter, to decide whether compromise is acceptable, and if so, to negotiate. The counselor is in a position to support the parent who negotiates in good faith and who sets appropriate limits.

SUMMARY

This chapter focused on some of the key structural issues facing families in recovery. The emphasis has been on parents as family leaders. The counselor can help families by helping parents develop their leadership skills. The decline of the extended family, along with the proliferation of single-parent and dual-career households, has the effect of isolating parents at a time when they need a great deal of support. The counselor can help with this, both through direct involvement and through providing opportunities for parents to support one another. Parent support groups function as a surrogate extended family. The family with integrity—with clear standards, firm sources of support, and a sense of direction and purpose—is a family that can cope effectively with virtually any crisis.

Families who face conflicts and work them out through negotiation and compromise are much like couples who do this: They are close, resistant to external influence, and adaptable in the face of change.

15

Group Treatment
of Adolescents
and Young Adults:
The Therapeutic Tribe

Adolescence is the time in life when the group exerts its most powerful influence on development. Prior to adolescence the parents are the most influential people in a child's life; later on individual, intimate relationships are more important. But the essence of adolescence is the peer group.

Contrary to the way many adults stereotype it, the adolescent subculture is not monolithic. The adolescent subculture can be likened to Native American tribal cultures as they existed prior to westernization: Despite some commonalities, they varied a great deal in language and customs. Adolescent groups, moreover, function not unlike tribes: They have leaders and rituals, rites and rules, even their own dress codes and languages; and like tribes they frequently coexist, more or less peacefully, within the same space. They exist within almost every school and community and are known to each other by tribal labels: preppies, deadheads, jocks, acid heads, etc. Movies such as *Rebel Without a Cause*, *The Breakfast Club* and *Dead Poets' Society* and books like *A Clockwork Orange* have addressed not only the phenomenon of adolescent tribal behavior, but also some of its more frightening aspects and potentials.

It is virtually inevitable that each and every adolescent will search for a tribe to join—individuation demands this. Given this fact of life, the major issue then becomes this: Will the group have a positive or negative effect on character development? Put differently: Will the tribal experience be a healthy one or an unhealthy one?

Most adolescents who drift toward substance abuse, toward anti-social behavior, or toward satanic cultism, do so out of a combination of personal will and peer pressure. They "belong to" socially dysfunctional tribes. Still, they have their individual wills, albeit immature ones. Simply removing them from the group is ineffectual: It leads to arrested development at best, and usually is not sufficient to produce attitudinal or behavioral change, unless efforts are also directed at integrating the adolescent into a healthier peer group. This is where the concept of the "therapeutic tribe" fits into adolescent and young adult treatment.

Previous chapters have focused on working with the adolescent and the family; in this chapter we'll examine some of the issues that can best be worked on in a group treatment format. The goal is to facilitate the development of what can be thought of as a healthy (functional) "tribe". The tribal analogy works well with teens and young adults, who intuitively relate to it, probably because it speaks to where they are developmentally and because it captures the reality of their lives. It is also a useful analogy for the counselor, who needs to think in terms of creating a tribe, rather than merely a group. In effect, counselors need to think about how they might provide a "culture" that is an important factor in adolescent development. The essential elements of a tribal "culture" are discussed in the following sections. As we examine each of them, consider how counselors can work toward establishing a group (social) environment that will lead to a therapeutic tribal experience for adolescents and young adults.

RITES OF ENTRY

Every member of a tribal group needs at some point to be judged and either accepted or rejected by the group. In actual tribes this rite usually takes place at birth or shortly thereafter; in a therapeutic tribe it should take place following a brief period of "orientation." Efforts by counselors to circumvent this fundamental group process usually lead to problems. Whenever a group's integrity is compromised — for example, by a counselor's efforts to impose on it members who are not truly accepted — group cohesiveness suffers. These groups quickly cease to be therapeutic, though counselors may not realize this at first, and consequently may try to make up for it through more and more strenuous interventions.

Obviously, the counselor hopes that each and every new member introduced into a group will win acceptance; on the other hand, the counselor needs to respect the integrity of the group and not impose members on it. There is no guarantee (or reason to think) that one group will be right for everyone. It is helpful, therefore, to establish rites of entry in a formal way, rather than trying to avoid the issue.

Rites of entry, or initiation, can be simple, but they should take place. In group work with young people who have substance abuse problems, a simple and direct rite of entry can be built around the act of preparing and sharing a personal chemical history. This should take place within the first week in an inpatient treatment setting or within the first several weeks of outpatient treatment.

Chemical histories were discussed in Chapter 11. Within the group, one or two members who have been there longer can be appointed "sponsors" for a new member. Better yet, sponsorship can be elevated to a position of status that is earned by fulfilling specific expectations. As in any tribal organization, leaders play a role in establishing social position; but they do not usurp the power of the group, which must agree by consensus on matters regarding social status. Therefore, individuals should be elevated to sponsor status only through group consensus and with the support of the leader (or counselor).

Sponsors may have the task of helping new members prepare for their rite of entry: to prepare their personal histories of involvement with mood-altering chemicals and plan how this information will be presented to the group. The sponsor can be a source of information, feedback, and advice. If the new member's efforts satisfy the sponsor, then he or she can advocate for the new member when the time comes to apply for formal entry to the group.

This example of sponsorship also illustrates how a social hierarchy can be created. Successful sponsorship of one or two new members can be part of the criteria for moving to yet a higher level of social status. This kind of social hierarchy provides a foundation for group cohesiveness. At the same time it allows for accelerated developmental growth: for becoming more socially responsible and internally controlled.

New members should be prepared in advance of their first group meeting for the rite of entry, and how they will be guided through it. They should be told exactly what is expected, and what will happen:

"You will prepare a careful and detailed history of involvement with mood-altering chemicals; a sponsor, who is a member of the group, will help you with this; you will present your history to the group, who may ask you questions. Afterward, you will ask the group to either accept (or not accept) your work, and to accept (or not accept) you into the group. Your sponsor can speak up for you then. To remain in the group, however, your history must be accepted."

New members who pass the rite of entry should be formally welcomed to group membership. A brief induction ceremony is appropriate, as is some symbol of membership, such as a medallion. Members who are not admitted — whose work is not accepted — need to be counseled immediately as to why, by a counselor as well as by the sponsor. Often this rejection will be due to perceived denial (minimizing, etc.) by the group. Group consensus in this regard needs to be taken very seriously. The new member can be given the choice of either asking the group for permission to repeat the rite or being referred to alternative treatment.

Rites of initiation build group cohesiveness and enhance treatment motivation. Through its rites and rituals, its expectations and its social hierarchy, the group not only becomes cohesive, but also represents a powerful force for recovery. The role (and power) of the counselor is balanced by this power of the group, which is a desirable balance for purposes of individuation.

In addition to rites of entry, essential elements of culture include a social hierarchy and traditions. In the last section, the beginnings of social hierarchy — the use of sponsors — was discussed. In a working (therapeutic) community, control of individual behavior, as well as developmental growth, is a function of the culture as much as of "therapy." To be effective, a social hierarchy must be based on group consensus and tradition.

In tribes, social hierarchies traditionally are based on sex and age. In therapeutic groups and communities, meaningful hierarchies can be established on the basis of age and accomplishment. Social status — and along with it, power — should accrue to those who have accomplished more within the group, who have demonstrated their responsibility and commitment to the group, who are older, and who have been there longer.

Many behaviorally oriented treatment programs have "hierarchies," but they do not account for differences in age or longevity; in other words, they are not developmentally organized. The same things are expected from 18-year-olds as from 14-year-olds, and there is an exaggerated emphasis on compliance as opposed to judgment. This is a mistake. It is not the way healthy families are organized, and it's not the way tribes are organized. More should be expected from the older adolescent — more responsibility, more self-control — in order to establish a developmentally corrective environment. In treatment programs that are not structured in this way, the typical result is regression: 18-year-olds will act like 14-year-olds. Another result is the absence of "culture": Social hierarchy is unstable, group cohesiveness is erratic, and counselors end up devoting a great deal of time and energy to controlling behavior (usually through punishment). Under these conditions relapse is highly likely as soon as environmental controls (restraints) are removed.

The fact is that adolescents and young adults often adjust their behavior to meet external expectations. If you expect impulsiveness and irresponsibility from youths, you usually will get it. Older adolescents in treatment, therefore, should be held to higher expectations simply by virtue of their age. This is a rule that is intuitively followed in most families, where older siblings are routinely held to somewhat more demanding standards than younger ones, and where older children assume some degree of responsibility for younger ones. So should it be in a therapeutic community or group. This places older members in the position of models. It gives them greater social responsibility, which is consistent with their closer proximity to adulthood and the expectations and obligations they will soon face. Interestingly enough, they will often rise to these expectations.

Though age matters, age alone cannot be the basis of a social hierarchy, especially among substance abusers whose development has been arrested. Similarly, focusing on younger members and their problems cannot he allowed to evolve into a form of denial. That's why achievement of specific goals and completion of specific tasks also need to be associated with passage to higher levels within the tribal community.

The counselor's role within this system is critical and should not be left to chance. The counselor plays a key role in establishing the criteria for movement within the social hierarchy, for establishing procedures for this to happen (rites), and for setting group norms (ethics). The counselor does not, on the other hand, need to make all the decisions for the group or monitor the process singlehandedly.

To evolve into therapeutic tribes, treatment groups and programs also need to become traditionalized. Contrary to many adults' expectations, following an initial period of adjustment most youths feel comfortable in this kind of social environment; indeed, they find it difficult to leave. While actual tribal traditions usually have seasonal and/or religious significance, it is possible to establish traditions in the context of a treatment program. Semi-annual reunions for "graduates" is one example of a viable tradition. In addition, within the program itself traditions can be established, such as the following:

- The group leader (and/or co-leader) always sits in the same place.
- Meetings always begin with a specific reading or meditation, or some other specified format.
- Days begin with a specific ritual.
- Meetings end with a reading of the Serenity Prayer.
- The group co-leader assumes the role of leader when the leader graduates.

These and other traditions build group cohesiveness and strengthen individuals' commitment to group values and ethics. They also play an important role in reestablishing a healthy individuation process in young persons in recovery.

ETHICS

All tribes have ethics: rules and norms that define the limits of acceptable behavior, and which control social interactions. Within the confines of group treatment — be it long-term residential or outpatient care — rules and norms need to be explicitly defined. Some rules that are useful are discussed below.

Punctuality

Continued involvement in the group, as well as maintenance of social status, should be contingent on punctual participation in all activities.

Sobriety

Members should never be permitted to participate in a group session if they are under the influence of any mood-altering chemical. The issue of coming to a meeting high or intoxicated needs to be confronted immediately, and the offending member asked to leave. If necessary, safe transportation or supervision may need to be arranged, but the member absolutely cannot be permitted to remain in the group. Consequences for this behavior should be imposed. The limits of those consequences can be broadly defined by the counselor, but the consequences themselves should be determined and delivered by senior members of the group and supported by the entire group. In general, more than one such instance should be sufficient grounds for exclusion from the treatment program for a specified period of time. This is necessary to preserve the integrity and motivation of the group.

No Drug Glorification

In recovery there is no room for "teasing": for talking or dressing in ways that invite or glorify substance use. This includes the following:

- Wearing clothing associated with substance use or that glorifies use in any way.
- Listening to music that in the past has been reliably associated with substance use.
- Talking in titillating ways about substance use or sharing exploits ("war stories") about using. Youths who are observed to be talking in a group about substance use should be confronted, since they are essentially getting high without the use of substances.

Respect

Respect for others should govern all group meetings. This includes listening to peers when they are speaking, making eye contact, and not speaking out of turn. Peers can be asked to raise their hands for permission to speak and to wait for recognition from a peer leader before speaking. This reinforces the tribal hierarchy. The counselor and more senior members of the group should intervene as necessary to point out disrespect and keep the group on task. Repeated confrontation of the same individual for lack of respect can be cause for some appropriate consequence, such as exclusion from a meeting for a period of time. Again, it's best if senior members of the peer group are able to confront these issues and impose consequences.

No Aggression

Verbal or physical aggression, including threatening another group member in any way, cannot be tolerated. Expressions of anger may be appropriate—indeed therapeutic—but not if they are directed at other group members in a threatening way. Obviously, physical aggression cannot be ignored. Even a single incident of physical violence is sufficient grounds for the group to exclude a member. Peers need to be encouraged to protect one another from intimidation or threat—inside or outside the group. There is strength in numbers, and in mutual support.

Sexuality

This is as integral a part of the adolescent experience as any other. Friendships and attractions among youths can't be avoided, though they can be regulated by the group. The goal of treatment is recovery. Within that context, preoccupation with a single relationship within the group is counter-therapeutic. On the other hand, attractions and romances can't be avoided altogether. Outside relationships, especially romantic and sexual ones, can create tensions and jealousies that threaten group cohesiveness. Rather than attempting to forbid such relationships, it is probably better to have them be publicly known within the group. At the same time, one group norm should be that such relationships not be permitted to compete with commitment to the group.

VALUES

Another thing that binds groups together, especially tribal groups, is their value system. This is the spiritual core of the tribe. Be it violence or passivity, compliance or rebelliousness, competitiveness or cooperation, faith or hopelessness: Every tribal group, good or bad, is guided by a set of common values that defines its outlook on life, its ideals, and its goals. Much of the collective behavior of groups is simply a reflection of their shared values. Morally, adolescents and young adults are in a state of developmental transition: from external control based on expected consequences (situational morality) to internal control by personal values (cultural morality).

Values were the subject of considerable discussion in earlier chapters. Certain values—such as naturalness over artificiality or social interest over self interest—are conducive to a chemical-free lifestyle; others are invitations to hedonistic or compensatory substance use and abuse. The group or program leader needs to be prepared to assume the role of moral leader, establishing and defending the values by which the group will be guided. These values should not be left implied, but should be discussed openly as they are represented by the group's behavior, attitudes, and decisions.

RITES OF PASSAGE

Rites of passage are rituals that mark the "passage" of the individual to a new social role (e.g. adulthood, parenthood), a higher social status, or both. Typically, higher social status is associated not only with added privileges—the right to marry, the right to vote—but also with added social responsibilities.

Within the therapeutic tribe, rites of passage can mark milestones in treatment, at the same time that they are gateways to higher levels of status. For instance, much like the act of preparing and sharing a personal chemical history, which can be a rite of entry, the preparation and sharing of a treatment contract can be the focus of a rite of passage in treatment. A "recovery plan" (see Chapter 8) is a set of individualized goals, along with specific, concrete plans for achieving them. A good recovery plan includes goals (and methods) relative to physical health and well-being, social health, spiritual health, and vocational/educational health. It is prepared with the assistance of the counselor, and possibly higher status members of the peer group.

Like the chemical history, the recovery plan is eventually shared with the entire community, which either accepts or rejects it by consensus. Acceptance is duly celebrated and marked by "passage" to a higher social status in the community: one associated with more power and responsibility. Part of this higher status may include "voting rights" on issues such as determining consequences for infractions. Along with power, though, there should also be greater social responsibilities, such as orienting new members to the group or community.

Should passage be denied (which should happen rarely if the event is properly organized and prepared for), this needs to be dealt with immediately. The individual needs to have a clear idea about what needs to be worked on to improve his or her chances of acceptance in the future.

In some residential treatment programs, members of the community are responsible collectively for maintenance of the house, including cooking, cleaning, and basic repairs. This kind of social structure lends itself to a social hierarchy based on work. This can be effective, although it will be more therapeutic if movement within the hierarchy is tied to recovery-related milestones as well as to work-related accomplishments. As members advance in this kind of community — moving, for example, from basic worker to team supervisor — privileges and power (and responsibility) within the community also increase.

Rites of passage should always be built around assuming greater leadership and social responsibility within the group. Becoming a sponsor (or a "foreman" in a work-oriented community) can be one such rite of passage. In order to apply (qualify) for this status, specific goals and tasks should have been accomplished. Examples of such tasks include the following:

- Leading a discussion of one of the 12 steps of AA or NA: what it is, what it means to each person, and how group members are "working it" in their recovery plans.
- Orienting one or more new members to the group or community: explaining rules and limits, etc.
- Assisting a new member in the preparation of his or her chemical history.
- Having a good performance record on all job assignments.

Rites of passage should be ritualized, and they should be community events. Counselors, working together with the group or community, can be as creative as they want in creating traditions and in ritualizing rites of passage. Whatever they are, however, they need to be taken seriously. Celebration should be appropriate to the occasion, and the focus should be congratulatory, not flip or silly.

The final rite of passage in any group treatment program is that of passage out of the group. At some point, all members of a group or therapeutic community will leave. Some will leave having achieved and grown a great deal; others will have come less far, but still hopefully some distance; both will need to be bid farewell.

The rite of passage out of the group should be as carefully constructed as any other rite. By the same token, the individual who leaves after having accomplished and contributed a great deal should leave not only with confidence and self-esteem, but with due recognition. This person will be missed.

Rites of passage are not only for those who leave; they are also for those who must stay. The group will experience the loss of any member, but especially one who has achieved and contributed a great deal to it. The rite of passage out of the group therefore has a decided element of grief inherent in it. This can and should be permitted; in fact, it should be ritualized in some way. The group needs to be able to express sadness at the same time that it expresses best wishes to the departing member. It is often helpful not only to give the parting member some concrete token of the group, but also to allow that person to leave something of him or herself behind.

TASKS AND GOALS

All groups function better—and more cohesively—when they have collective tasks to work on, collective goals to achieve, and collective challenges to overcome. Tribal cultures typically recognize adolescence as a developmental stage and make certain allowances for it; however few, if any, provide no goals for their youths. This should be true in group treatment as well.

Group treatment of young people works best when it is structured. The focus of that structure can vary—the community can be centered around work, around recovery, or even around adventure as it is in Outward Bound programs—but it needs to be there. In programs aimed at recovery from substance abuse and addiction, therapy should also be structured. Group sessions should not be freewheeling; they should have specific agendas that deal with various issues relevant to recovery. This helps to build self-discipline. Group meetings can be "directed" by senior members of the peer group, with the counselor serving as a guide or monitor of the group process. Some of the issues that can be regular agendas for adolescent group sessions are discussed below.

Steps

The Twelve Steps of AA and NA are important subjects for ongoing discussion. A single session can focus on just one step: on what it means to each group member,and how they can apply it to their own situation. The Twelve Traditions of AA can be used in a similar way.

Symptoms and Effects of Chemical Dependency

All persons in treatment for substance abuse should become knowledgeable about the process of addiction: its symptoms, its physical effects, and how chemicals affect development and mental functioning. An early task for new group or community members should be a careful personal assessment of their level of substance involvement. This can be done with the aid of symptom checklists or reading assignments, and should then be shared with the group as a whole; group members can ask questions and challenge denial if and when it is perceived.

Denial

A subject and issue in itself, denial (like enabling) is the prime enemy of recovery. The recovering addict can never afford to let down his or her guard—to indulge in denial in any form. Group members need to become "experts" in identifying denial and confronting it in each other. When confronting this most basic defense against loss of control, a direct approach is best: Simply describe what you see, and why you think it is denial.

Enabling and Codependence

Young people in recovery should be able to articulate the patterns of codependence and enabling in their lives. How, for example, was their own substance use enabled, and by whom? What role did they play in encouraging this enabling? Have they enabled someone else's use or addiction? How have others been affected by their substance abuse?

Sexuality and Relationships

At times it may be more appropriate to separate males and females for discussions of sexual issues. This would be true, for example, when the focus of discussion is sexual abuse, and where the agenda is for group members to share these experiences for the first time. At other times, though, productive discussions can take place in coed groups on subjects such as:

- Making opposite-sex friends (without getting high)
- Making same-sex friends (without substance use as the agenda)
- Socializing without getting high
- Choosing partners (boyfriends and girlfriends)
- Healthy relationships
- Sex and love

Same-sex groups, on the other hand, can be used to focus on issues such as:

- Body-image
- Sexual abuse and assault
- Alcohol, drugs, and sex
- Sex education

Coping and Socializing

Young people in recovery know surprisingly little about how to have fun or how to cope with stress without using substances. If they have done anything — bowling, playing ball, dancing, or skating — they probably haven't done it straight in years, if ever. They probably also haven't been to a movie or a party sober in years, if ever. In sobriety they should be encouraged to be creative in thinking of ways to have fun and given opportunities to act on them, without the use of mood-altering chemicals.

Coping is another area where peers can be helpful. A repeating agenda for the group can be "problem-solving": identifying individuals' most difficult situations, how they dealt with them in the past, and how they can deal with them better in the future.

Grief and Gratitude

These emotions play keys roles in recovery. Teens and young adults who've become entangled with substances usually have experienced many losses: They've lost social status and friends, have probably experienced failure in school, and perhaps worst of all, they've lost self-respect. Being capable of experiencing and expressing both grief and gratitude is a powerful antidote to shame and can be vital in sustaining motivation for recovery. Specific work on both grief and gratitude should be an integral part of the agenda for adolescent groups.

ON LEADING ADOLESCENT GROUPS

When working with adolescents or young adults in a therapeutic context, the counselor must be willing and able to articulate and enforce group norms until such time as peer leaders emerge and a group culture evolves. Observations of therapeutic communities and therapy groups for youths reveal the basic dynamics of adolescence: the struggle to individuate. This struggle is acted out in the group context in the form of competition between the peer group and the counselor for leverage, commitment, and influence. This is to be expected and is not in itself unhealthy; on the contrary, the presence of a moderate amount of such tension should be interpreted as meaning that a therapeutic group environment has been created.

Occasionally, the counselor may attempt to overcontrol the group process. In this case the group will be characterized by excessive amounts of rebellion, a failure of natural peer leadership to emerge, and cohesiveness that is built around opposition to the counselor rather than around a shared commitment to recovery. This group will not evolve an effective culture.

The other extreme is represented by the counselor who is overly laissez-faire, who essentially sits back passively, waiting for the group to "structure itself." This will prove to be a long and unproductive wait, during which the youths will lose interest in the group and lose faith in the counselor. Again, no meaningful or effective culture will emerge.

In starting new groups, as well as in working with existing groups where members are intensely antisocial and uncontrolled, the counselor will need to be a more active "enforcer," for a longer period, than in groups of relatively better socialized youths. In either case however, success can be measured by the ability of the group, over time, to focus on its primary goal (recovery) as opposed to process issues (coming on time, etc.), and by the emergence of peer leaders who are committed to group norms and ethics, as well as to their own recovery.

When attempting to enforce group norms, the best approach is a direct one: State the rule and ask the individual(s) who are noncompliant to get in line. This intervention should be done the first time the counselor notes an infraction of the rules, since ignoring an infraction invariably invites a second one (usually by more than one person). Also, one warning is sufficient before consequences are imposed. One of the best consequences is a brief "time-out": either having the group member turn his or her chair around, facing away from the group for a few minutes, or having him or her leave the group entirely for a brief period of time. Some infractions (for example, arriving for a group meeting high or drunk) do not require any "warning" at all: These should be sufficient grounds for asking the member to leave, period. Care should be taken, of course, to assure safe transport, and the member should be invited to return for the next session, assuming that he or she is sober and straight.

In more advanced or "mature" groups, confrontations will come from peers as well as from the counselor. This should be encouraged, as it is one sign of "tribal" growth. In such groups, consequences can also be imposed, to a greater or lesser extent, by the community and/or its leaders.

SUMMARY

This chapter described the main characteristics of a therapeutic treatment milieu for adolescents and young adults in recovery. Using a tribal analogy, some of the more important dimensions of such a treatment environment were described. Change and developmental growth occur most quickly in an environment that is characterized by age-appropriate expectations, social hierarchy, and structure, and where control of behavior rests as much with the group as a whole as with its leadership. In this social environment individuation moves ahead along healthy lines. The therapeutic tribal experience promotes the development of values that are prosocial and the development of self-esteem based on achievement and responsibility. Though in some ways it represents a departure from contemporary treatment models, the therapeutic tribe experience actually reflects a return to basic principles of socialization.

16

Relapse Prevention

In one sense relapse prevention should not be the subject of a separate chapter of this book, the reason being that recovery from substance abuse and addiction can be thought of as one continuous process of relapse prevention. In other words, persons are either in recovery or in some stage of relapse—they are opposite sides of the same coin. As previous chapters have shown, recovery involves changes in attitudes, behaviors, and personal values. It means breaking many old habits and establishing an equal number of new ones. It means building a different self-image and identifying with a different peer group.

Given the above definition of recovery, one can see how relapse begins well before the first drink is taken, the first joint is smoked, or any other mood-altering chemical is used to manipulate feelings. Relapse ends in substance use, but it begins much sooner than that. Relapse begins when attitudes and behaviors change and become more like those associated with using than with recovering.

Relapse is most likely to occur early in recovery, when the habits and attitudes that sustain recovery are not yet well established, when the skills needed to replace substance use are not yet well developed, and when identity with a functional peer group is not yet strong. The greatest risk is that young persons in recovery will place themselves in situations that invite use or which evoke emotions that have triggered substance use in the past—with results that naturally surprise no one but themselves. In this chapter we'll look at some of the factors that pose the greatest threats to recovery and how the counselor can work with recovering teens to sustain it and prevent relapse.

COPING WITH RISKY SITUATIONS

One approach to relapse prevention that teens and young adults appreciate involves teaching them to identify risky situations, especially those associated with trigger emotions, and to plan ways of avoiding or coping with them.

Identifying High-Risk Situations

Adolescents and adults in recovery intuitively understand what we mean when we talk about "risky" situations. Substance use does not occur in a vacuum. For most teens it is associated with certain people, certain kinds of interactions, certain places, certain times, certain music, certain talk, even certain clothing. Resistance to letting go of the trappings of use is part of denial. Adolescents who maintain that they will keep the same friends, go to the same places, listen to the same music, and wear the same clothing they wore when they used—but somehow not use—are fooling no one, except perhaps themselves. Placing themselves in situations which have strong associations with use is sure to evoke strong urges to use. Add to this the likelihood that old friends, who are probably still using, will actively encourage use, and soon the recovering teen is recovering no more.

Corrective group experiences, such as those described in Chapter 15, can be used in part to help teens identify risky situations and plan ways of avoiding them. As part of group norms and expectations, teens can be encouraged to "pull each other up": to confront one another whenever they detect a peer "slipping" into old patterns of dress, talk, etc., or drifting toward a using peer group. The more a teenager looks, talks, dresses, and thinks like a user, the closer he or she is to being one. This is the "addict" personality emerging. By the same token, the more time teens spend around users, the closer they are to using. They are walking a psychological tightrope. This may appeal to their adolescent adventurousness, but it's risky business. It should be confronted, by peers if possible as well as by a counselor. Its riskiness should be openly discussed, and the denial it represents should be confronted. The teen can be "pulled up" by being asked to take responsibility for his or her actions and to make a specific commitment to do something different; the group and counselor must later follow up to see that he or she kept this commitment.

Along with avoiding "dangerous" people, places, and things, the recovering youth must develop alternative relationships and interests, as well as many other new habits—basically, a new lifestyle. This is the recovery plan. It includes commitments to maintaining physical health, spiritual health, and social health. These are more than statements of intent: To be effective they need to be backed up by concrete plans on a practical "how-to" level.

Not only a great deal of effort but also a great deal of support is necessary to keep the recovery process alive. Adolescents should not be expected to do this without guidance, encouragement, and when needed, confrontation. Avoiding any evidence of relapse—any evidence at all of the reemergence of faulty thinking or the addict personality—is to flirt with disaster. Recovery requires constant vigilance, openness, and honesty.

Identifying Trigger Emotions

Teens relapse not only when they place themselves in dangerous situations, but also when they are confronted with emotions that once motivated substance use. These "trigger" emotions differ from person to person, but anger and frustration are high on the list for males, while depression and shame are common triggers for females. Meanwhile, grief, resentment, boredom, and anxiety are frequent triggers for substance use for both sexes.

Trigger emotions are associated with particular situations: with people, places, and/or things. Keeping this context in mind can be helpful when trying to identify trigger emotions, since the situation can can easily trigger the feeling.

Teens can construct their own personal lists of trigger emotions by talking about times (situations) when they used regularly. Who were they with? What were they doing? What was happening? What were they feeling? These will usually be feelings that substances are used to compensate for. Boredom, for example, might be relieved by a chemical that makes a teen feel good. Anger and stress can be compensated for by something that anesthetizes them. Shame and anxiety can be dealt with through chemicals that create temporary feelings of well being and self-confidence. And so on.

PROBLEM-SOLVING

Young people need to appreciate the fact that they can effectively "relapse" well before they have actually used any mood-altering chemical. The following sections address specific strategies that counselors can use in relapse prevention work. Many of these strategies work best in a group treatment format, such as that described in the last chapter.

Internality

Substance abuse can be motivated out of a desire to avoid problems rather than confront and try to solve them. Since recovery is fraught with challenges, dilemmas, and problems to be solved, any tendency toward avoidance poses a major threat.

Successful problem-solving depends on several factors, the first of which is a basic attitude that problems can be solved—in other words, a hopeful attitude about the outcome of confronting problems. In lay terms this could be called self-confidence; in the professional literature it is sometimes referred to as an "internal" orientation toward life: a belief that the individual can make a difference and determine the outcome of events through personal effort and intervention.[1] The opposite is an "external" orientation: the belief that what happens to the individual is the result of chance or external forces that cannot be significantly influenced by personal action. It's obvious which of these orientations is more conducive to recovery. Relapse can occur simply because the individual believes it is inevitable.

Repeated experiences with victimization, chronic deprivation, frustration, or an objective lack of real-life opportunities can lead to an external orientation that is reality-based and therefore resistant to change. On the other hand, an external attitude toward life can be modeled, in which case it can be influenced by exposure to respected persons (including peers) who model an alternative outlook. When it's based in experience, an external orientation can usually be changed only through remedial experiences. Therapeutic adventure programs, remedial education, and vocational training programs are most helpful in this regard. Being vigilant for such experiences and pointing them out to the teen or young adult is an important aspect of counseling. However it is done, external outlooks need to be challenged and "converted" to internal attitudes as much as possible.

Techniques

Following a few basic rules can help build skill and confidence in problem-solving.

RULE 1: DEFINE THE PROBLEM

Surprisingly, this is often the most difficult rule of all to follow. We let our emotions get ahead of our thoughts and end up spending a lot time and effort being angry or resentful, instead of trying to define clearly what it is that is frustrating us. Adolescents who have an external outlook are more in touch with their frustration or anger than they are with their thoughts; as a result they will act impulsively (and ineffectively). They will run away from problems — or attempt to "lose" themselves (avoid the problem) in alcohol or drugs.

The essence of rule one is this: *Stop and think*. The teen needs to be coached to react to anger or frustration not with immediate, impulsive action or with avoidance, but with pause. He or she needs time to think before acting. This may mean having the courage and self-control necessary to leave the situation that is causing the anger or frustration. Starting with the emotions he or she is feeling, the adolescent needs to answer the following questions for him or herself:

- What exactly am I feeling: anger, frustration, sadness, boredom?
- What is causing this?

Self-statements that can help this process are:

- "Calm down."
- "Take time out."
- "Stop and think."

The teen can be coached in using these self-statements, at first by literally saying them out loud, to help cope with trigger emotions. This is best done in the context of discussing a real-life problem: a "risky situation". Doing this in counseling will increase the chances that these statements will be used in similar situations outside of counseling.

RULE 2: EVALUATE THE PROBLEM

Just how dangerous or threatening is this situation? Exactly what potential consequences am I faced with? These are important questions. Lacking reasonable answers, the individual is likely to overestimate the severity of the problem. This in turn will encourage avoidance or impulsiveness, both of which undermine effective problemsolving. Again, asking these questions out loud, with the guidance of a counselor or a functional peer group, can help "transfer" the learning from counseling to day-to-day living situations. The counselor (or group) can help the individual learn to evaluate problem situations realistically, by learning to stop and think.

RULE 3: GENERATE ALTERNATIVES

Impulsive children, teens, and young adults do not take the time to consider alternative ways of solving an interpersonal problem; instead, they act on the first idea that comes to mind. Often, this idea will be inappropriate and ineffectual. They will let their feelings guide them—thoughtlessly. Typically, their impulsive solutions will involve either fight or flight: They will argue, lash out, have a tantrum, or get into a physical confrontation; alternatively, they may run away, get drunk, or get high.

Recovery demands that youths develop greater self-control. To do this they must have the confidence that they can solve problems, plus the skills necessary to do so. They need to be able get in touch with their feelings, but not to be ruled by them. In achieving this goal, the counselor and the peer group provide vital support and encouragement, as well as practical ideas. They reinforce "stopping and thinking" and they help generate ideas for how to solve problems—ranging from how to get a job, to how to stay away from old friends who are still using, to how to deal with a parent who is using. The message that enables this to happen is hope; the confidence that it is possible to change your life and find ways of dealing with even the most difficult situations.

RULE 4: CHOOSE THE HEALTHIER (NOT EASIER) SOLUTION

Once a problem has been realistically defined and evaluated, and alternative solutions have been generated, the issue boils down to what to do. Solutions can always be divided into two categories: those that support recovery and those that don't. The difference has a great deal to do with integrity and character. The person in solid recovery is a person who has learned the importance of making the right choice, day after day. He or she appreciates the fact that it takes strength and integrity to make the right choices, and that making those choices in turn builds character. In this light I recall vividly the words of a colleague at a celebration of his eleventh year of sobriety: "It's something that I'm very grateful for. I guess if I've learned anything in these past 11 years, it's that if I know who I am, what I want for myself, what I believe in, and what I stand for, I can make it through anything, one day at a time." This is an important message. Young people—in or out of recovery—need living models of people who have learned to live this way, who believe that ideals can lead to a better life, and who are willing to share their wisdom and their mistakes, their successes and their failures. Despite the alienation that is so prevalent among young people today, it is still possible to inspire many of them. Inspiration has its place in treatment.

In learning to solve problems of living, adolescents should be encouraged to explore the alternatives that are open to them, as well as their implications. They should be challenged to identify the values— and the self-image—associated with each course of action.

- What does running away from a difficulty, or getting high to avoid it, say about your values and about how you feel about yourself?
- What are your values? What do you stand for? Whom do you admire?
- Given the above considerations, what should you do in this situation?

ANGER MANAGEMENT

There is probably no emotion that gets teens into as much trouble as anger. Learning to deal effectively with anger is a task that requires maturity, which is precisely what the adolescent lacks. Accepting that limitation, there is still a lot the counselor can do to help the recovering teen manage his or her anger in ways that are not self-destructive.

Chronic frustration or resentment, along with anger that cannot be effectively expressed, invites substance use. The first line of defense against this is effective problem-solving. As discussed in the previous section, confidence built from experience in solving problems of living reduces anxiety and along with it the temptation to flee into substance abuse. In addition, there are some other helpful strategies.

Your Right to Be Angry

Nothing inflames an angry person more than being told that he or she has no right to his or her feelings. Dysfunctional families often invalidate emotions that are very appropriate to the situation. The motivation for this is simple denial: an unwillingness on the part of parents, or the entire family, to accept an emotion, usually because it points to a problem that they cannot (or else don't want to) deal with. Living in this kind of family, with its chronic frustrations, is an invitation to all kinds of avoidance, including avoidance through substance abuse.

The counselor cannot afford to join any conspiracies of silence; instead, the counselor needs to validate the adolescent's anger. The message is this: If you're angry, chances are you aren't crazy. Maybe the problem is family denial. The next step is to help the teen figure out what the denial is about.

Dealing with Anger

Once anger is acknowledged and legitimized, the counselor can help the young person deal with it. This process joins client and counselor, who has the advantage of having already validated the youth's feelings. Even the angriest adolescents can be engaged in a constructive dialogue once their feelings are validated.

There are many strategies for dealing with anger, but first the teen must be helped to see how he or she has dealt with anger in the past and to evaluate whether that has been healthy or unhealthy. Anger that is drowned in mood-altering chemicals or diverted into self-destructive or aggressive behavior is anger that is not being handled well.

Problem-solving skills can be used to help teens develop healthier ways of dealing with anger. Assertiveness training can be very useful to teens who have been raised in families that either avoid conflict or deal with it through aggression. The recovering teen should not be encouraged, however, to believe that he or she can singlehandedly reverse family denial or solve longstanding family problems. On the other hand, teens can be supported in their refusal to join denial and in detaching from the family to the extent that this is necessary for their own psychological health.

Detaching

The concept of detaching is an important one within the recovery movement. It's an idea that is captured in the spirit of the Serenity Prayer:

> God, grant me the serenity
> To accept the things I cannot change,
> The courage to change the things I can,
> And the wisdom to know the difference.

The wisdom in detachment has to do with the effects that resentment and hatred have on the human spirit. Anger, it seems, needs either to lead to effective expression, confrontation, and change, or to be let go of. Let go of, you say? How does one do that? The answer is this: detachment.

Detaching has to do with accepting what one cannot change—with reconciling oneself to that—and learning to live with it. It means letting others be responsible for living their lives, while you live yours. It means accepting differences between yourself and someone else, instead of trying to change the other person. Detaching, in short, requires respect. It is not at all like alienation, which is at heart a form of anger, much like resentment. On the contrary, detaching can actually allow for affectionate or warm feelings to emerge.

Detachment can also be thought of as the final stage of grief: when one has pretty much come to terms with a loss and decided to move ahead instead of dwelling on it. People can reach this point only after they have been able to work through other aspects of grief, including denial and bargaining.

Sheila was a tall 18-year-old young woman with short brown hair, hazel eyes, and a sad, tense face. I was a "professional in residence"—a kind of participant-observer—in a weeklong program at a treatment center in the midwest. Sheila was there because her father was in treatment—for the third time—for cocaine addiction. I found myself observing Sheila a lot that week, partly I think because something about her reminded me of my own daughter. I was touched by her sadness, and struck by the tenacity of her love for her father.

Because of the way the program was designed, Sheila was able to see her father for only a short time each day, mostly at mealtimes. She would meet him at the cafeteria; they would find an empty table and sit together, talking intensely as they ate. Then all the sadness would disappear from Sheila's face, and she would be animated and very obviously happy.

Through the program we—those of us who were in training, and those who were there because they had family members in treatment — explored many issues, including "detaching." Supported primarily by each other, and living together more or less as an extended family, we were able to look at some of the disappointments, losses, frustrations, and resentments in our lives. During one of our informal meetings, Sheila made a casual comment about how good it felt to "really open up, for the first time," about her father. I asked her what she meant. This was the first time, she replied, that she'd been with people who did not criticize her (for loving her father), judge him (for being an addict), or encourage her to walk away from him.

Sheila was, in reality, frustrated, angry, and resentful toward her father. His addiction had taken him away from her, physically and emotionally. It had broken up their family. She had not shared any of these feelings with him, however; and sadly, she'd started using marijuana and alcohol quite a bit in the past year.

After finding a receptive audience among our extended family, Sheila went off one afternoon to meet with her father and a counselor. My heart went with her, as did many others'. When she came back her eyes were red, and she looked drained. We respected her when she said she needed to be alone for a while and went off to her room. She went to bed early that night, and I didn't see her until the next morning, though my thoughts turned to her as I lay in bed on the edge of sleep.

The next day, Sheila still looked tired, but I thought I detected less tension in her face. I told her so. She smiled, and in that instant I caught a glimmer of light in her eyes that I will never forget.

Sheila and I left the program on the same afternoon. We rode the van together to the airport, and by chance we had an hour to kill before our respective planes would take us to different parts of the country. She suggested we have some coffee. As we sat together, I told her how I had been struck by her when I first saw her, and how different her face had looked these last two days. Yes, she said, she felt that she'd changed, too. I asked her what had made the difference. She told me that she knew now—truly knew, and accepted— that her father was an addict. She had accepted that as a fact, and stopped trying to deny it, for the first time in her life. She had told him, she said, how much she'd hated him for that, how much it frightened her, and how she'd been burdened by resentment and guilt for years. "Now he knows about all those terrible feelings I was keeping inside," she said. "And he knows that I still love him, but that there's nothing much I can do about his addiction. It's his illness. That's an incredible relief—like a thousand pounds being taken off my shoulders."

Then, suddenly, it was time to go. Sheila got up. I rose with her. We paused, looking at each other. Then she did the nicest thing: she reached out. We hugged—right there in the middle of that crowded airport cafeteria—and then we went our separate ways.

The best way to teach detaching—as Sheila taught it to me—seems to be to model it. People who must live with chronic frustration or with situations that understandably make them angry and resentful can benefit not only from developing skills like assertiveness and problem-solving, but also from the wisdom of a someone who can teach them about detachment.

SUMMARY

Preventing relapse means supporting recovery. Recovery can be supported by teaching adolescents skills and by involving them more and more in the monitoring—and protection—of their own recovery. Indeed, recovery requires a certain amount of vigilance and protection. Teens and young adults need practical guidance and emotional support in order to make (and sustain) the changes in their lives that recovery demands. As difficult as this may sound, it is not at all impossible to attain. Beyond learning to express feelings, confront conflict, change their lifestyles and stand for values, young persons in recovery—like all of us—must learn when to let go.

Notes

CHAPTER 1

1. *National Household Survey on Drug Abuse: 1985.* Rockville, MD: National Institute on Drug Abuse, 1985.
2. *National High School Senior Survey, 1986.* Ann Arbor, MI: University of Michigan, Institute for Social Research, 1987.
3. Clayton, R.R., Ritter, C. The epidemiology of alcohol and drug abuse among adolescents. *Advances in Alcohol and Substance Abuse*, 1985; 4:3–4, 69–97.
4. Holland, S., Griffin, A. Adolescent and adult drug treatment clients: Patterns and consequences of use. *Journal of Psychiatric Drugs*, 1984; 16:1, 79–89.
5. Yamaguchi, K., Kandel, D. Patterns of drug use from adolescence to young adulthood: II. Sequences of progression. *American Journal of Public Health*, 1984; 74:7, 668–672.
6. Donovan, J.E., Jessor, R. Problem drinking and the dimension of involvement with drugs: A Guttman scalogram analysis of adolescent drug use. *American Journal of Public Health*, 1983; 73:5, 543–551.
7. Krupka, L., Knox, L. Enhancing the effectiveness of alcohol and substance abuse prevention programs for children. *The International Journal of the Addictions*, 1985; 20:9, 1435–1442.
8. Marijuana. *Psychiatric Annals*, 1986; 16:4, 209–212.
9. *Summary of substance abuse data/information.* Hartford, CT: Connecticut Alcohol and Drug Abuse Commission, 1986.
10. Hafen, B.Q., Fransden, K.J. *Youth suicide: Depression and loneliness.* Evergreen, CO: Cordillera Press, 1986.

CHAPTER 2

1. Johnston, L.D., Bachman, J.G., O'Malley, D.M. *Highlights from student drug use in America, 1975-1981.* Rockville, MD: National Institute on Drug Abuse, 1980.
2. Krupka, L., Knox, L. ibid.
3. Burns, C., Geist, C. Stressful life events and drug use among adolescents. *Journal of Human Stress*, 1984; Fall, 135–139.
4. Jalali, B., Jalali, M., Crocetti, G., Turner, F. Adolescence and drug use: Toward a more comprehensive approach. *American Journal of Orthopsychiatry*, 1981; 51:1, 120–130.
5. Newcomb, M., Maddahian, E., Bentler, P.M. Risk factors for drug use among adolescents: Concurrent and longitudinal analyses. *American Journal of Public Health*, 1986; 76:5, 525–531.

235

6. Pandina, R., Schuele, J.A. Psychosocial correlates of alcohol and drug use of adolescent students and adolescents in treatment. *Journal of Studies on Alcohol,* 1983; 44:6, 950–973.
7. Kandel, D.B., Raveis, V.H. Cessation of illicit drug use in young adulthood. *Archives of General Psychiatry,* 1989; 46, 109–116.
8. Seligman, M.E.P. *Helplessness.* San Francisco: W.H. Freeman, 1975.

CHAPTER 3

1. Holland, S., Griffin, A. ibid.
2. Piaget, J. *The moral judgment of the child.* M Gabain, trans. New York: Free Press, 1965 (Originally published 1932).
3. Hartshorne, H., May, M.A. *Studies in the nature of character. Vol. I. Studies in deceit.* New York: Macmillan, 1928.
4. Kohlberg, L. *Essays on moral development. Vol. I. The philosophy of moral development.* New York: Harper & Row, 1981.
5. *Twelve steps and twelve traditions.* New York: Alcoholics Anonymous, 1952.

CHAPTER 6

1. Kobasa, K.C. Stressful life events, personality, and health: An inquiry into hardiness. *Journal of Personality and Social Psychology,* 37:1, 1–11, 1979.
2. Fossum, M., Mason, M. *Facing Shame.* New York: Norton, 1986.

CHAPTER 7

1. Holland, S., Griffin, A. ibid.
2. Newcomb, M., Maddahian, E., Bentler, P.M. ibid.
3. Marcus, A.M. Academic achievement in elementary school children of alcoholic mothers. *Journal of Clinical Psychology,* 1986; 42:2, 372–376.
4. Foster, H.L., Broadfoot, M. Children of drug disturbed parents. In *Critical concerns in the field of drug abuse. Proceedings of the Third National Drug Abuse Conference.* New York: Marcel Dekker, 1978.
5. Holland, S., Griffin, A. ibid.
6. Mayer, J., Black, R. Chad abuse and neglect in families with an alcohol or opiate addicted parent. *Child Abuse and Neglect,* 1977; 1:1, 85–98.
7. Black, R., Mayer, J. *An investigation of the relationship between substance abuse and child abuse and neglect.* Washington, DC: National Center on Child Abuse and Neglect (DHEW), 1979.
8. Breger, E. Relationship between alcohol misuse and family violence. *Military Family,* 1983; 3:2, 5.
9. Behling, D.W. Alcohol abuseas encountered in 51 instances of reported child abuse. *Clinical Pediatrics,* 1979; 18:2, 87–91.
10. Black, R.M., Mayer, J., Zaklan, A. The relationship between opiate abuse and child abuse and neglect. In *Critical concerns in the field of drug abuse. Proceedings of the Third National Drug Abuse Conference.* New York: Marcel Dekker, 1978.

11. Wilson, C.A., Trammel, S., Greer, B.G., Long, G. *An exploratory study of the relationship between child abuse-neglect and alcohol-drug use*. Memphis, TN: Tennessee State Dept. of Human and Social Services, 1977.
12. Cohen, F.S., Densen-Gerber, J. A study of the relationship between child abuse and drug addiction in 178 patients: Preliminary results. *Child Abuse and Neglect*, 1982; 6:4, 383–387.
13. Pandina, R.J., Schuele, Y.A. ibid.
14. Parke, R.D., Slaby, R.G. The development of aggression. In E.M. Hetherington (Ed.), *Handbook of child psychology*. New York: Wiley, 1983.
15. Radke-Yarrow, M., Zahn-Waxler, C., Chapman, M. Children's prosocial dispositions and behavior. In E.M. Hetherington (Ed.), *Handbook of child psychology*. New York: Wiley, 1983.

CHAPTER 11

1. *Narcotics Anonymous*. P.O. Box 9999, Van Nuys, CA: NA World Service Office, 1982, p. 15.

CHAPTER 13

1. *Alcoholics Anonymous*. New York: Alcoholics Anonymous World Services, 1976 (Originally published 1939).

CHAPTER 16

1. Rotter, J.B. Generalized expectancies for internal versus external control of reinforcement. *Psychological Monographs*, 1966; 80:1.

Index